BLOCKCHAIN FOR BUSINESS WITH HYPERLEDGER FABRIC

A complete guide to enterprise blockchain implementation using Hyperledger Fabric

by

Nakul Shah

M000272145

FIRST EDITION 2019

Copyright © BPB Publications, India

ISBN: 978-93-88511-650

All Rights Reserved. No part of this publication may be reproduced or distributed in any form or by any means or stored in a database or retrieval system, without the prior written permission of the publisher with the exception to the program listings which may be entered, stored and executed in a computer system, but they can not be reproduced by the means of publication.

LIMITS OF LIABILITY AND DISCLAIMER OF WARRANTY

The information contained in this book is true to correct and the best of author's & publisher's knowledge. The author has made every effort to ensure the accuracy of these publications, but cannot be held responsible for any loss or damage arising from any information in this book.

All trademarks referred to in the book are acknowledged as properties of their respective owners.

Distributors:

BPB PUBLICATIONS
20, Ansari Road, Darya Ganj
New Delhi-110002
Ph: 23254990/23254991

DECCAN AGENCIES
4-3-329, Bank Street,
Hyderabad-500195
Ph: 24756967/24756400

MICRO MEDIA
Shop No. 5, Mahendra Chambers,
150 DN Rd. Next to Capital Cinema,
V.T. (C.S.T.) Station, MUMBAI-400 001
Ph: 22078296/22078297

BPB BOOK CENTRE
376 Old Lajpat Rai Market,
Delhi-110006
Ph: 23861747

Published by Manish Jain for BPB Publications, 20 Ansari Road, Darya Ganj, New Delhi-110002 and Printed by him at Repro India Ltd, Mumbai

About the Author

Nakul Shah is the founder and director of Sate Development, a leading blockchain and software development company. He is a regular speaker at conferences across the globe on topics like blockchain technology, Hyperledger, and Distributed ledger technology. As a longtime creative thought leader in financial markets, technology, and innovation, he has worked with startups and multinationals across the world.

Nakul has multiple years of experience in research, development, and deployment of solutions using blockchain technology. Besides creating enterprise solutions, he also provides training, consultancy, and development services, helping clients demystify the technology and understand how organizations can leverage its key features.

Nakul has conducted lectures for banks, universities, and governments on various topics covering platforms and use cases of blockchain technology.

Nakul has played a significant role in the adoption and application of blockchain technology. He started his career at State Street Corporation in Boston, which is one of the biggest and oldest providers of mutual fund, pension processing, and asset custody services. He used advanced statistical and technical tools in the field of socially responsible investment. He also served as a product specialist for the wealth management team at Charles River Development. While executing independent consulting assignments, he has advised a leading sustainability firm that helps Fortune500 companies.

Nakul holds a master's degree in financial engineering from the University of Michigan, Ann Arbor, USA.

Acknowledgements

Translating your knowledge of a subject into a book is not as easy as it sounds. I realized this as I started writing the first chapter of this book. I am really grateful to my family for their love, support, and encouragement, which kept me going. The experience, though challenging, was quite rewarding once the book was complete.

My vision with this book is to educate students and professionals about the advantages of blockchain technology and equip them with skills required to develop solutions using Hyperledger Fabric. The use of blockchain technology could ultimately assist businesses to operate in a safe and trusted manner. Blockchain technology represents an opportunity to mutualize data-driven infrastructure across entities spanning diverse industry sectors like banking, insurance, media, and more, thereby translating into huge cost savings and capital growth.

I am overwhelmed in all humbleness and gratefulness to acknowledge my deep gratitude to all those who have helped me put these ideas well above the level of simplicity and into something concrete. I would like to take this opportunity to thank everyone who supported me while I embarked on this journey of following blockchain technology into a new future.

Preface

I was motivated to write this book to help the industry understand the use of blockchain technology and recognize its potential in revolutionizing the way businesses work. In 2016, enterprise blockchain was a new concept. There were very few players in the private permissioned blockchain space. The advent of Hyperledger Fabric has since brought this technology in front of the likes of multinational companies across various sectors like banking, insurance, retail, and more. Corporations and startups across the globe have started moving towards Hyperledger Fabric to find new use cases to support business requirements efficiently. As a result, relevant technical expertise and knowledge are required to build and support solutions on Hyperledger Fabric.

This book aims to equip you with enough knowledge on enterprise blockchain platforms in conjunction with skills to use Fabric in order to succeed as a blockchain developer or subject matter expert.

The book starts with a brief introduction to the world of blockchains. It covers all aspects of Hyperledger Fabric, ranging from network setup, use case deployment, to testing. Several examples have been covered in this book to provide readers with hands-on understanding of the subject. Readers will also learn to use the basic functions, libraries, and packages required in Fabric business network deployment.

The book is aimed to address readers from disparate backgrounds ranging from entrepreneurs to C-level leaders and the entire software development community. This book will serve as a tutorial for understanding and building business solutions using Hyperledger Fabric.

Errata

We take immense pride in our work at BPB Publications and follow best practices to ensure the accuracy of our content to provide with an indulging reading experience to our subscribers. Our readers are our mirrors, and we use their inputs to reflect and improve upon human errors if any, occurred during the publishing processes involved. To let us maintain the quality and help us reach out to any readers who might be having difficulties due to any unforeseen errors, please write to us at :

errata@bpbonline.com

Your support, suggestions and feedbacks are highly appreciated by the BPB Publications' Family.

Table of Contents

1. Blockchain and Decentralization 1

Definitions 2

   Cryptocurrency 2

   Bitcoin 3

   Blockchain 3

   How Bitcoin works 4

Wallets 5

Basics of blockchain 6

Mining in blockchain 6

Cryptography 8

Building blocks of blockchain 9

   Blocks 9

   Transactions 9

   Smart contracts 10

   Virtual machine 10

   Nodes 10

   Peer-to-peer network 10

   State machine 11

   Consensus 11

Structure of blockchain 11

Working of Blockchain 13

Fundamentals of secure transaction processing 14

Decentralization 15

   History of decentralization 16

      OpenBazaar 17

      Popcorn time 17

      Lighthouse 17

      Gems 17

Decentralization using blockchain 17

Decentralized ecosystem 18

   Storage 18

   Communication 18

Computation *19*

Blockchain for enterprise.. 20

Enterprise blockchain platforms 20

Considerations for using blockchain.. *22*

Distributed systems... 23

Byzantine Generals problem... 23

Types of blockchains.. *24*

Summary... 25

2. Introduction to Hyperledger and Composer **27**

Blockchain for business 29

Advantages of Hyperledger Fabric.. 31

Problems with existing blockchain technology..................................... 31

Hyperledger Fabric architecture 32

Consensus in Hyperledger.. 32

Hyperledger tools... 33

Hyperledger Explorer *33*

Hyperledger Cello *34*

Hyperledger Composer *34*

Hyperledger Caliper *34*

Hyperledger Quilt *35*

Hyperledger URSA.. *35*

Hyperledger Composer 35

Hyperledger components *36*

Hyperledger application using Composer *38*

Step 1: Create a business network structure............................... *39*

Step 2: Define a business network *39*

Modeling assets, participants, and transactions *39*

Step 3: Generate the business network *41*

Step 4: Deploy the business network *41*

Step 6: Generate a boilerplate angular application.................... *43*

Composer query language *43*

Step 1: Update the business network... *43*

Step 2: Create a query definition file... *45*

Step 3: Regenerate the business network archive *46*

Step 4: Deploy the updated business network 46

Step 5: Generate a REST server 47

Step 6: Generate a skeleton angular application 47

Fabric Composer Playground 47

Summary 51

References 51

3. Basics of Hyperledger Fabric **53**

Hyperledger and blockchain 54

Blockchain for enterprises 55

Hyperledger frameworks and tools 57

Burrow 57

Fabric 57

Indy 57

Iroha 57

Sawtooth 58

Caliper 58

Cello 58

Composer 58

Explorer 58

Quilt 59

Fabric and its components 59

How does a transaction happen in Hyperledger Fabric? 65

Difference between Bitcoin, Ethereum, and permissioned blockchain 67

Public versus permissioned networks 67

*Differences between Hyperledger Fabric by Linux Foundation, Corda by R3,
and Quorum by JP Morgan* 69

Permissioned parties only 69

Chaincode/smart contracts 69

Hyperledger Fabric releases and differences 70

Fabric 0.6 72

Fabric 1.0 74

Fabric 1.1 75

Fabric 1.2 77

Fabric 1.3.. 80

Fabric 1.4 LTS 81

World state and states 83

Membership service provider (MSP)... 84

    Generate MSP certificates and their signing keys 87

Node.js SDK for Hyperledger Fabric... 89

Peers returning transaction proposal 93

Chaincode in Node.Js... 94

    Init(stub) Asynchronous 95

    Invoke(stub) Asynchronous... 96

Summary.. 99

References.. 99

4. Frameworks, Network Topologies, and Modeling........................... **101**

Unlisted company network in Hyperledger 101

Hyperledger network and application model................................ 102

    Blockchain network... 103

    Build a sample network 103

    Creating network from scratch 104

    Certificate authority 105

    Network administration node... 105

Consortium definition 106

    Channel for consortium 107

    Adding peers and ledgers to network 108

    Client/application and chaincode... 109

Exploring Hyperledger frameworks 110

    Hyperledger Sawtooth 110

    Hyperledger Fabric 111

    Hyperledger Indy... 112

    Hyperledger Burrow 113

    Hyperledger Iroha.. 114

        Iroha architecture 114

    YAC consensus algorithm 116

Transaction privacy and security 116

Understanding pre-requisites 117

Docker 118

Process of creating Hyperledger network 125

Hands-on with network 127

Summary 143

References 143

5. Chaincode in Hyperledger Fabric **145**

Demystifying chaincodes 145

Chaincode for developers 146

Deploying and testing the chaincode 159

Chaincode best practices 164

Creating a token using Convector tool 166

Writing unit tests for chaincode 170

Chaincode development using IBM blockchain platform 172

Chaincode for operators 177

Packaging the chaincode 177

Creating the package 178

Package signing by other owners 178

Installing package 178

Instantiating the chaincode 179

Upgrading, starting, and stopping the chaincode 179

System chaincode 180

Summary 181

References 181

6. Fabric SDK: Interaction with Fabric Network **183**

Prerequisites 184

Start Fabric network 184

Install Node.js and NPM 187

Create a Node.js SDK project 187

Install Fabric npm modules 187

Fabric client 187

Fabric CA client 188

gRPC module 188

Process of working with the network.. 188

Enrolment and registration of admin and user using CA server..................... 188

Registration and enrolment of the user 196

Chaincode invoke and query... 202

Invoking createProperty from the chaincode 202

Invoking ChangePropertyOwner from Fabric SDK................................... 219

7. Fabric SDK: Building End-to-End Application with Fabric Network 229

Prerequisite.. 230

Creating the API project 230

Using Fabric SDK for advanced use cases... 277

Creating a channel using Fabric SDK... 277

Joining the channel using SDK.. 279

8. Fabric in Production 283

Fabric deployment using Swarm 283

Integrating solution for monitoring Hyperledger Explorer........................ 290

Step 1: Set up Hyperledger Fabric... 290

Step 2: Set up Hyperledger Explorer. 291

Step 3: Install PostgreSQL. 291

Step 4: Generate the Hyperledger Fabric network.............................. 292

Step 5: Configure Hyperledger Explorer on Fabric............................. 292

Step 6: Build Hyperledger Explorer.. 293

Step 7: Run Hyperledger Explorer. 293

Hyperledger Fabric in Clouds 294

Fabric in AWS... 294

Hyperledger Fabric in Azure Cloud 300

IBM blockchain platform 305

Summary.. 305

CHAPTER 1

Blockchain and Decentralization

After World War II, organizations started leveraging databases for their operations. As the use of databases increased, companies realized there was a need to share this data—both, within an organization as well as across companies all over the globe. The Internet revolutionized the process of sharing data by making it seamless to exchange information. It also opened doors for new possibilities in the world of digitization, like Internet banking, social media, online ticketing, and more.

However, since the inception of the Internet, there has always been a need for real-time, low-cost connectivity and exchange of money (or value) through some form of the Internet of trust.

Trust has always been a missing element within the Internet. *Trust* is what the banks and other financial institutions laid their foundations on. Since people couldn't trust each other with their money, they would go to the banks hoping that the bank would keep their money safe and give it back when requested. This trust shook up during the global meltdown of 2008. As banks began to collapse, people started losing their trust in banks and realized the need for a reliable e-cash system through which two people could exchange value without the need for a central counterparty, to mitigate fraud. Thus, people wanted to exchange money the way they exchange information over the Internet. This hope became a reality in 2008 when a white paper went viral over the Internet. The paper described the working of Bitcoin, which was a protocol that allowed people to exchange value (in the form of cryptocurrency) without the need of any central authority and outside the control of any government or jurisdiction. Since its early days, Bitcoin has always stayed in the grey area, with central authorities debating about its legality and a surge in Bitcoin's use on the dark web.

While this parallel debate was going on regarding the legality of Bitcoin, some financial institutions started looking under the cover. They wanted to understand the technology that was making their existence moot—a technology that enabled people to transfer value, across borders, without the need for central authorities like banks, and with no failures or frauds. Thus, blockchain came to the forefront. Blockchain is the technology that underpins Bitcoin. It is a decentralized distributed transaction database to which you can write new data, but you can never edit or delete it. It is immutable!

In this chapter, we will focus on the following key topics:

- Background of Bitcoin and blockchain
- Working of blockchain and its key concepts
- Operation of wallets and the role played by mining in running a blockchain network
- Building blocks of a blockchain and structure of a block
- Decentralization and distributed systems
- Enterprise blockchain networks
- Difference between public and private blockchain

This would help lay the foundation as we move towards Hyperledger, which is one of the most widely used enterprise blockchain platforms.

Definitions

Let us start by defining certain important terms that would be used repeatedly in this book. These terms are used as common jargon while discussing blockchain and would thus benefit you in understanding the chapters better:

Cryptocurrency

It is defined as any digital or virtual currency leveraging cryptography for security. Many researchers, financial institutions, academics, and others are considering cryptocurrency as the *money of future* or a *twenty-first-century unicorn*. Cryptocurrencies are based on blockchain technology using decentralized systems.

A striking feature of cryptocurrencies is they are neither issued by a government authority nor controlled by any organization. This makes them immune to third-party interventions or manipulations. The first blockchain-based cryptocurrency, conceptualized in 2008, was bitcoin.

Main features of a cryptocurrency are as follows:

- It serves as a digital asset that is used as a medium of exchange.

- It controls supply and secures transactions by use of advanced cryptography. These cryptography techniques are comprised of hash functions and digital signatures.

- It is a subset of alternate currencies.

The underlying technology that enables the exchange of digital coins or assets between individuals is termed as **blockchain**.

Bitcoin

The term *crypto* refers to encryption algorithms and techniques like public key/ private key pairs. These technologies were combined with hash functions to develop the first well-known (and currently most popular) cryptocurrency called **bitcoin** that was launched in 2008–09 by an individual/corporation under the pseudonym "Satoshi Nakamoto." Bitcoin was released as virtual money or token with an intent to disrupt the financial markets and as an alternative to paper-based currency. It leverages a collection of cryptographic concepts and blockchain technology to store and transmit value among users.

Bitcoin's modus operandi is a combination of the following key components:

- Proof-of-Work (PoW) consensus algorithm that serves as a decentralized peer-to-peer network.

- Blockchain technology that is used as a transaction ledger.

- A decentralized and mathematically bound mining and token issuance method.

- A verification method used with the help of transaction scripts.

Blockchain

The best way to define a blockchain is by drawing an analogy between a blockchain and a commuter train. We are all aware of how a train moves to transport people — it is structured in the form of multiple compartments and each compartment is linked to the next. Thus, if one compartment is removed from the middle of a train, the entire train will collapse because of loss of connectivity. A blockchain operates in a similar manner. It consists of blocks (instead of compartments) that are connected in a linear fashion such that each block, apart from carrying its own data, also has a signature (in the form of a hash function) to the previous block. This ties a new block to the previous one. If one of the blocks is removed from the blockchain, the entire chain will collapse because of loss of connectivity, just like in a train.

The first type of blockchain, that is, Blockchain 1.0, comprised of simple ledgers that could only record transactions. This basically refers to the Bitcoin blockchain that was implemented to simply record transactions in an immutable manner. As Bitcoin gained popularity, the industry realized that a blockchain is capable of much more. Thus, Blockchain 2.0 evolved where *smart contracts* were created. **Smart Contract** is a framework that enables users to execute logical code for various programs on a blockchain. Thus, several operations can run on this new technology. This concept came to market with the advent of Ethereum. Now, enterprises are looking at leveraging blockchain and distributed ledger technologies to create enterprise-grade applications. One of the most widely used environments for this is Hyperledger, which we will cover in detail in the later chapters of this book.

Following are some of the commonly used definitions of blockchain:

- A blockchain is a distributed database of records or public ledger of all transactions or digital events that have been executed and shared among participating parties.

- A blockchain is referred to as a peer-to-peer distributed ledger that has a cryptographically calculated algorithm with consensus (like PoW) that makes it immutable.

- A blockchain is defined as a data structure with a linked-list-format connecting blocks of transactions.

How Bitcoin works

Bitcoin allows people to send money (or value in the form of tokens) in a way that is similar to sharing information via an email or text—that is, online! To understand how a transaction takes place within the Bitcoin network, let's consider an example. User A wants to transfer 5 bitcoins to User B. Following are the steps that need to be followed to settle the transaction:

Step 1: User A and User B need to create their wallets. Thus, each user will have their own unique public and private key pair (also called **addresses**).

Step 2: User A (sender) requests the public key/address of User B (receiver) and sends bitcoins (or any other cryptocurrency).

Step 3: The transaction is confirmed and recorded within the blockchain ledger.

These transactions are recorded using a large distributed set of computers over the Internet. This network is neither closed nor under the control of one party. As soon as User A (from the preceding example) initiates the transfer of bitcoins to User B, a transaction message is generated and sent across the blockchain network. The transaction message contains the time, date, participants' unique wallet addresses, and the amount. This message is encrypted using the sender's unique private key known only to the sender. When the new transaction is sent to the network, each node verifies the transaction using a complicated state-of-the-art technology, which is based on mathematics. Each node of the blockchain tests the signature by trying to decrypt it. If successful, they know that the true account owner created the signature. The mathematical principle also ensures that nodes automatically and continuously reach consensus about the current state of the ledger and every transaction in it.

The nodes are distributed all across the globe, and each node contains a copy of the exact same ledger. The maintainers of these nodes are called miners. Thus, when a new message with a valid signature is sent, each miner updates their personal ledger with the transaction information. Since these ledgers are distributed, traffic delays lead to differences in the ledger. Thus, for the world to decide which version of the ledger to use, a kind of voting system is followed. But unlike traditional voting, which involves ballot boxes, blockchain technology relies on mathematical puzzles that each miner has to solve. The first miner to solve the puzzle broadcasts the solution and everybody updates to that solution, making the vote a mathematical race.

The private keys serve like signatures on a cheque book. But instead of relying on handwriting, it relies on mathematics to ensure the integrity of the blockchain. Thus, if someone tries to send an unauthorized transaction, the nodes will not reach consensus, refusing to incorporate the concerned transaction into the blockchain. This way every node of the blockchain contains the entire copy of the ledger right from the genesis block (which is the first block ever mined) to the most recent block. Thus, everyone has access to a shared single source of truth called **blockchain**, which we can trust with the authenticity of all the transactions ever made.

Bitcoin is not similar to traditional banking or payment systems. In the traditional transaction method, a centralized authority keeps track of money, but in the Bitcoin system, there is no issuance authority. Instead, all tracking and settlement are achieved by cryptographic concepts and blockchain technology over a network maintained by the participants themselves.

Wallets

Before using bitcoins, the user needs to install a wallet. A digital wallet is required because bitcoins only exist in a digital, and not physical form.

Following are some types of wallets:

- **Software wallet**: It is a Bitcoin application that can be downloaded on the computer and allows users to control and secure their bitcoins.

- **Web wallet**: Web wallets refer to wallets owned by third-party platforms like exchanges. Web wallets are more convenient than software wallets since they can be accessed from any device by use of your private key or password.

- **Cold wallet**: Cold wallet refers to any wallet that is not connected to the Internet. It can be a piece of paper with your private key on it, or you can have wallets on USB drives, and so on.

- **Hardware wallet**: There are companies who have created hardware devices to store private keys. Every time a user wants to transact, they need to plug the hardware wallet into the computer so the private key gets connected to the Internet, thereby allowing the user to access their bitcoins. When unplugged, the connections breaks, and bitcoins can no longer be transacted.

- **Multi-signature wallets**: In this kind of wallet, one wallet has multiple private keys, and only a combination of those keys can open that wallet. Thus, it serves as an escrow account.

Basics of blockchain

A blockchain serves as a ledger that collects and records transactions validated by the network in elementary units called **blocks**. Once validated by the network's consensus mechanism, these blocks are added to an existing sequential chain of cryptographic hash-linked blocks, to ensure the integrity of the data—thus the name blockchain. Often people get confused between Bitcoin and blockchain and use the terms interchangeably. However, this is a misconception! Bitcoin is a cryptocurrency that uses the blockchain technology to record all valid transactions across the network. Thus, Bitcoin is merely one of the applications of blockchain.

Mining in blockchain

The process of creating a block, validating transactions, and recording the block with transaction details is referred to as mining. These transactions are recorded in a block through hashing, which is a method of converting text (or any data) of any length to a fixed-length value. All the transactions in a blockchain are hashed using the SHA-256 algorithm. SHA-256 always consists of 64 symbols and is 256 bytes in size.

Figure 1.1 shows the word **Hello** with different hash values:

Input	Output
Hello	185F8DB32271FE25F561A6FC938B2E264306EC304EDA518007D1764826381969
Hello	2CF24DBA5FB0A30E26E83B2aC5B9E29E1B161E5C1FA7425E73043362938B9824

Figure 1.1

The purpose of mining is to calculate the hash for every block that is generated. However, the rise in miners increases the computing power required to create an individual block. The maximum time for generating a block within the Bitcoin blockchain is 10 minutes. The level of mining difficulty is automatically calculated and adjusted every 2016 blocks. This has been ingrained within the Bitcoin code.

Each block includes the following fields:

- A random number (hash value), block size, block header, a transaction counter, and transactions that contain information about all transactions confirmed in the block.

- The block header has the following components: version, previous block header hash, Merkle root hash, timestamp, difficulty target, and nonce value.

- Merkle root is the topmost hash in the block of transactions and is calculated using the Merkle tree algorithm, also called a binary hash tree. The steps to compute the same are as follows:

- **Step 1**: Compute hashes for all the transactions in a block.

- **Step 2**: Divide the transactions into pairs, and calculate the hash for every pair.

- **Step 3**: Continue the above step until a single hash code is created, which is called the root.

Figure 1.2 is a Merkle binary hash tree:

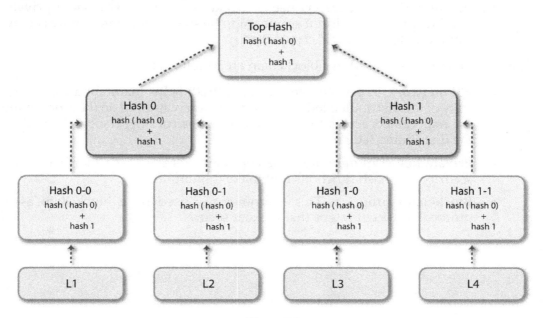

Figure 1.2

Cryptography

All information/data in Bitcoin, Ethereum, and other blockchain platforms is verified by a signature produced using the **Elliptic Curve Digital Signature Algorithm (ECDSA)**. This algorithm uses cryptography as the main asset.

The method of signing and verifying a transaction is executed through cryptography keys. There are two types of keys—a private key that is used for signing a transaction and a public key used to verify it. A private key is randomly generated when a wallet is created. A public key is mathematically derived from the private key using elliptic curve multiplication on a finite field. The private key is meant to be known only to the person who signs the transaction. The public key, on the other hand, is available to anyone who wants to verify the same.

Let's consider an example:

Two people A and B want to transfer some information through the Internet. Each holds a private key/public key pair. The prime use of cryptography is to create a secure digital transaction. Thus, A will send the information to B using B's public key. Upon receiving this encrypted information, B will decrypt the same using her private key. Encryption is the core concept used in cryptography as it renders the message unreadable for others on the network, who lack appropriate permission. Two types of encryptions are **symmetric cryptography** and **asymmetric cryptography**:

- Symmetric cryptography uses one key for both encryption and decryption.
- Asymmetric cryptography needs two keys—a public key and a private key. The private key is not supposed to be shared, making it more secure compared to symmetric cryptography.

The major components used in a blockchain are as follows:

- **P2P network**: A peer-to-peer network (P2P) helps maintain a consistent copy of the distributed ledger. All transactions captured on the blockchain are maintained across the network of nodes running the blocks within the distributed ledger.
- **Private key cryptography**: This component is used by a blockchain for security and hash functions that make it immutable.
- **Blockchain program**: This component is used by a blockchain as a protocol to execute steps that make it secure.

Building blocks of blockchain

Let us understand the concept one by one.

Blocks

If we consider a blockchain to be a ledger or a book, each block would represent a table or a page, respectively, which records a collection of confirmed transactions.

Each block stored in the blockchain is uniquely identified by a hash and is composed of a header and body.

Figure 1.3

The header contains information about its creation like time stamp, Merkle root, nonce, difficulty target, version, and a reference to the previous block. The body is a collection of approved transactions. Once a block is successfully validated (mined), it becomes part of the main chain:

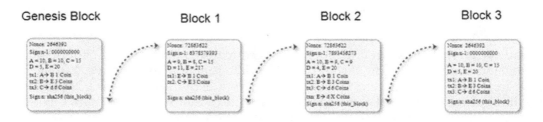

Figure 1.4

Transactions

Transactions are the most fundamental building blocks of the blockchain system. They represent the transfer of value (cryptocurrency) within the blockchain network between two addresses.

Before creating a transaction, the sender signs it using her private key (managed by their wallet) and specifies the destination address. Digital signatures and public keys are used to enable network users to validate the transaction and check whether the sender has the right to spend the bitcoins held by a specific address.

Smart contracts

Smart contracts are one of the most exciting concepts in blockchain technology, representing self-executing scripts stored on the blockchain itself. A smart contract takes the blockchain concept to the next stage, enabling it to translate business logic into inviolable contract terms, which can be autonomously executed without relying on a broker, lawyer, or other intermediaries.

Virtual machine

A virtual machine is a logical element implemented as part of a node application that every participant in the ecosystem runs. In order to understand the concept of virtual machine, let's draw an analogy with our regular computer. When a physical computer runs a computer program, the instructions in the program tell the computer to change its *state*. The change of state is identified by the user either by a dialog box, sound, or other means of transmission. A virtual machine is a representation of a machine (real or imaginary) created by a computer program and operated with instructions embodied in code. It is an abstraction of a machine, held inside a machine. Ethereum is a blockchain ecosystem that, like Bitcoin, implements a virtual machine. The virtual machine lives in the Ethereum node application called a wallet, and unlike Bitcoin, it can understand a wider range of instructions, making it possible to manage the state of digital contracts.

Nodes

A **node** is referred to as a device on the blockchain network, that forms a foundation for the technology, allowing the entire network to function and survive. Nodes are distributed across the network and carry different activities and tasks. Nodes are the individual sections of the larger data structure that is a blockchain. Owners of nodes have the chance to collect the transaction fees and earn rewards for a transaction.

Peer-to-peer network

When compared to centralized systems that are widespread, a peer-to-peer (P2P) network brings in decentralization to the blockchain. Each peer (a *peer* being a computer system on the network) is considered equal and is commonly referred to as a node. A peer makes a portion of computing resources such as disk storage, processing power, or network bandwidth directly available to other participants without the need for any central coordination by servers or stable hosts. The main advantage of using a P2P network is the absence of a central point of access or storage. Thus, there is no authority to take control.

State machine

State machine refers to the set of concepts that are used for designing programs or the logic for programs. There are two types of state machines—a finite state machine and an infinite state machine. A finite state machine comprises a set of states and transitions and can be modeled into a flow diagram, whereas an infinite state machine uses logic to develop a path of the concept with conditions. In a blockchain, finite state machines are used to develop the set of programs and logic to get the required results. State machines have a pre-configured graph structure such as topology, which blockchain technology uses to connect the network.

Consensus

It is used to confirm the transactions and produce new blocks within the network. Miners try to solve the mathematical puzzle by verifying each block. Thus, consensus serves as a receipt for the miners to show that they have added a block successfully.

Structure of blockchain

The structure of a blockchain is very similar to that of linked lists, where every block points to the previous block's header. Thus, a blockchain forms a collection of blocks that are linked to one another and are connected with hash pointers. This makes blockchains tamper-proof.

Any block in a blockchain consists of three parts: header, Merkle, and transaction list. *Figure 1.5* shows an example of the structure of a single block. The structure of all blocks within the same blockchain is similar:

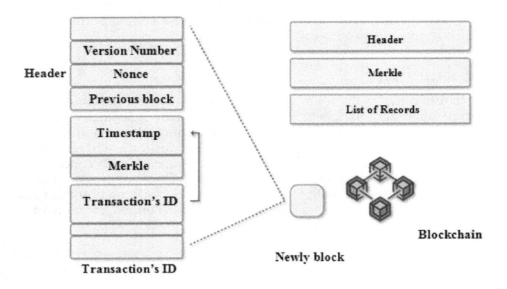

Figure 1.5

Let us understand each of the three elements:

- **Header**: It contains the version information of the block, the nonce, the previous block ID, timestamp, and a hash value.

- **Merkle root**: It is a hash built from the block's transaction identifiers.

- **Transaction list**: It represents the transactions themselves. It's a list of identification hashes of all transactions validated by the block and included in its Merkle tree.

Merkle tree is also known as a binary hash tree. It's a data structure used for summarizing and verifying the integrity of large sets of data. It keeps track of what's happening in the block. It is integrated and cannot be tampered as it contains cryptographic hashes, which are used to make sure that integrity is maintained across the block. It's an upside-down tree where the root is at the top and the leaves are at the bottom. Merkle trees are similar to binary trees.

If any change or tampering occurs in any part of the transaction data, it can be clearly identified in the Merkle tree, and further transactions or hashing will be stopped.

Hence, a Merkle tree is important in the implementation of blockchain technology and forms a major contributor to making sure that blockchain data has not been tampered with. The above information is combined together to create a new block.

This newly created block gets added to the blockchain, thus confirming all the transactions within that block.

Working of Blockchain

Let us consider an example to understand how a blockchain works.

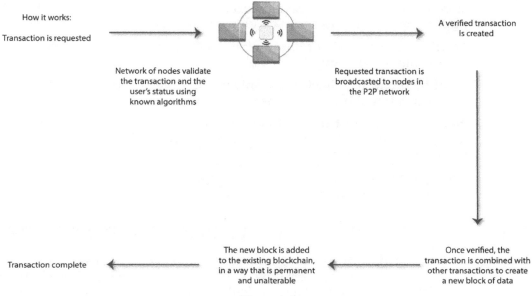

How it works:

Transaction is requested

Network of nodes validate the transaction and the user's status using known algorithms

Requested transaction is broadcasted to nodes in the P2P network

A verified transaction Is created

Once verified, the transaction is combined with other transactions to create a new block of data

The new block is added to the existing blockchain, in a way that is permanent and unalterable

Transaction complete

Figure 1.6

Let's assume that person A wants to send bitcoins to person B. This request is broadcasted to the P2P network, consisting of computers known as nodes, which are spread across the globe. Once the transaction is propagated, the transaction is picked up by the network of nodes. Each node, which picks up the transaction, validates it using an algorithm that is common to all the nodes. Upon validation, the transaction is combined with other validated transactions and placed in a pool called the memory pool. These validated transactions from the memory pool create new blocks of data for the ledger and get added to the existing blockchain. With this block added to the blockchain, the transaction is complete.

The features of the blockchain technology are as follows:

- **Secure**: It is practically impossible for anyone to tamper with transactions or ledger records present in the blockchain, making it secure and reliable.

- **Global reach**: Blockchain operates across borders and has no central authority or government controlling it, making it a globally accepted technology stack.

- **Automated operations**: Private companies are not needed to handle operations, which eliminates the need for mediation to carry out the transactions.

- **Open source**: Blockchain is an open source technology, where all operations are carried out by the community.

- **Distributed**: Blockchain works in a distributed model where records are stored in every node of the network. If one node goes down, it doesn't impact the other nodes as data is globally distributed across all the nodes.

- **Flexible**: Use of basic programming concepts and semantics makes the blockchain technology very flexible.

- **Double spending**: Blockchain prevents double spending, which is the case of sending the same tokens to two parties.

- **Non-repudiation of transactions**: In the blockchain world, one cannot make a transaction and go back on it, unlike the banking world where it's possible to reverse transactions.

- **Anonymity**: Blockchain provides complete anonymity by hiding the identity of users through cryptography.

Fundamentals of secure transaction processing

The most important part of a secure transaction in a blockchain is that all the components of the network are inter-linked with the ledger using a Merkle Tree. In the Merkle Tree, every leaf node has a calculated hash value. This provides data integrity as the network cannot change the hash value that was previously created.

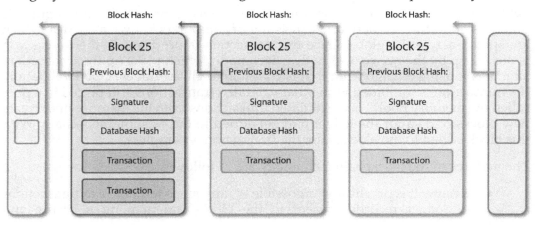

Figure 1.7

All the transactions are cryptographically connected through a Merkle tree. If any block is modified, the entire blockchain network will be notified about the attack. There is no way of changing the Merkle tree root in the blocks' header as the network will be notified about the malicious attack.

Decentralization

Decentralization is a building block for both permissioned and permissionless blockchain networks. Decentralization is not a new concept or idea that came into being with blockchain technology. In fact, it has been used in the development of various software applications. A centralized system or model is most widely used for software applications. This model directly controls the operation of individual units and the flow of information from a singular point. All information has to be sent and received from a central location. It is commonly referred to as a *client-server* model. Decentralization, as the name suggests, has no central authority controlling the network. All nodes are distributed across the network, and each node is responsible for its own activities.

In a distributed model the computation is spread across several nodes and a copy of all the information is stored with every node. However, the decision in a distributed model may still be centralized using complete system knowledge:

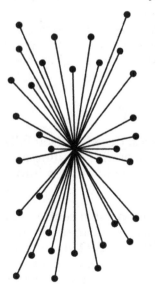 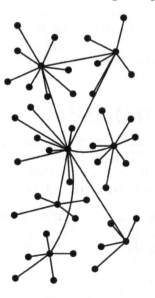 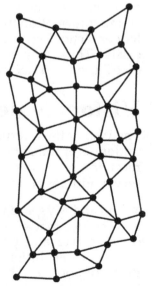

Figure 1.8

The differences between a distributed model and a decentralized model are listed in the following table:

Distributed model	Decentralized model
• Processing is started across multiple nodes but decisions may still be centralized.	• There is no central point of decision-making. All the nodes have equal responsibility in making the decision.
• Responsibilities are shared among multiple nodes.	• Each and every node is responsible for their activities within the network.
• System information is shared among nodes in the network.	• System information is not shared among nodes in the network.

One question that might arise is, can a system have both distributed and decentralized models?

The answer is, yes, a system can have both distributed and decentralized network models. In fact, blockchain technology leverages the same. Blockchain is referred to as *a distributed decentralized ledger*. To make it simple, let's take Bitcoin as an example—it operates in a distributed network model because it has its own time stamp information that is entered in the public ledger. Thus, it uses the distributed ledger technology but is built on a decentralized model where no single authority exists. Thus, any app using blockchain technology will be leveraging both distributed and decentralized models.

History of decentralization

The Web or the Internet, which has been in existence for several decades, itself falls under decentralization. The HTTP protocol connects the network for sending and receiving messages using a trusted server that translates the web address into a server address and is also controlled through centralized servers.

Yahoo and Myspace were the most popular network applications on a centralized server. They made it seamless for individuals or groups to pay for the maintenance of the server and profile of the users that utilize the software. **BitTorrent** was created as a solution to download huge media files within no time, making this protocol popular. The modus operandi was that if there is a file that a user wants to download, the BitTorrent protocol would find the file on various sources so that the user can download it through multiple servers providing faster speed and higher reliability. This was one of the first examples of decentralized systems.

Following are some decentralized applications:

OpenBazaar

OpenBazaar is a decentralized version of eBay. No middle man determines the cost of a product. Instead, the seller decides the price of his product. The only issue is that the seller has to host the store on their own server that needs to be bought. OpenBazaar uses a protocol similar to BitTorrent and leverages bitcoin as a currency for the transaction between sellers and buyers.

Popcorn time

This is another app that works on BitTorrent protocol and helps in streaming videos and TV shows, similar to Netflix. However, it has its own system file that has to be downloaded onto the user's system to watch the videos anytime, anywhere.

Lighthouse

It is a Bitcoin wallet embedded with a series of smart contracts. These smart contracts help in pledging money to certain projects similar to Kickstarter. Once the goal is reached, it becomes possible to retrieve funds out of the project wallet.

Gems

Gems is a social messaging app that is trying to create a business model similar to WhatsApp. Gems is issuing its own currency and letting advertisers pay users directly with it for their data rather than acting as a middle man.

Decentralization using blockchain

Let us consider a simple example where one user wants to transfer funds to another user. Typically, the user would transfer the funds from her bank account to the recipient's account. This kind of transaction is governed and controlled by centralized servers, and a transaction fee is charged by the bank. Thus, the bank plays the role of an *intermediary*. Using blockchain technology, funds can be transferred without the need for intermediaries. This is termed as **disintermediation**. Elimination of intermediaries is the core concept of decentralization used in blockchain technology.

Now let's understand how this decentralization works in a blockchain:

- In decentralization, storage of information is across the network, thus eliminating the risk arising from central storage or central point of failure.

- The system uses a cryptographic technique where a public key is used for authentication and is available to all and the usage of the key depends on mathematical processes.

- Ad-hoc message passing and distributed networking are used.
- Every node in the network duplicates the blocks of the blockchain. Data equality is maintained by data replication, which means no official copy exists. Every user is treated equally and has the same copy of the data. Using software, the transactions are broadcasted into the network.

The three main features of **decentralization application (Dapps)** are as follows:

- Not owned by anyone
- No downtime
- Cannot be shut down

Decentralized ecosystem

In order to achieve successful decentralization, the environment around a blockchain should be decentralized.

Storage

In a blockchain, data is stored in blocks distributed across the network. However, this storage is restricted to a small amount of data like transaction hashes. Large data files cannot be stored in a similar fashion.

Thus, an alternate method to store the information is using the distributed hash tables, which leverages file sharing within a peer-to-peer system. Two key factors that would make storage possible include availability and stability—data should be available for retrieval when required and network link should be accessible. **Interplanetary file system (IPFS)** possesses both these properties. It replaces the HTTP protocol by using the Merkle **directed acyclic graph (DAG)** for storage and search.

Communication

In a decentralized system, seamless communication is required to enable the network and nodes to send and receive messages without any failure or miscommunication. Thus, a decentralized method is created for every user without a central hub for communication. Thus, there is no authority to shut down the system and take control.

Computation

Decentralization is achieved through computation by using cryptographic methods such as hashing.

Figure 1.9 explains the ecosystem for decentralization:

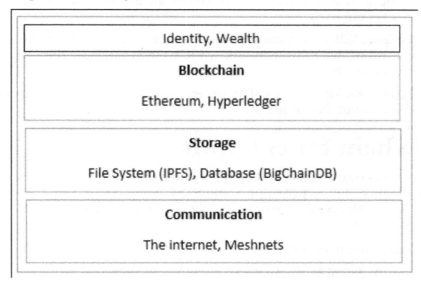

Figure 1.9

A decentralized autonomous organization (DAO) is the most complex form of a smart contract that aims at decentralizing a company's bylaws by embedding it into the smart contract code. Historically, the Bitcoin blockchain network was considered the first autonomous corporation. It was coordinated using a distributed consensus protocol and could be adopted by anybody. Eventually, DAOs have evolved their technology stack to become completely virtualized. Thus, DAO is a smart contract executed on top of a distributed network that uses consensus technology. It can also be seen as a business or an organization whose decisions are made electronically by written computer code or through the vote of organization members.

The requirements of a decentralized application are as follows:

- The Dapps should be written as an open source program and be autonomously controlled and executed through tokens. All the changes must be transparent and based on consensus.

- Data and records of the organization and its operations must be secured by cryptography and stored in a public ledger.

- If a token is generated by the decentralized application, it must follow cryptographic standards. These tokens are usually provided as miner fees.

The disadvantages of decentralization are as follows:

- **Miners**: A 51% attack is considered an inherent setback for a public blockchain.

- **Eclipse**: Eclipse is a network-level attack on a blockchain. Attackers take control of the entire network while trying to tamper the node from the blockchain network.

- **Money-making scams**: The decentralized public blockchain has given rise to a number of scams.

Blockchain for enterprise

Blockchain technology has been gaining significant traction within the corporate world. A number of enterprise applications are being researched and developed. Enterprises are interested in leveraging the following capabilities of blockchain technology:

- Reduction in cost and time for transactions

- Improvement in product and system security

- Prevention of fraud/counterfeiting

- Increased transparency

- New revenue streams

Enterprise blockchain platforms

As we have seen, cryptocurrency is just one application that runs on blockchain technology. However, the technology is capable of offering much more. The true potential of this technology is being researched and tested across various industries by developing solutions and running operations on the same. Following are some of the other blockchain-/DLT-based platforms:

Ethereum: Ethereum has been around since 2014 and has played a major role in understanding the paradigm of decentralized applications. It has robust smart contracting functions and a flexible architecture. Ethereum is being used for various cross-industry projects and business applications. It is a permissionless (or public) platform that was developed with a vision to create advanced applications using blockchain technology. The consensus algorithm used in Ethereum is **PoW**, with a possibility of changing into **Proof-of-Stake** in the future.

Hyperledger Fabric: Hyperledger was founded by Linux Foundation and was launched in 2017. It is an open source platform for cross-industry enterprise solutions. Hyperledger has over 185 collaborations with organizations across the globe. The main contributor to Hyperledger Fabric was IBM.

R3 Corda: Corda is a new platform developed primarily for banking and financial services industry, launched in 2015. R3 is a consortium of some of the world's biggest enterprises that came together to create an open source distributed ledger platform called **Corda**. Corda does not require any token or cryptocurrency for its process and transactions. It is a permissioned blockchain that restricts access to data to only the network participants.

Ripple: Ripple is an enterprise blockchain solution for global payment systems. The primary objective of Ripple is to connect banks for seamless payment processing.

Quorum: Quorum is developed by one of the world's leading investment and financial companies, JPMorgan, who forked the Ethereum blockchain code to develop Quorum. Instead of using the PoW consensus algorithm, it uses a vote-based algorithm that enables it to process hundreds of transactions per second, depending upon how the smart contract and network are configured.

The following table provides a comparison of different enterprise blockchain systems:

Name	Type	Throughput
	Enterprise blockchains	
Hyperledger Fabric	Permissioned DLT	3.5k – 110k tx/s
Quorum	Modified Ethereum blockchain	25 – 200 tx/s
R3 Corda	DLT	15 – 1700 tx/s
	Public blockchains	
Bitcoin	Bitcoin blockchain	7 – 10 tx/s
Ethereum	Ethereum blockchain	15 – 20 tx/s
Stellar	Stellar blockchain	1000 – 2000 tx/s

As we can see in the preceding table, enterprise blockchains typically have much higher throughput, lower latency, and often less complex consensus protocols than standard public blockchains like Bitcoin or Ethereum. Some of the key features of enterprise blockchain platforms include the following:

- A distributed ledger
- A consensus mechanism
- Smart contracts
- Identity management

- Permissioning
- Access control
- Tokens/cryptocurrency (in some cases)

Considerations for using blockchain

Many businesses and organizations have started using blockchain technology for their operations. It is not necessarily important to implement this technology in every business. In a recent survey, it has been proved that many businesses utilize it without understanding the underlying concept. A number of organizations have started releasing their own crypto tokens using ICOs in which 80% of the ICOs researched turned out to be scams.

Following are some considerations one should keep in mind before implementing blockchain technology into their business:

- **Transparency**: A striking feature of blockchain technology is transparency, which makes it open to scrutiny. Anyone permissioned to use the network can view the transaction history. Participants can view the information but cannot modify/delete the same. Thus, businesses interested in making a transparent statement for the entire network can consider blockchain technology.

- **Efficiency**: Blockchain technology's immutability avoids the need for manual verification, thereby improving operational efficiency.

- **Integrity**: Entire network is integrated through consensus, with every portion of the blockchain network programmed under certain conditions. Thus, no one can change the conditions or operate independently, thereby enhancing integrity.

- **Security**: Advanced cryptography concepts ensure complete security. Thus, companies seeking to keep their transaction data secure can leverage blockchain technology.

- **Disintermediation**: If an organization needs the data to be distributed, then blockchain technology is an appropriate choice because blockchains are completely disintermediated and distributed, unlike central databases where a central authority controls everything.

- **Robustness**: Blockchain technology's robustness is primarily attributed to its distributed nature, thus avoiding a single point of failure.

Distributed systems

A distributed system is defined as two or more systems or nodes that are connected to work together in a coordinated fashion in order to achieve a common result. The node/system can be defined as a separate or individual entity connected such that each node is able to send and receive messages.

Each node has its own core memory or processing unit. These nodes can become fault tolerant, thereby behaving in a random manner, which also results in a Byzantine node or system.

These types of nodes can become malicious, causing the entire network to display faulty behavior. The main challenge in a distributed system is to ensure all the nodes coordinate and avoid fault tolerance. However, it is difficult to overcome this as distributed systems require consistency, availability, and partition tolerance simultaneously.

Blockchain technology has been able to cater to these three important requirements simultaneously by using a method referred to as the Byzantine generals problem. To understand this problem, first, let's understand the major requirements that have been achieved.

Fault tolerance is the challenging part, as the node may crash unexpectedly, which may lead the entire network to behave in a random fashion, or the full node will be rendered inactive.

Byzantine Generals problem

In order to create a secure transaction system using consensus protocol, the system should be fault tolerant. Now we will take a brief look at the Byzantine generals problem.

Two generals problem: This problem states that there are two generals in an army base station: General 1 and General 2. General 1 is the leader, and General 2 is the follower. The situation under consideration is that both generals are camped at different places and there is an enemy base station between the two.

Now, General 1 sends a messenger with a message to General 2 with a plan of attack.

But there are chances that the messenger, before reaching General 2, may get trapped and killed by the enemies.

Even if the messenger reaches General 2, an acknowledgment message has to be sent via the messenger to General 1 confirming the receipt of the attack plan.

This brings inconsistency to the network. To avoid this, the Byzantine Generals solution is proposed.

Types of blockchains

There are two broad categories of blockchains:

1. **Public blockchain**: A public blockchain encapsulates platforms like Bitcoin and Ethereum where anyone can join the network, anyone can transact on the network, and everyone has the same set of data on the network. There is no permission required. Every party on the network is treated alike and has the same copy of the ledger.

2. **Private blockchain**: A private blockchain, as the name suggests, comprises certain parties who are nominated to join a particular blockchain network and all transactions as well as data will only be restricted to these parties. The rest of the chapters in this book will cover Hyperledger, which operates on the concept of private blockchain.

The following table shows the differences between public and private blockchains:

Characteristic	Public	Private
Data Access	Anyone can access the data as all data is public.	Only certain restricted parties that are part of the network have the right to access the data.
Performance	It is slower than private blockchains.	It is faster than public blockchains but slower than central databases.
Security	It is fully reliant on consensus algorithms for data security.	In addition to consensus, the presence of pre-approved entities as nodes adds an additional security layer.
Anonymity	Participants have pseudonymous or are completely anonymous.	Participants are known.

Summary

With all the cryptocurrency buzzwords flying around, it is hard to get to the core of the technology. The essential piece that serves as the underlying mechanism of all these technologies is blockchain technology, which is a decentralized, trustless, distributed ledger popularized by Bitcoin. In the first chapter, we covered the fundamentals of blockchain technology, including its core layers and various types of blockchains used in the market. We also developed a strong grasp of some of the core concepts of blockchain technology by understanding how it works and reviewed certain key vocabulary and concepts commonly used when discussing the technology. In the next chapter, we will move onto Hyperledger, which is the most widely used network to deploy decentralized applications for enterprises.

Chapter 2

Introduction to Hyperledger and Composer

When moving from Ethereum to Hyperledger, the first question you might ask is, why was something like Hyperledger created in the first place?

In order to understand the vision behind creating Hyperledger, it's important to understand a key drawback of Ethereum that made it unusable for enterprise-level applications. Let's assume that an Ethereum network comprises of four nodes—**Node 1**, **Node 2**, **Node 3**, and **Node 4**. When a smart contract is deployed on the network, it gets propagated to all the four nodes. Thus, a distributed system is formed. In the example, let's assume that a transaction takes place; we will refer to the transaction as Tx1, initiated by **Node 1**. Even though Tx1 is initiated by **Node 1**, owing to the distributed nature of the Ethereum public blockchain, Tx1 is propagated to all the other nodes on the network:

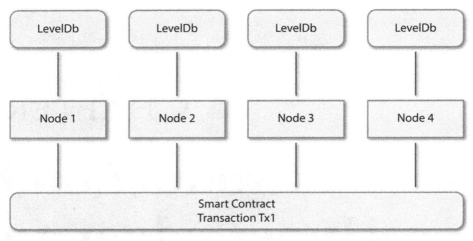

Ethereum Blockchain

Figure 2.1: Ethereum Blockchain

Though the transactions are encrypted and their identities are hidden, every node at least knows that a certain transaction has taken place. Thus, all the other nodes can reverse engineer the transaction (not the exact details but at least the basic information) to estimate the transaction details, thereby being able to conclude what the transaction is trying to achieve. This kind of system worked well in the world of cryptocurrencies like Bitcoin and Ethereum, which operate on public blockchains that need transparency.

However, in the banking world, this concept cannot work. Banks (and institutional organizations) require privacy. If a person has been banking with a certain institution for long, it is possible that the bank might offer better credit card fees or interest rates on loans, especially compared to another person who has no past working relationship with the bank. These scenarios are platitude within the banking world. Thus, complete transparency would cause issues for the banks as they would not prefer information like this being public.

Moreover, there is also an issue pertaining to competitors. All banks are basically competing with each other in order to create a better market for themselves. Thus, they prefer keeping their transaction details, strategies, and policies confidential to ensure that other banks do not leverage their competitive advantages. This kind of a confidential and private system is not possible on public blockchains like Ethereum. Thus, Ethereum was unsuited for enterprise applications.

This is where the Hyperledger project entered. Hyperledger was all about promoting the use of blockchain technology within enterprises.

Hyperledger is governed by the Linux Foundation, which is known for its open source projects. A number of companies had submitted their platform code to

Linux Foundation, and the foundation then invited other industry experts and organizations to join, develop, and test these platforms together by creating consortiums.

Hyperledger itself is not a blockchain platform. It has various platforms and projects under its umbrella.

The vision of Hyperledger was to promote the use of blockchain technology within enterprises. One of the most widely used project under Hyperledger is called Fabric, which we will discuss in later chapters of this book.

In this chapter, we will focus on the following key topics:

- Blockchain for business
- Advantages of Hyperledger Fabric
- Problems with existing blockchain
- Architecture and consensus in Fabric
- Hyperledger tools
- Composer Playground

Objective: This chapter would help the reader understand the purpose behind creation of Hyperledger, along with some of the key components of Hyperledger. The reader will get a grasp of Composer Playground, a tool commonly used for quick deployments of business networks.

Blockchain for business

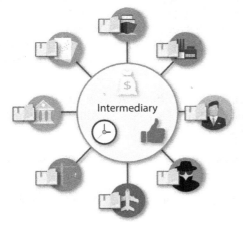

Traditional Business Network   Blockchain Business Network

Figure 2.2

Figure 2.2 shows a traditional business network that comprises a huge number of intermediaries. These intermediaries exist in every business. For example, in the process of stock trading, we have depositories, traders, transfer agents, and more. These kinds of intermediaries delay the process, add to the cost, and create bottlenecks. Blockchain technology provides a way to overcome dependency on these intermediaries. It is providing a way to write these processes in the form of smart contracts that can be executed on a distributed platform. Hyperledger is one such platform that can be permissioned to ensure privacy and security.

The other issue with traditional business networks is that each maintains its own record and they need to continuously reconcile the same to ensure that both parties have made corresponding updates to their individual records to reflect all activities.

However, in blockchain technology, parties maintain one ledger with a copy of the same available to all. Thus, all organizations in a blockchain business network have the exact same copy, thereby overcoming the need for reconciliation. Moreover, its distributed nature makes the copy immutable.

A few advantages of blockchain business networks are as follows:

1. It is highly efficient owing to the elimination of intermediaries, thus overcoming any bottlenecks.

2. It allows for the codification of business transactions. Since ages, business is conducted either by word of mouth or through legal agreements that are usually paper-based and are signed by all counter-parties. However, in the blockchain world, smart contracts are created that can execute their instructions autonomously. As such, legal agreements could become moot if the conditions are executed automatically without third-party intervention. Of course, legal aspects are an entirely different topic, and beyond the scope of this book. Moreover, currently, there is no precedence of using smart contracts to settle a legal dispute. But it certainly automates the process and eliminates most of the manual labor required in traditional business networks.

3. It also eliminates the need for trusting each other because all terms are on smart contracts operating on a blockchain network, which serves as a transparent and immutable system.

Thus, a blockchain-based business network comprises the following four concepts:

1. **Shared ledger**: Blockchain network creates a shared ledger between different parties.

2. **Smart contracts**: They help in automated execution of the terms and conditions.

3. **Privacy**: The network can have additional privacy by use of permissioned blockchains that keep the data secure from the outside community.

4. **Consensus**: It forms the basis for approving or rejecting a transaction.

Hyperledger was created with the aim of promoting enterprise use of blockchain technology. Following are some of the goals of Hyperledger:

1. It's primarily targeted towards enterprise applications.

2. The idea is to create a community around it and utilize the community to build different blockchain applications.

3. Through collaboration, the community can even test out different **Proof-of-Concepts** (**POCs**) and use cases on the various blockchain platform.

4. The goal is also to educate people about blockchain technology and its potential.

Advantages of Hyperledger Fabric

1. **Rich queries**: One can run these queries to find the transactions that have been executed on the blockchain platform.

2. **Modular architecture**: Modular means that various modules can be used either together or on-need basis. Thus, it is different from Ethereum where you have to utilize the entire blockchain. In Hyperledger, you can use a module that you require.

3. **Protection of digital keys and sensitive data**: Hyperledger works on the same distributed ledger concept and keeps your digital keys and data secure from tampering.

4. **Permissioned data**: A party can view/use the data only if it is permissioned to do so. Unlike Ethereum and Bitcoin blockchain, everyone cannot see all the data. This is essential for enterprise applications.

5. **Performance and scalability**: Hyperledger is better than many other public blockchain networks when it comes to performance and scalability, as its target audience is enterprises who have stringent performance requirements. Moreover, it is undergoing further improvements in order to make it more efficient and scalable.

Problems with existing blockchain technology

1. **Slow transactions**: Ethereum and Bitcoin blockchain transactions are slow.

2. **Anonymity**: In public blockchains, you have no clue who the other miners are (or network participants). Hyperledger resolves this issue with the concept of a private permissioned network where a set of members can join a particular instance of the network following due diligence through

membership services. We will learn more about membership services in later modules.

3. **Cryptocurrency**: Public blockchains like Ethereum and Bitcoin rely heavily on their native cryptocurrencies. Since enterprises are not interested in the concept of cryptocurrencies, public chains do not meet their requirements. However, Hyperledger does not need any kind of cryptocurrency for its operation, thereby, making it a go-to platform for institutional clients.

4. **Lack of privacy**: Public blockchains lack privacy when it comes to transactions. All transactions can be seen by everyone because of the transparent nature of the blockchain. However, Hyperledger prevents this from happening. In the coming modules, we will see how Hyperledger Fabric ensures the privacy of transactions among limited participants.

Hyperledger Fabric architecture

Following are the layers in the architecture of Hyperledger:

1. The first one comprises APIs and SDKs that are used to integrate the Hyperledger blockchain with user applications.

2. The next block is the membership services. Hyperledger provides the concept of membership services to ensure that only certain permissioned parties can transact on a business network and access its data. Every member needs to register with the membership services of the corresponding business network to participate in the same. Every new business network that is set up on Hyperledger would have its own business network.

3. The blockchain and transactions block is collectively called the blockchain services, and it handles all the B2B protocol, distributed ledger, and the consensus algorithm.

4. The chaincode in Hyperledger is analogous to the smart contract in Ethereum. The chaincode comprises the business logic and programming that determine how the participants will interact with each other.

5. Lastly, it has Hyperledger services that are basically different projects in Hyperledger like Cello, Explorer, and so on.

This is a brief overview of the Hyperledger architecture. In the coming modules, we will discuss each of these in further detail.

Consensus in Hyperledger

Consensus on a blockchain determines how to come to a certain conclusion or decide whether a transaction is valid or no. In Hyperledger, it is determined by the action of two nodes:

1. Ordering node
2. Validating node

The concept of the orderer is unique to Hyperledger. Let's understand this concept with an example.

Let's say there is a company X that is using blockchain technology for its internal purposes. X has three departments: QA, engineering, and production department. Thus, X has three validating peers: QA peer, engineering peer, and production peer. Each of them forms a node of the blockchain business network used by X. In addition to these, it also has an ordering node.

Each of these three teams will mandatorily run a node for themselves, and each member of their team has to get their identity by registering with the membership services. Only then will they be allowed to use the concerned node. Each of these nodes has different permissions.

Now, let's assume that the company X is using a smart contract that is running on this blockchain shared by the three departments. The smart contract is available on the entire network, and each node has a copy of the same. We will assume the contents of this smart contract to be an equation: $A = A + 1$.

Let's assume that the first transaction for this specific chain code is initiated by the QA node. QA node will generate a read-write pair for this transaction, which is $A=0/A=1$. A similar pair is generated by all the other nodes in the network, except the orderer.

Once the transaction has propagated to all the nodes and each of them has done their computation to generate a read-write pair, each node will send their value to the orderer. The orderer will review the values to reach a consensus, and accordingly, it will send the final result to all the peers so they can commit it to their database. Thus, a consensus is achieved on the platform.

Hyperledger tools

Hyperledger Explorer

Just like Ethereum uses an explorer (https://etherscan.io/), Hyperledger Explorer is used to explore important metadata like block details, network details, transaction metadata, and more. This data is useful for analyzing the network and various ledgers.

It is hosted on (https://github.com/hyperledger/blockchain-explorer) GitHub and can be configured to work with different blockchain platforms like Hyperledger Fabric, Sawtooth, and so on.

It is also very useful in understanding the metrics used in a blockchain network.

Hyperledger Cello

From administrative viewpoint, it becomes increasingly difficult to manage multiple parallel-running blockchain platforms and their lifecycles. Therefore, Linux Foundation created Hyperledger Cello to provide blockchain as a service to make it easy to deploy, manage, and terminate the blockchains. This is a great tool to handle multiple blockchain platforms.

It was contributed by IBM and is hosted in GitHub at https://github.com/hyperledger/cello.

This currently supports Hyperledger Fabric.

Hyperledger Composer

Developing and managing the chaincode and business logic natively, with previous and initial versions of Hyperledger Fabric, was difficult and complex. Composer was introduced to reduce the complexities around the development of a business network for Hyperledger Fabric.

A number of tools and modules for node.js were introduced as part of this to develop end-to-end applications over Hyperledger Fabric. Composer was widely used to develop business networks.

It is hosted at https://github.com/hyperledger/composer and the documentation is hosted at https://github.com/hyperledger/composer.

This also provides the user interface to develop business models and network in the web browser itself (https://composer-playground.mybluemix.net/).

Hyperledger Caliper

There are some important performance indicators for any blockchain platforms. It is necessary to have a tool to measure the performance of the blockchain through these indicators. Hyperledger Caliper was created to measure the performance using indicators like transaction per second, latency, utilization of resources, and more. We can specify a number of parameters against which the platform will be tested.

It is hosted at https://github.com/hyperledger/caliper/.

Hyperledger Quilt

There are multiple blockchain platforms storing value and assets. It is essential to make these platforms interoperable such that transfer of value can take place between them, e.g., payments between Ethereum and Bitcoin blockchain. Thus, Quilt was developed to implement interoperability. It is hosted at https://github.com/hyperledger/quilt.

Hyperledger URSA

Cryptography is a prime component of blockchain technology. However, there seems to be no common repo to host all the common crypto-related resources and libraries to be used by different blockchain platforms, thus making it standard and secure. Cryptography required for common operations like signing the transactions, hashing, **zero-knowledge proof** (**ZKP**), and so on is intended to be stored and developed here at https://github.com/hyperledger/ursa.

Hyperledger Composer

Hyperledger Composer is an open source framework used for developing and testing blockchain-based decentralized applications in an easier and faster manner. By using Hyperledger Composer, we can create and execute applications on Hyperledger in just a few days as opposed to weeks or even months. Composer helps us model the business network. It leverages the Hyperledger Fabric blockchain infrastructure. The pluggable consensus protocol in Fabric ensures that users are identifiable throughout the network, making the transactions valid. Thus, Composer is a tool that can be leveraged for quick development and deployment of Fabric-based blockchain networks.

Following are a couple of advantages of Composer:

1. It increases understanding of blockchain business networks and Hyperledger. Those interested in learning more about blockchain business networks with a limited amount of coding can utilize this platform and leverage it to understand how these networks operate.

2. It saves time as it allows for rapid development and deployment of business networks.

Let's dive into the architecture of Hyperledger Composer.

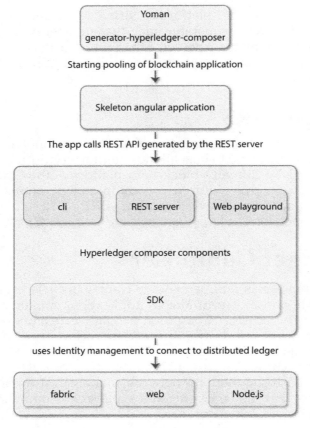

Figure 2.3

Hyperledger components

Following is a list of the components that make up Hyperledger Composer:

- Execution runtimes (Fabric, web, Node.js)
- Connection profile
- JavaScript SDK
- Command line interface (CLI)
- REST server
- LoopBack connector
- Playground web user interface
- Yeoman code generator

- VSCode and Atom editor plugins

Let's learn about these components in a little more detail:

Execution runtime: Composer supports multiple pluggable components:

- Hyperledger Fabric, for storing the ledger in a distributed fashion
- The web, used by Playground and States, stored in the browser's local storage
- Node.js, used for implementing business logic and testing. States are stored as an in-memory key-value store.

Connection profile: Connection profile in Hyperledger Composer specifies connection with execution runtime. Various configuration options are used for different types of execution runtime. For example, Hyperledger Fabric requires cryptographic certificate, IP address (host address), and port to connect with a peer.

Javascript SDK: Fabric has a number of APIs that enable developers to create and manage the application as well as interact with the blockchain network. These APIs are split into two sub-divisions. These are NPM modules as listed below:

- **Composer-client**: It helps submit a transaction to the network. It also helps in querying and running operations like READ, CREATE, UPDATE, and DELETE on assets and participants (peers).
- **Composer-admin**: This division or module manages the blockchain network and can perform operations like INSTALL, START, and UPGRADE.

Command line interface: It enables developers and admins to deploy and manage business networks.

REST server: REST server creates an open API (Swagger) for business networks by default. REST server changes the composer model for a blockchain network into an open-API definition, and it implements CREATE, READ, UPDATE, and DELETE operations for assets and participants at runtime. This operation allows the transaction to be submitted for further business logic processing or retrieval.

LoopBack connector: The LoopBack connector is used by Hyperledger Composer's REST server for customizing REST-API. This supports the LoopBack framework natively.

Playground web user interface: It's a web-based user interface used to define and test business networks. With its use, business analysts can quickly import samples and prototype business logic that executes on the web Hyperledger Fabric at runtime.

Yeoman code generator: It's an open source framework for generating skeleton projects:

- Angular web application
- Node.js application
- Skeleton business network

Hyperledger application using Composer

In this section, we will create and run Angular 2 application that interacts with the blockchain network. We will be executing a transaction in Hyperledger Fabric blockchain network.

We would initially need to install the prerequisite that is essential to run a Composer-based application, which includes the following:

- Ubuntu 14.04 or higher with (4 GB RAM)
- Docker-engine
- Docker-compose
- Node.js v8.0 or higher (< v9.0 or less is required)
- NPM v5.x
- Git
- Python: 2.7.x
- A code editor (VScode or atom)

The instructions to install Composer on Linux OS are as follows:

- Initiate install as a normal user—don't be a sudo user or root user.
- Use CURL while installing pre-requisite and unzip it using sudo.
- Avoid using npm with sudo or su to root to use it.
- Avoid installing node globally as root.

Use the following commands to download the pre-requisite on Ubuntu:

```
curl -O https://hyperledger.github.io/composer/latest/prereqs-ubuntu.sh
chmod u+x prereqs-ubuntu.sh
```

Now, run the following script:

```
./prereqs-ubuntu.sh
```

Install other pre-requisites as well, which have been previously mentioned.

Now let's start the process of creating the application.

Step 1: Create a business network structure

Business network definition (BND) is the key concept in a Hyperledger Fabric network. BND defines the data model for the application, access control rules of the blockchain, and transaction logic. We have to create a project structure on the disk to generate BND. This can be done by using the Yeoman generator for generating a skeleton business network. This skeleton includes components of the business network.

- Yeoman is a popular tool for generating business networks. The following command will ask for a business network name, description, author of the project, email address of the author, license, and namespace:

```
yo hyperledger-composer:businessnetwork
```

- Enter "testNetwork" for network name and other information like description, author email, and author name.
- Choose Apache-2.0 as License.
- Select org.example.myNetwork.
- Select No if asked to generate an empty network.

Step 2: Define a business network

A business network contains assets, participants, transactions, access control rules, and events and queries (optional). A standard business network, created in the previous step, contains a model (.cto) file that comprises the class definitions for participants, assets, and transactions happening within the business network. The boilerplate business network includes an access control (permissions.acl) document with basic access control rules, script (logic.js) file containing transaction processing functions, and a package.json file containing the metadata pertaining to the business network.

Modeling assets, participants, and transactions

Model (.cto) file is a primary file required to update the document. This file is written with the help of Hyperledger Composer modeling language. Model file has the definition for each class of asset, transaction participant, and event.

Open the org.example.myNetwork.cto model file.

Replace the content in the file as follows:

```
namespace org.example.myNetwork
asset Car identified by manufacturer {
    String carType
        String description
```

```
    String price
    String color
Seller owner
    }
        Participant Seller identified by sellerId {
    String sellerId
        String sellerName
    }
    Transaction Sell {
          Car car
              Seller newSeller

                                                                          }
```

Save the changes.

JavaScript transaction logic:

Go to the model file where a trade transaction was defined and provide a relationship between asset and participant. Transaction process function file has the JavaScript logic that executes transactions specified in the model file.

The trade transaction receives an identifier of the manufacturer asset that is being traded, and the identifier of the trader participant is set as newSeller.

Open the logic.js file and replace the code with the following:

```
            async function tradeCar(trade){
                  trade.car.owner = trade.newSeller
                  let assetRegistration = await
getAssetRegistry(org.example.myNetwork.manufacturer)
          }
```

Save this logic.js file.

Add access control list:

Open permission.acl and replace the rules defined as follows:

```
 rule Default {
                                description: "Allow all participants access
to all resources"
participants: "Any"
operation:  All
```

```
resource: "org.example.mynetwork.*"
action: ALLOW
            }
            rule SystemACL {
                                description: "System ACL to
permit all access"
                                participant: "ANY"
                                operation: ALL
                                resource: "org.hyperledger.
composer.system.**"
                                action: ALLOW
            }
```

Save the changes to permission.acl file.

Step 3: Generate the business network

The preceding files must be defined and packaged into a deployable business network archive (.bna) file. In order to do so, follow the below steps:

Using command line navigate to testNetwork (tutorial-network) directory.

Run the CMD, mentioned as follows, from the testNetwork (tutorial-network) folder:

```
composer archive create -t dir -n .
```

Output of the preceding command will be an archive file called testNetwork@0.0.1.bna or tutorial-network@0.0.1, which has been created in the current directory.

Step 4: Deploy the business network

Once the business network is ready (as shown in *Step 3*), you can deploy the same on an instance of Hyperledger Fabric. Information from the Fabric administrator is needed for creating PeerAdmin identity with privileges to install chaincode on the peer and start chaincode on composerchannel. While setting up development environment installation, PeerAdmin identity gets created. Upon completion of the business network installation, the network can be started. After deployment, a new identity is created, referred to as network admin.

Getting correct credential:

Deploying the business network to Hyperledger Fabric requires a composer business network to be installed on the peer. Then, the business network can be started, and with a new participant, identity and associated card should be imported. Testing of the network can be done by pinging and checking the response:

1. Install business network from the testNetwork (tutorial-network) directory and run the following command:

```
composer network install --card PeerAdmin@hlfv1 --archiveFile tutorial-
network@0.0.1.bna
```

Composer network install command needs PeerAdmin business network card. In our use case, it is already imported and the file path of .bna is defined as a business network.

2. Start the business network with the following command:

```
composer network start --networkName tutorial-network --networkVersion
0.0.1 --networkAdmin admin --networkAdminEnrollSecret adminpw --card
PeerAdmin@hlfv1 --file networkadmin.card
```

The Composer network start command needs the following:

- A business network card
- Name of the admin identity for business network
- Name and version of the business network
- Name of the file to be created, ready to be imported as a business network card

3. Import network administrator identity as a usable business network card:

```
composer card import --file networkadmin.card
```

4. To check that the business network is deployed successfully, run the following command to ping the network:

```
composer network ping --card admin@tutorial-network
```

It requires the business network card to identify the network to ping.

Step 5: Create a REST server

Navigate to testNetwork (tutorial-network) directory and run the following command:

```
composer-rest-server
```

- Give admin@testNetwork or admin@tutorial-network as card name.
- Select Never use namespaces when it asks if you would like to use namespaces in generated API.
- Select No to secure the generated APIs.
- Select Yes to enable event publication.

- Select No to enable TLS security.

Step 6: Generate a boilerplate angular application

Navigate to tutorial-network or testNetwork directory and run the following command:

```
yo hyperledger-composer:angular
```

- Connect to a running business network by selecting YES.
- Enter package.json description like (project name, description, author name) and other parameters.
- For business network card, enter admin@testNetwork.
- Then choose Connect to an existing REST API.
- Enter REST API server address as http://localhost and use port 3000 (or any other).
- Select Namespaces are not used.

To run the angular application, go to the angular project directory and run npm start.

Our rest API is running at http://localhost:4200.

Thus, we have successfully set up a Composer-based application and network from scratch.

Taking this forward, let's look into the Composer query language and REST-API.

Composer query language

It is used for invoking transactions for operations like updating or removing assets on result sets. These queries are located in a query file (.qry) in the root directory or parent directory of the business network. These queries have a WHERE clause that gives the criteria that can be used to choose assets and/or participants.

Following steps depict the process for the same.

Step 1: Update the business network

We need to evolve/change/modify the created business network. There are two events and an additional transaction in the updated business network.

Update the model file:

To have an event and a new transaction, update the model file.

- Open model (.cto) file for testNetwork or tutorial-network.

- Add the event and transaction mentioned in the following code:

```
event TradeNotification {
    Car car
}

transaction RemovePriceCar{

}

event RemoveNotification{

    Car car

}
```

- Save the changes in your model

Update transaction logic for queries and events:

After updating the model file, we can write additional business logic that runs when a transaction is submitted for process. Here, we shall add events and queries to the business logic:

- Open transaction processor function file lib/logic.js.

- Replace the transaction logic with the following code snippet:

```
async function tradeCar(trade) {
    trade.car.owner = trade.newSeller;
    let assetRegistry = await getAssetRegistry('org.example.mynetwork.
Car');


    // emit a notification that a trade has occurred
    let tradeNotification = getFactory().newEvent('org.example.
mynetwork', 'TradeNotification');
    tradeNotification.car = trade.car;
    emit(tradeNotification);


    // persist the state of the car
    await assetRegistry.update(trade.car);
}


/**
 * Remove all high price car
```

```
*/
async function removeHighPriceCar(remove) {


    let assetRegistry = await getAssetRegistry('org.example.mynetwork.
Car');
    let results = await query('selectCarWithHighPrice');


    for (let n = 0; n < results.length; n++) {
        let trade = results[n];


        let removeNotification = getFactory().newEvent('org.example.mynet
work','RemoveNotification');
        removeNotification.car = trade;
        emit(removeNotification);
        await assetRegistry.remove(trade);
    }
}
```

- Save the logic.js file.

The second function calls a query named selectCarWithHighPrice (defined in queries. qry) that will return all car asset records with price greater than 1000, emit an event, and remove the car from the AssetRegistry.

Step 2: Create a query definition file

Queries used in transaction processor logic are given in a file called queries.qry. Each query entry defines the resources and qualification for which the query is running.

- In tutorial-network folder create a new file named as queries.qry.

- Paste the following code into the queries.qry file.

```
query selectCar {
  description: "Select all car"
  statement:
      SELECT org.example.mynetwork.Car
}
```

```
query selectCarWithHighPrice {
  description: "Select car based on quantity"
  statement:
      SELECT org.example.mynetwork.Car
         WHERE (price > 60)
}
```

- Save this file.

Step 3: Regenerate the business network archive

Now we have to repackage the business network archive (.bna) after changing the files in a business network and redeploy the Hyperledger Fabric instance. We have to upgrade the deployed network that requires a new version number.

- In testNetwork or tutorial-network directory, open package.json file.
- Modify the version parameter from 0.0.1 to 0.0.2.
- Navigate to testNetwork or tutorial-network directory.
- Run the following command:

```
composer archive create --sourceType dir --sourceName . -a
tutorial-network@0.0.2.bna
```

Step 4: Deploy the updated business network

Now we have to deploy the changed/modified network to make it the latest version in the blockchain. We are using the newly created business network archive file to update the existing deployed business network:

- Navigate to the directory that contains the folder comprising tutorial-network@0.0.2.bna or testNetwork@0.0.2.bna.
- Run the following command to upgrade the network with a new version:

```
composer network upgrade -c PeerAdmin@hlfv1 -n tutorial-
network -V 0.0.2
```

- Now, ping the current version of the business network using the following command:

```
composer network ping -c admin@tutorial-network | grep
Business
```

Step 5: Generate a REST server

Following are the steps to create REST-APIs:

- Navigate to tutorial-network directory and run the following command:

    ```
    composer-rest-server
    ```

- Enter admin@tutorial-network as the card name.
- Select Never use namespace when asked whether to use namespace or not in API generation.
- Select No when asked whether to secure the generated API.
- Select Yes when asked whether to enable event publication.
- Select No when asked whether to enable TLS security.

The generated API is connected to the deployed blockchain and business network.

Step 6: Generate a skeleton angular application

Following are the steps for creating an Angular 4 application:

- Navigate to tutorial-network directory and run the following directory:

    ```
    yo hyperledger-composer:angular
    ```

- Select Yes when asked to connect to a running business network.
- Enter standard package.json arguments.
- Enter admin@tutorial-network for the business network card.
- Select Connect to an existing REST-API.
- Enter http://localhost for REST server address.
- Enter 3000 for server port.
- Select Namespace are not used.

Fabric Composer Playground

In this section, we will review the user interface of Composer. The intent here is to get familiarized with the user interface in order to perform some common tasks.

Playground is available for both online and local development. You may want to do it locally for reasons like data security, availability, and more. Here we will provide a walkthrough of the online version as both look similar.

First, open the following URL in the browser: https://composer-playground.mybluemix.net. Once opened, you will see an online development portal for modeling your business network, as shown in *Figure 2.4*:

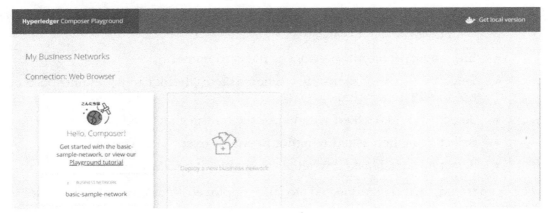

As you can see, one sample network is already available for you to explore. When you click on **Deploy a new business network**, you will see a number of templates available for you to explore and modify:

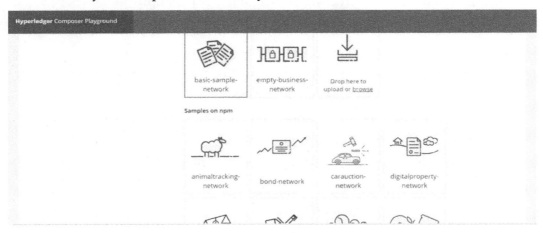

Figure 2.5

Here, the models are created using UI, and they are stored in the local storage of the browser.

This will open the default UI with two tabs—one will be used to define your model and the other to test your model.

You will also see some of the default files created for you, like README.md, sample. cto, sample.js, and permissions.acl:

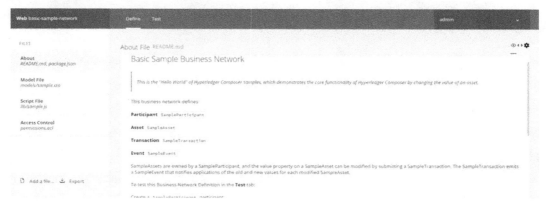

Figure 2.6

You can create a new file by clicking on Add a file button. This will list various formats available to create.

In the Test tab, you can create different entities defined in your model file. For example, in the sample.cto file, you will see a sample participant:

```
participant SampleParticipant identified by participantId {
    o String participantId
    o String firstName
    o String lastName
}
```

Now, in the Test tab, you can create a sample participant by clicking on Create New Participant.

This will open a popup with the .json structure, and you can provide details inside it, like firstName, lastName, and more. Once the details are entered, click Create New.

This will show a new participant in the table.

Figure 2.7

As you add new entities, the transactions get logged in the network, and you can view these transactions in the **All transactions** tab.

You can click the **All Transactions** tab and view the records. A popup with additional information, as shown in *Figure 2.8*, can be seen:

Figure 2.8

You can see the transaction and events details. You can also submit a transaction by clicking on the **Submit** button. You can use the *export* button to export the model, change it, and import it back for a new deployment.

The typical steps for development are as follows:

1) Develop locally using the code editor and Yeoman.
2) Using the command line interface, generate the BNA and import it back to the UI.
3) You can conduct simulated testing on the same.
4) You can also import the previous code and upload it to the network.

Summary

In this module, we learnt about the basics of Hyperledger and Composer, a tool within the Hyperledger suite. It enables us to write a business network in a fast and seamless manner. It also assists in generating the front end and back end for creating end-to-end applications. In this chapter, we also performed a walkthrough of the Composer UI to help develop the business network model in the browser. In the next chapter, we will review the Hyperledger in further detail.

References

- https://hyperledger.github.io/composer/latest/tutorials/tutorials.html

CHAPTER 3
Basics of Hyperledger Fabric

In *Chapter 1*, *Blockchain and Decentralization*, and *Chapter 2*, *Introduction to Hyperledger and Composer*, we understood the current landscape of blockchain technology and how Hyperledger fits in this space. Now, we will learn about Hyperledger in further detail along with the role of the Linux Foundation. We will also learn about Hyperledger Fabric, which is one of the most widely used platforms within the Hyperledger umbrella.

The key topics covered in this chapter are as follows:

- Use of blockchain technology for enterprise applications
- Various Hyperledger frameworks and tools
- Fabric, the most widely used platform within the Hyperledger umbrella
- Various components of Fabric
- Creation and execution of transactions in Hyperledger Fabric
- Chaincode and smart contracts
- History of Hyperledger Fabric
- Chaincode in Node.js and SDKs

Objective: This chapter is intended to introduce readers to Hyperledger Fabric and its evolution over time. Readers will also be introduced to the concept of chaincode (or smart contract) deployed on Fabric to run various business operations.

Hyperledger and blockchain

Blockchain technology is perceived as the next big thing that has been built on the Internet since the world wide web. A blockchain is technically defined as a distributed decentralized ledger or database where records are immutable, unlike traditional databases.

Data is immutable because it is chronologically stored and is linked to each other by cryptography such that an attempt to change any previous records will make the whole chain invalid. Here, immutable doesn't mean you cannot change the data. For instance, let's assume you are the owner of a car, and in the blockchain ledger, ownership is assigned to you. Once you decide to sell it, you can update the buyer as the owner of the car in the blockchain. However, you cannot change the historical data of the previous owners of the car if it is stored in the blockchain, because the chain will become invalid as the cryptographical link will be broken.

Data is distributed as it is replicated and stored on all the nodes that are part of the network, similar to traditional cloud distributed databases. Moreover, it is decentralized as no single party controls the data, unlike a bank where data is controlled by the bank and one can only see it through net banking. Therefore, blockchain significantly strengthens risk management for bank customers.

In simple terms, it is just a big, almost hack-proof database that can store valuable details. Since it is almost hack-proof, it becomes a single source of truth and can then be used in varieties of applications where trust is an issue.

The great crypto apocalypse and blockchain problems:

If you have heard of bitcoin or cryptocurrency recently, you are possibly aware of the crypto apocalypse or the bitcoin bubble burst that happened in 2018 where most of the cryptocurrencies fell more than 80% in value. This created negative ripples among the blockchain enthusiasts, thus causing a steep drop in the popularity of bitcoin and even blockchain, as seen on Google Trends. It is estimated that a number of blockchain start-ups have already stopped their operations or are on the verge of shutting down. Many have argued that this is a natural phenomenon in the hype cycle of disruptive technology and that only about 10% of the initial projects survive the hype. This also has to do a lot with the number of problems a public blockchain presents, including scalability, latency, and data and transaction privacy, and they simply aren't ready for enterprises or for global audiences yet.

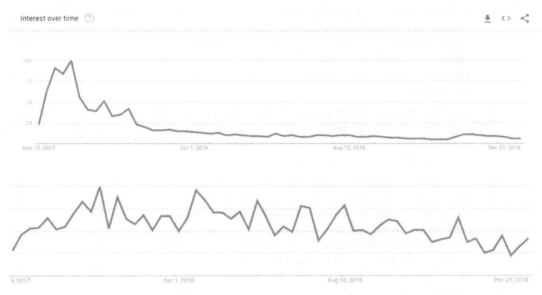

Figure 3.1

Nonetheless, amidst all this, there are definitely bright spots in blockchain that have kept the hype around it alive. This is evident from the preceding Google Trends pattern where the first graph shows the massive dip in interest in Bitcoin and Ethereum or any other public blockchain. However, Hyperledger has been able to survive the crypto onslaught, while public blockchain networks have been struggling with the mainstream adoption for various technical and social reasons. This year has seen progress with respect to permissioned blockchains. In fact, many firms have tried the popular public blockchain platform Ethereum and have decided to move to permissioned blockchain networks like Hyperledger Fabric. They are looking for an enterprise blockchain solution to their problems, and have decided to keep only the incentives or transaction part in the Ethereum, in the form of ether tokens.

So, in a holistic view, the business world and enterprises are looking at the permissioned blockchain, optimistically, to solve their problems after trying public ones.

Blockchain for enterprises

It is important to understand that enterprises work in a standard framework when it comes to technical, legal, and business aspects, and so on. There are certain considerations that they need to take care of before adopting and incorporating any technology in their existing frameworks, including the following:

- **Value it brings into the enterprise**: The return on investment (ROI) is one of the most important considerations for enterprises. The technology should either help in cutting down the cost of operation or provide new means of revenue. Mere adoption of the technology for transparency or process improvement may not necessarily provide an economic edge to an enterprise.

- **Long-lasting, robust solution**: Enterprises thrive on industry-standard solutions built on robust technologies. Thus, any naive solution that requires huge maintenance and support will cost a huge amount for enterprises in the long run.

- **Scalability, latency, and flexibility**: The blockchain network used by enterprises has to be scalable. Platforms like Ethereum and Bitcoin public blockchains do not even remotely match an enterprise's standard. While Ethereum can process around 15 tps (**transactions per second**), Bitcoin is even slower with a very high block or confirmation time required for a transaction to be confirmed or mined. While trust in trade is definitely an issue among enterprises, the trade-off that comes with these public blockchains is huge.

- **Interoperability and integration with current systems**: One thing that blockchain got completely wrong is believing that it can disrupt existing centralized systems within enterprises or even outside. Most of the systems built over cloud solutions, SAP, and ERP systems are scalable and robust. The incoming solution should aid and integrate with these existing systems. When it comes to the existing system of records, the solution should provide adapters or connectors to them instead of replacing them.

- **Regulatory compliance**: Enterprises also need to understand that whatever comes out should be compliant with existing regulatory frameworks. This is one major challenge that public blockchains have been struggling with.

- **Technical and skill requirement**: Most of the enterprises have technical standards and frameworks, and each solution has to conform to these to be adopted. Enterprises tend to follow standard programming languages, tools, consensus algorithms, frameworks, UX designs, and so on. Also, the enterprises have to make sure they have enough skilled resources available to support such disruptive technology.

- **Identity management and security**: Enterprises have extensive investment and infrastructure in place for various identity management solutions within their organization. Thus, any incoming solution should be interoperable with these existing, well-tested, and highly secure systems. In later chapters, we will see how Hyperledger's identity management system in the form of membership provider is robust such that we can implement our own or even plug the existing systems through the interfaces provided.

- **Data privacy**: Enterprises seek comprehensive data privacy for their transactional information. We will see how Hyperledger implements logical channels in their network to facilitate these kinds of private transactions among different parties.

Many tech giants like IBM, Intel, and may other companies had foreseen and sensed the drawbacks of public blockchain networks, and started working on more constrained blockchain solutions that may not be open to all but to the interested parties only. But such research and development initiatives were fragmented among different organizations, which was not ideal for blockchain technology's future. Then Linux Foundation came to the fore to host such enterprise blockchain development, continuing its dominance in the open source community.

Hyperledger frameworks and tools

Following are some of the frameworks within Hyperledger:

Burrow

Hyperledger Burrow, hosted by the Linux Foundation, is a blockchain framework implementation. The framework was contributed by Monax and co-sponsored by Intel. Burrow is a permissioned smart contract application engine partially developed in accordance with the specifications of **Ethereum Virtual Machine (EVM)**.

Fabric

Hyperledger Fabric's framework was contributed by Digital Asset and IBM. Fabric works as a foundation for developing applications with a modular architecture. The framework utilizes container technology to host smart contracts (chaincode), comprising the system's application logic.

Indy

Hyperledger Indy is a distributed ledger and utility library built for decentralized identity. The distributed ledger provides tools, libraries, and reusable components to create and use independent digital identities based on blockchains. They are interoperable across administrative applications, domains, and any other *silo*.

Iroha

Hyperledger Iroha, hosted by the Linux Foundation, is another blockchain platform implementation. The framework was contributed by Soramitsu, Hitachi,

NTT Data, and Colu. Written in C++, Hyperledger Iroha incorporates a unique algorithm on chain-based Byzantine fault-tolerant consensus. It provides a small set of fast commands and queries, covering most common operations for digital asset and identity management.

Sawtooth

Hyperledger Sawtooth is a blockchain platform implementation that builds, deploys, and runs distributed ledgers. It is a modular platform that provides a digital record without a central authority or implementation.

Hyperledger tools are as follows.

Caliper

Hyperledger Caliper, hosted by the Linux Foundation, is a blockchain benchmark tool. It allows measuring the performance of a particular blockchain implementation against predefined use cases. It will produce important reports having a number of PI, for example, transactions per second and so on.

Cello

Hyperledger Cello, hosted by the Linux Foundation, is a blockchain module toolkit. The blockchain toolkit was contributed by IBM, with sponsors from Soramitsu, Huawei, and Intel. Hyperledger Cello aims to reduce the effort required for creating, managing, and terminating blockchains by bringing the on-demand *as-a-service* deployment model to the blockchain ecosystem.

Composer

Hyperledger Composer is a set of collaboration tools that help business owners and developers to create smart contracts and blockchain applications to find the solution to their business problems. Built with JavaScript, utilizing modern tools such as Node.js, NPM, CLI, and popular editors, the tool offers business-centric ideas as well as sample applications to create robust blockchain solutions.

But this tool has been recently frozen, and Hyperledger Fabric doesn't provide compatibility to it from v1.3, which is going to impact its use. So it's better that we switch to native implementation for now.

Explorer

Hyperledger Explorer, hosted by the Linux Foundation, is a blockchain module. The blockchain tool was contributed by IBM, Intel, and DTCC. Aimed at creating a user-friendly web application, Hyperledger Explorer can view, deploy, invoke, or query blocks, transactions and associated data, network information, chaincodes, and transaction families, or any significant information stored in the ledger.

Quilt

Hyperledger Explorer, hosted by the Linux Foundation, is a business blockchain tool. Hyperledger Quilt was contributed by NTT Data and Ripple. The blockchain tool offers interoperability between ledger systems by implementing the **Interledger protocol (ILP)**. The ILP is basically a payments protocol designed to transfer value across distributed and non-distributed ledgers.

Fabric and its components

Hyperledger Fabric uses a modular architecture by separating consensus, ledgers, nodes, and MSP nodes into separate services. It is a highly scalable architecture and built on the principle of microservices.

We will first understand the technical stack of Fabric:

Golang: Fabric modules are written in Go language, which is a highly performant programming language developed by Google developers. A basic understanding of Golang will help to debug the components profoundly when required. However, it is not necessary to write the applications on it, as you can write chaincodes in Node.js and Java as well. Chaincode is usually written in Node.js because of the support it has for Fabric.

Node.js: Node.js, introduced by Ryan Dahl in 2008, has quickly captured a decent market in the software industry. The ability to write JavaScript on the back end has changed the way we see JavaScript now, its asynchronous and event-driven behavior owed to the v8 engine. It also boasts a great community, probably the biggest among the programming languages. You can find all the packages available at https://www.npmjs.com/. It is heavily used for writing chaincodes and client applications and will be using angular 7/REACT for writing the front end, which is also based on JavaScript. So, knowing JavaScript is definitely a prerequisite when looking to build a career in this space.

Also, note that there is significant support in terms of modules available for Hyperledger Fabric in npm modules. The Node.js SDK, which we will talk about later, is also quite stable for interacting with the Hyperledger Fabric network.

Fabric CLI and chaincode runtime support Node.js for writing chaincodes, apart from Go language and Java.

Docker: Fabric heavily uses Docker for all its microservices, and therefore it is very important to understand the basics of Docker to work with the Fabric network. It also uses Docker Compose for orchestration, and you can use Docker Swarm or Kubernetes to deploy this into a multi VM production environment. Later in this book, we will also be discussing how you can customize and build production Fabric network.

Also, it will be really helpful for you to have an account on https://hub.docker.com/.

We will also be using https://labs.play-with-docker.com/ for some quick demos of the network. Subsequently, we will work on a more standard environment when we build a POC for a use case in Fabric.

Note: If you already have a Docker set up in your machine, you can use that as well. I suggest trying hands on the Play with Docker website with some modules as it will not require any installation on your machine and you can learn it through the web. At a later stage, we will be detailing the steps for installing all the tools required for working with Hyperledger Fabric.

gRPC and protobuffs: Generally, services communicate with each other using REST APIs, even in traditional client service models. For example, front end talks to back end using REST APIs and the data is sent across in JSON format, which is just a key-value pair. But this has downsides and Google's gRPC has given a better way to communicate among different services, where the data is transferred in binary format or as proto puffers, giving great performance and latency. Hyperledger Fabric uses gRPC and protobuffs heavily for communication.

Apache Kafka and Zookeeper: Apache Kafka is a high-throughput, fault-tolerant distributed messaging system. It is used by Fabric to implement an orderer, which is a component of Fabric that achieves consensus and orders the transactions, building them in blocks and sending it to the peers. It is a highly useful stream process and messaging system used by thousands of companies all over the world.

Also, note that we need Kafka for the orderer node in Fabric, but that is in the real Fabric network. However, in local development setup, we can use solo implementation, which does not use Kafka.

Another thing to note here is that you don't need to use only this implementation since Fabric allows you to use your own orderer implementation for achieving consensus by implementing the interface provided in the consensus package (https://github.com/hyperledger/fabric/blob/master/orderer/consensus/consensus.go). The modular and plug and play implementation is a robust architecture.

These are some of the important technologies used in Fabric. Equipped with this knowledge, let us understand the following in detail:

What are the different nodes in the Fabric network?

- How does a transaction and block creation happen in Hyperledger Fabric?
- How is consensus is reached in the network?

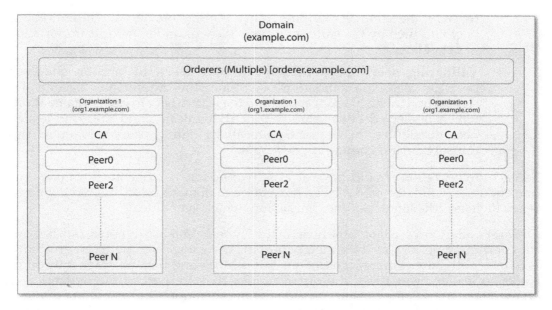

Figure 3.2

From *Figure 3.2* we can also understand the naming of all the nodes in the Hyperledger Fabric network. It is crucial to understand these as they are defined in Docker Compose files by these names and are discoverable by these names and ports, which we will see in detail in the next section.

So **Peer2** is named as **peer2.org1.example.com** referring to *Figure 3.2* and other peers or client or even the orderers will use this to identify them.

The nodes in the Fabric network can be broadly categorized as follows:

Peers: Peers in Hyperledger maintain the chaincode, endorse a transaction, and validate the transaction and block. Each member organization of the network needs to have these peers set up. These peers can be further divided as follows:

- **Anchor peer**: Each organization must have one anchor peer in their network setup before they can join the network. This anchor is the node that communicates with the other nodes in the network outside the organization in a channel, so it should be discoverable. We will know more about it once we see the journey of a transaction in Hyperledger.

- **Endorser peer**: Each organization should have at least one endorser peer that the client application can send a transaction to, in order to get it endorsed. This is to generate a valid read-write endorsed response that the client application can then send to the orderer node to order this transaction into the block and send it to validating peers. The endorsing peer hosts the chaincode too. It executes the chaincode to validate the transaction and generate a read-write set. Thus, the chaincode is executed twice for the same set of inputs from a transaction, once by the endorsing peer and then by the validating peer. We will understand its importance in detail later.

- **Validating peer**: They are like endorser peers. In fact, an endorser peer can also be a validating peer. Once the orderer has ordered the transaction in the block, it sends it to the leader peer in each organization, which is elected either statically or dynamically, and then the leader peer distributes the transaction to all validating peers to validate the transaction and commit to the ledger.

So each organization should have at least two nodes, i.e., one anchor node and one endorser (validator) node. It can have more than that as well, but having more peers increases the latency of the transaction, which is not ideal.

Orderer node: Orderers are at the heart of the Hyperledger Fabric network. They are the connecting pieces for all the members of the network. Their main responsibility is to order all the incoming transactions into a block and then message it through Kafka to leader peers of all the organizations that are part of the network. As shown in *Figure 3.2*, they can be outside the organization's infrastructure and are discoverable by all the client applications within the organization. They receive the endorser response from the client SDKs, validate the signatures, and order them, and then send them to validating peers via leader peers.

They do not host any data or chaincode and are used to achieve consensus and logical ordering of the transactions into a block. As per our earlier discussion, this implementation of the orderer is pluggable and you can implement your own orderer too, as long as it implements the interface. The development-based implementation is known as solo, which is a mock orderer that does not really take part in consensus.

MSP and CA services: Membership service provider (MSP) nodes provide the necessary certificate infrastructure for nodes to be identified in the network. We will study in depth about MSP in the next module. This is also a pluggable component, and you can replace it with any existing CA (certificate authority) infrastructure using the hooks provided in the network. We will also see how CA services can be reached out by client SDKs to get certificates to send a transaction, handle channel lifecycle, and more.

Services: Apart from the preceding nodes, there are other nodes that may not necessarily be a part of the network but help in providing certain services:

- **CLI**: This is a key component in the network, which is basically a Docker container that can be used to do necessary operations in the network, like creating a channel, installing chaincode, upgrading chaincode, and more. From a network administrator's perspective, it is a very crucial component to be mastered. But for most of the operations in the network, we can use SDKs to do it, using code instead of doing it manually.

- **CouchDB**: Hyperledger provides level DB for key-value storage of the contract states by default. But for advanced queries and storage, CouchDB implementation is also available. This stores the ledger information and is implemented along with the peer in a network. So, every peer in the network has a CouchDB available for storing the ledger data. They are declared along with the peer service in Docker compose files of the same subnetwork.

Now, let's get a feel of this network by running a simple example. In the next section, we will understand this network in detail when we will be building our first network. However, you can just follow these simple steps to understand the fundamentals:

- Go to https://labs.play-with-docker.com/ in your favorite browser and log in with your Docker account. Play with Docker is a Docker educational platform for running Docker-based applications quickly. Feel free to use your own Docker setup if you have one locally.

- Once you have logged in the platform, click on the **DD NEW INSTANCE** button on the left side panel. This will start a new instance for you to start playing with Docker:

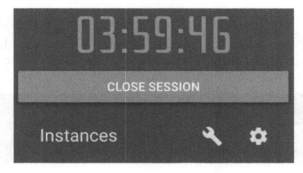

Figure 3.3

Run the following commands in the order:

```
sudo su
        mkdir ~/fabric-dev-servers && cd ~/fabric-dev-servers

        curl -O https://raw.githubusercontent.com/hyperledger/
composer-tools/master/packages/fabric-dev-servers/fabric-dev-servers.
tar.gz
```

```
    tar -xvf fabric-dev-servers.tar.gz
    cd ~/fabric-dev-servers
    ./downloadFabric.sh
    ./startFabric.sh
docker ps
```

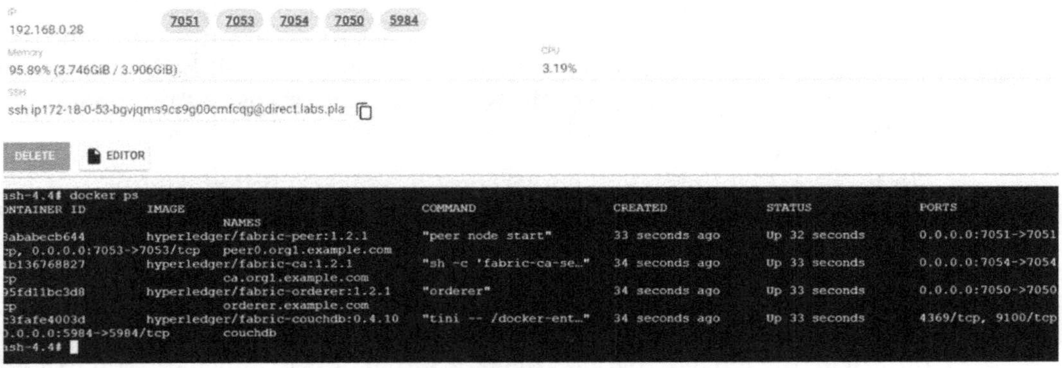

Figure 3.4

```
docker images
```

If the preceding commands are executed correctly, you should see the following output of Docker images command that lists all the local Docker images available in the local system:

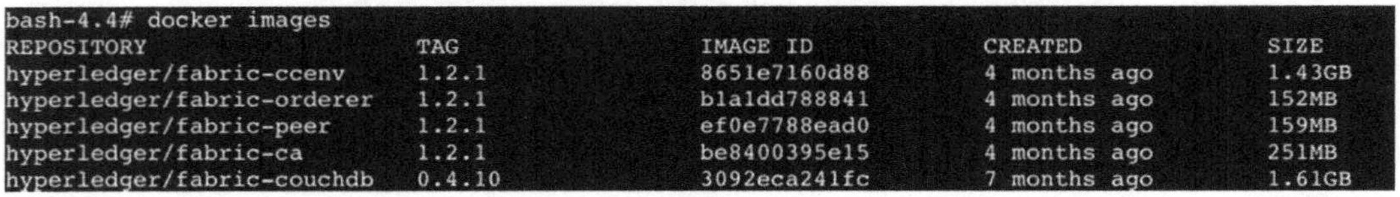

bash-4.4# docker images

REPOSITORY	TAG	IMAGE ID	CREATED	SIZE
hyperledger/fabric-ccenv	1.2.1	8651e7160d88	4 months ago	1.43GB
hyperledger/fabric-orderer	1.2.1	b1a1dd788841	4 months ago	152MB
hyperledger/fabric-peer	1.2.1	ef0e7788ead0	4 months ago	159MB
hyperledger/fabric-ca	1.2.1	be8400395e15	4 months ago	251MB
hyperledger/fabric-couchdb	0.4.10	3092eca241fc	7 months ago	1.61GB

Figure 3.5

Above, we have pulled the Fabric network starter code from GitHub, from an open source repo. Then, we pulled all the Docker images required to run the Fabric network.

Docker containers are like **virtual machines** (**VM**) you use to deploy applications, and Docker images are like templates of such VMs. Lastly, Docker Compose is the tool used to orchestrate all these VMs together.

Now run the following command to start the network:

```
./scripts/startFabric.sh
```

Congratulations! You have started the first simple network for one organization with one peer, one orderer with solo implementation, one CA, and one CouchDB. In a more complicated network with multiple organizations, we will see that there will be a large number of containers and port mappings. But it is important to understand that these four components form the base of any type of Hyperledger Fabric network.

How does a transaction happen in Hyperledger Fabric?

Now we have a fair bit of understanding of the base components in a Fabric network. Let us understand how the transaction propagates through the different network components to get committed in the ledger.

This is a multi-step process. We will discuss each step in detail, and *Figure 3.6* will serve as the base for understanding the journey of a transaction from a client app to the block in peer:

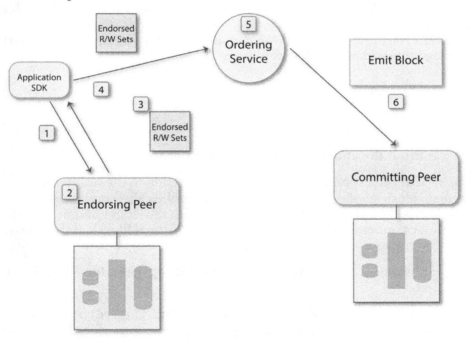

Figure 3.6

Client SDK sends the transaction:

Let's understand this with a simple example. We will be explaining states in detail in the next section when we will talk about Hyperledger data structure, but for brevity sake, we will be explaining it in simple terms now. Let's assume we have a state in the ledger named as carOwner denoting the current owner of the car and it's stored as a key-value pair in a peer of organization.

```
(k,v)=> carOwner : owner1
```

Now owner1 has decided to sell the car to owner2 and has submitted a request to the Node.js back end from the car ownership dashboard.

The Node.js SDK client takes this newly proposed state and sends a proposal to all endorsing peers of the organization as per the endorsing policy defined in the channel configuration as shown in *Figure 3.6*. This includes a proposal request to invoke the updateOwner function described in the chaincode deployed in the fabric peer.

Endorsement of the transaction proposal:

The endorsing peer takes the proposal and validates whether it conforms to the endorsement policies agreed upon by the peers of the organization. Once it's validated for the basic policies, the endorsing peer then executes the invoke method of the chaincode such that its invocation doesn't update the ledger. It's more like a simulated transaction carried out to flush out erroneous or compute-intensive transactions. The result of invoking the transaction is a read-write set that can be represented roughly as follows:

```
Read set (k,v) => carOwner,owner1
Write set(k,v1)=> carOwner,owner2
```

This read-write set is returned to the client SDK again as shown in *Figure 3.6*:

- **Submit the endorsed proposal to the orderer**:

The client SDK then submits this endorsed transaction to the orderer for inclusion in the next block of the ledger. The orderer verifies the signatures of all these endorsed responses for inclusion of transactions in the ledger and then orders it in a chronological manner based on channels in the form of blocks. It then broadcasts it to the leader peers of all the organizations.

- **Submitting the transaction to committing peer for inclusion in the ledger**:

This is the last step in the lifecycle of a transaction. The orderer broadcasts the batch proposal or block to all the leader peers in the network for all organizations. The committing peer validates those transactions again by executing the chaincode one last time for the particular transaction before it gets committed in the ledger. This time the result of the execution of the chaincode is final, unlike the last time, which was merely for generating a read-write set. After this step, the state in the DB and read set becomes

```
set(k,v) => carOwner , owner2.
```

Difference between Bitcoin, Ethereum, and permissioned blockchain

In this section, we will be understanding the core differences between public networks and permissioned networks, which are quite obvious and easy to understand.

We will also understand the subtle differences between Hyperledger Fabric and other permissioned and private blockchain networks.

Finally, we will also understand how permissioned networks like Hyperledger are not similar to traditional database systems, which has been the main concern for blockchain enthusiasts who have been accusing Hyperledger networks as just modified distributed databases.

Understanding such differences will bolster the confidence of someone looking to offer business solutions using a Hyperledger network.

Public versus permissioned networks

In layman's terms, the difference is quite obvious. A public blockchain does not have any restriction on who can join them as nodes, and they are truly decentralized networks at a global level. On the other hand, a permissioned network requires that only nodes who are allowed to be a part of the network have the required certificates to identify themselves and can join.

Let's understand the differences at a low level.

Consensus: As discussed in the previous chapter, apart from traditional consensus algorithms like BFT, PBFT, and so on in distributed systems, the public network also needs algorithms like POW, POS, DPOS, and so on to achieve consensus in an anonymous network. The traditional PBFT consensus algorithm is not enough to maintain consensus and security in the network as the network has unidentified nodes too.

However, in networks like Hyperledger Fabric, where the nodes are identified, PBFT seems to be enough to achieve consensus. It also gives us several advantages in terms of scalability, latency, and so on as lesser number of nodes are required to reach the consensus. This is analogous to the real world, where if there are lesser number of friends, it takes lesser time to reach a consensus about where to go out for dinner.

In terms of tps (transactions per second), different performance tests have been carried out for varying loads and some companies claim they have reached a throughput of around 3,500 tps with latency less than 1 s. Many other independent researchers have claimed an average of around 1000 tps.

Ethereum, led by Vitalik Buterin and his team, have been working on a second layer solution—Sharding and Plasma—but their implementation is going to take time. Currently, Ethereum offers around 15 tps, which is very low compared to Fabric.

In Bitcoin, the tps is around 7, which is even lower than Ethereum.

Incentives: Permissioned networks are truly used for business purposes among multiple organizations who do not necessarily trust each other but would like to trade among each other or do some transactions. The idea of incentives is quite native to the public blockchain, where, in order to maintain the security and integrity of the network, you need several nodes available to mine and token incentives to be provided. This is not a requirement in a permissioned network, as the companies interested in doing trade will host their own node and take care of it after they join the network.

That's the reason Hyperledger doesn't have a cryptocurrency of its own.

Smart contracts:

In Hyperledger, smart contracts are described as chaincodes and are written in standard programming languages like Golang, Node.js, or Java. In a public Ethereum network, the smart contracts are written in a newly evolved language called **Solidity**.

Also, smart contracts in Hyperledger do not support non-deterministic transactions, while Ethereum does allow them. This is important to understand because of its inherent business implications.

Non-deterministic transactions are similar to calculating a random number or getting data from some API or doing a transaction depending on the current timestamp. These values may change every time the code runs, for example.

In Hyperledger, the contract execution happens twice: once to the read-write set, and second time to validate whether the execution of all transactions in the block was broadcasted by the orderers to produce the same result as before.

If you have a state depending upon some random function to generate the output, the first execution might result in a state value that may not necessarily be the same as the output of the next execution, and this will result in a failed transaction, which is going to be a problem.

Same is true for external API calls to fetch some time-bound data like the current weather data of a place. In Ethereum, we can use Oraclize solutions to query external APIs to fetch some time-bound data. However, this is not possible at a chaincode level in Hyperledger.

With this understanding in place, it's time to see the differences between permissioned networks. We will compare three major permissioned networks namely Hyperledger, Corda, and Quorum.

Differences between Hyperledger Fabric by Linux Foundation, Corda by R3, and Quorum by JP Morgan

In terms of innovation on permissioned networks, the Linux Foundation is not the only party involved.

R3 consortium has been working on creating a permissioned network for facilitating and automating legal contracts between multiple identifiable parties.

Quorum by JP Morgan is an enterprise version of Ethereum. Thus, if you know about Ethereum and Solidity, you are almost ready to use Quorum.

Permissioned parties only

In this regard, all three have the same principle—the parties should be known and identified in advance and there should be a mechanism in place to identify each of them.

Consensus:

In Hyperledger Fabric, we have already seen how the transaction goes through multiple steps of validation before getting committed into the block.

However, in Corda, *notaries* are responsible for validating, timestamping, and committing a transaction in an immutable chain. These notaries can be centralized entities like banks.

Quorum uses a consensus protocol called **QuorumChain**. It is straightforward in its approach and depends upon a majority voting mechanism.

So, in terms of tps, they have almost identical results, but in Hyperledger Fabric, this idea of consensus is plug-and-play owing to its modular architecture.

Incentives and tokens:

They do not support a cryptocurrency for their platform. However, in Hyperledger, it is possible to create such tokens whereas in others it isn't possible.

Chaincode/smart contracts

Hyperledger supports Node.js, Golang, and Java for writing chaincodes. These are a few of the most commonly used languages within the developer community, making the platform developer-friendly.

Corda supports Kotlin, which runs on JVM. Also important to note here is that the smart contracts in Corda have legal foundation, unlike Hyperledger or Quorum. Thus, Corda is not simply a code.

Quorum, similar to Ethereum, supports Solidity for writing smart contracts.

The clear distinction between Hyperledger Fabric, Corda, and Quorum is that while Corda and Quorum are focused and built primarily for financial institutions, Hyperledger Fabric is more of a general solution for almost all industry verticals.

Differences between Hyperledger Fabric and traditional databases:

Many proponents of public blockchains and critics of permissioned blockchains have accused it of being just another distributed database. So, it's important to understand the difference between them. It's true that traditional relational databases can be re-engineered to be distributed and immutable, but solutions like Hyperledger Fabric are built with the sole purpose of being totally decentralized among its parties where cryptography is used heavily to safeguard the chain data. All the transactions in a blockchain are linked cryptographically to its previous records, so changing any previous records will leave the chain broken. But this is not the case for databases, and this is one of the key differences.

Channels:

In order to facilitate private transactions between interested parties, Hyperledger uses channels that are like private sub-networks.

Channels provide transaction privacy in the multi-organization network.

Channel configurations are provided in YAML, specifying the participant organization, peers, anchor peer, and so on, and based on that, the network starts a channel.

Every organization has an anchor peer. These peers are discoverable from other organizations. We will see in the upcoming sections how these channels form the basis of a Hyperledger network. We will also see how we can use private data collection to reduce the number of channels to do private transactions within the channel itself, which is quite useful. We will be working with channels in detail using Fabric SDK for Node.js.

Hyperledger Fabric releases and differences

In this section, we will look into various releases of Hyperledger Fabric.

Hyperledger Fabric was the result of IBM's Open Blockchain project that was announced in the fall of 2015.

Hyperledger Fabric is an open source project hosted on GitHub. It has been in active development since 2016. The following graph, in *Figure 3.7*, shows a timeline of the different Fabric releases over the past two years.

On September 16, 2016, the first release of Fabric tagged as v0.6.0-preview was released. Since then, many stable versions have been released. The development of Fabric has taken off in the last six months, with as many as three major versions having been released. The latest version of Fabric (as on the date of writing of this book) is v1.4.0, which is an LTS production-ready release:

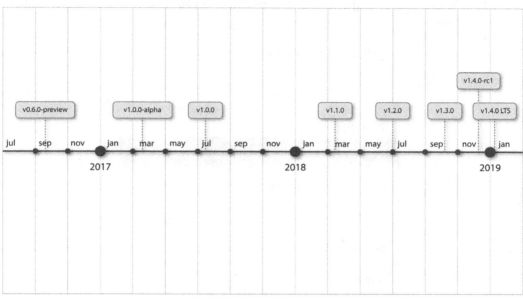

Figure 3.7

The project has more than 150 contributors on GitHub, whereas issues and features are being actively tracked in Jira.

The Hyperledger Fabric project on GitHub is being actively developed in collaboration with more than thirty companies and individual contributors.

In this section, we will look into the major differences and changes in major versions of Hyperledger Fabric.

Hyperledger Fabric has been very meticulous with their roadmap, and you can look and track all the features planned in their roadmap here:

https://jira.hyperledger.org/secure/Dashboard.jspa?selectPageId=10104.

Hyperledger has planned a major v2.0.0 release in the Q2 2019, which is being seen as a game changer in the permissioned blockchain space.

Fabric 1.4 is the first production-ready LTS release.

Though we will explain the key differences between different versions, most of these versions do not really differ much in terms of the architecture of the components of Fabric.

In the next section, we will dive deep into the modular architecture of Fabric, which is almost the same for 1.1+ releases and are not expected to change anytime soon because of its robustness.

If you are interested in the code bases and structure of the project of all these versions above, you can always switch to different branches based on the release as shown below:

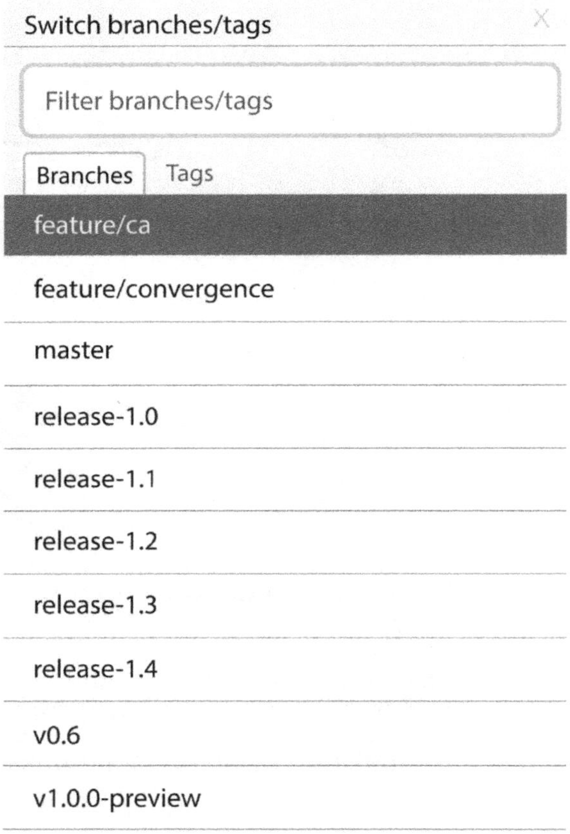

Figure 3.8

Fabric 0.6

The initial version of Fabric 0.6 was by no means ready for any real use cases since there were many missing pieces and issues to be resolved by the world enterprise community. But the effort by IBM in trying to develop an enterprise blockchain solution was appreciated.

Fabric architecture was based on the key building blocks of any permissioned blockchain network:

- A client SDK to transact with the blockchain
- A node or peer to hold the ledger and smart contracts

- A service to identify and enroll nodes in the network

- A consensus mechanism

Fabric underwent drastic changes from 0.6 to 1.0. Some of these included complete rewriting of components like peers, which were quite monolithic in design. *Figure 3.9* clearly illustrates the architecture of Fabric version 0.6:

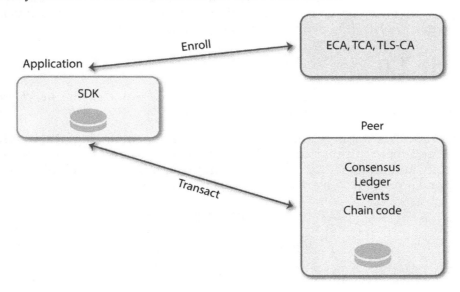

Figure 3.9

It had an MSP for enrolling the parties, so it was definitely permissioned, but it wasn't quite private. There are well-defined business use cases for companies to undertake a private transaction with different parties without revealing the details to other parties in the network (e.g., bidding process). So, these *channels* to facilitate such private transaction was a missing piece.

Also, another thing to note here is the issue with the monolithic design of the peers. The consensus, ledger, and events were all part of this and were against the basic principle of modular architecture. The consensus had to be separated from all this, or in other words, an *orderer* was needed.

There was also an issue with the non-upgradable and deterministic chaincode. For any long-term blockchain solution, the platform should allow upgrading of the smart contracts without having to redeploy them. Once you redeploy them, all the state data associated with them gets reset. Even in Ethereum, there is no way to enable this as of today.

- MSP implementation had to be more distributed as it was a candidate for a single point of failure.

- Flexibility in terms of adding more participants and scalability in terms of transactions were also an issue in this naïve version.

- Also, the communication between peers was still not secure with TLS causing serious issues.

Various working groups of Fabric, which included requirement teams, technical teams, functional teams, and others, decided to work on a more concrete blockchain solution that was useful beyond the experimentations and POCs.

Fabric 1.0

Fabric 1.0 was the first major release, solving some if not all the prevalent and grave problems of Fabric 0.6+ releases.

Figure 3.10 shows the new architecture. Notice a box appearing at the right end that was not there in previous versions. This was a necessary change to achieve modularity and pluggability in the platform. Also, MSP looks a bit different from the last one now with some new mechanisms added to it:

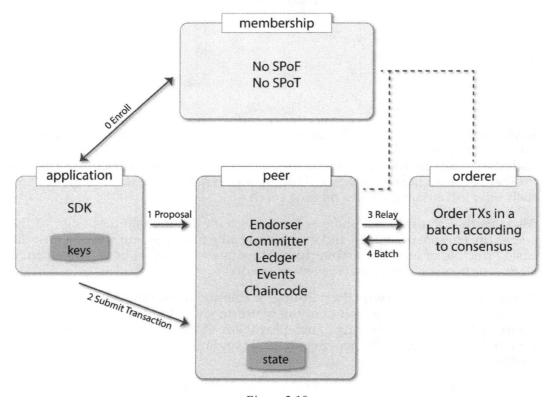

Figure 3.10

The key changes that were implemented were as follows:

- The ability to create channels and do private transactions in a permissioned network
- Separate ordering service for ordering of transactions and achieving consensus
- Ability to implement your own MSP or use an existing one
- Support Java for writing chaincodes

In short, it became less opinionated, more modular, with pluggable components, which were brilliant in the purview of software architecture.

Events: Now we will look at the concept of blockchain events like adding a block when a transaction is completed and more.

In Fabric 1.0, this implementation was not concrete and fine-grained. There was just one service for events named *event hub* that peers could connect to and get information. At the high level, for example when the block is *cut* by the orderer, there was still an issue with the events at channel level.

Though this was a major release, there were some key issues and pending features:

- Enabling TLS communication between peers, orderers, and clients for security reasons was pending.
- Another missing piece was the CouchDB indexed chaincodes for improved performance and to efficiently enable querying of the data from the CouchDB.
- Channels were not fully functional and needed some fixes.
- Better event handling mechanism was required.
- There was also a lack of important utility packages in shim package that Fabric provides, like encrypt and decrypt confidential ledger data before putting them on a ledger. *Out of blockchain* at client-level solution was not always secure in some use cases.
- Also, there was a popular demand from the developers' community to include JavaScript (Node.js) support for writing chaincodes.

Fabric 1.1

The fabric was an evolved version, solving a lot of problems that were either present in 0.6 or came as a result of architecture changes in Fabric.

There was no major architectural rewrite in Fabric 1.1, but it provided some fixes and implemented major proposals at that time from the enterprise or developer community.

Support for Node.js to write chaincodes was implemented. With this came the concept of writing connection profiles. This was very useful because you could write a YAML now and give it to the network, and it could configure all the important things for you like setting up a channel, as shown below.

Example:

```
channels:
  bankingChannel:
    orderers:
      - orderer1.banking.com
    peers:
      peer0.bankOfAmerica.example.com:
        endorsingPeer: true
        chaincodeQuery: true
        ledgerQuery: true
        eventSource: true
      peer0.royalBankOfScotland.example.com:
        endorsingPeer: true
        chaincodeQuery: false
        ledgerQuery: true
        eventSource: false
organizations:
  bankOfAmerica:
    mspid: bankOfAmerica MSP
    peers:
      - peer0.org1. bankOfAmerica.com
    certificateAuthorities:
      - ca- bankOfAmerica
    adminPrivateKey:
      path: …
    signedCert:
      path: …
```

```
royalBankOfScotland:
```

```
...continue
```

This profile YAML between two banks is self-explanatory. We are defining a channel profile providing the name, participants, and other configuration. We are also defining a connection profile for organizations, which defines two or more organizations and their MSPs, peers, and certificates.

- It also improved its shim package by adding entities for encryption and decryption of data etc.

- It also enabled TLS communication between peers, orderers, and clients. To facilitate the same, following environment variables were introduced, which can be injected in Docker containers through Docker Compose, for example:

```
CORE_PEER_TLS_ENABLED = true

CORE_PEER_TLS_CERT_FILE = fqp

CORE_PEER_TLS_KEY_FILE = fqp

CORE_PEER_TLS_ROOTCERT_FILE = fqp

CORE_PEER_TLS_CLIENTAUTHREQUIRED = true

CORE_PEER_TLS_CLIENTROOTCAS_FILES = fqp

CORE_PEER_TLS_CLIENTCERT_FILE = fqp

CORE_PEER_TLS_CLIENTKEY_FILE = fqp
```

As discussed before, events were an issue in the earlier versions of Fabric. Fabric 1.1 introduced events at a channel level. This was important for the participants to have a greater view of what is happening inside the channel and transactions.

This was better from the perspective of many use cases. For example, you can now access historical events in the network after joining it.

There were two services introduced in this version, namely *Deliver* and *Deliver Filtered*.

Fabric 1.2

One of the major features of this release was private data collection. It is different from channels in many ways. Careful consideration and designing of this private data collection can save you from creating a lot of redundant channels.

We will try to explain in detail private data collection when we use them in the sample application. But for now, let us understand them from an overview of what they are and what problem they solve.

Channels are basically used to keep the entire ledger private for the interested parties, but in these channels, there might be requirements for having some private transactions. For example, let's say companies A, B, and C are part of the channel, and A and C want to do a private transaction in this channel. In Fabric 1.1, we would have created a separate channel for this kind of a scenario, but this is not an ideal solution as channels are resource-intensive. Hence, private data collection was introduced to perform these kinds of private transactions in a channel.

There are two ways to send this private transaction in a channel:

- The first one involves the use of gossip protocol to send private data from one peer to another peer directly without ever bringing the orderer in the picture.

- The second approach is to use hashing to store only hashes of these private transactions, and this involves the orderer just like in a normal transaction lifecycle.

Incidentally, this might be the right time to explain what gossip protocol in Fabric is before we move on.

Hyperledger Fabric documentation defines gossip protocol as a scalable data dissemination (spreading) protocol. This is basically a protocol implemented in Fabric to achieve peer-to-peer communication.

Let us understand this intelligibly. In every organization, a leader is selected either statically or dynamically. This leader has two main responsibilities:

- Getting blocks from the ordering peer. Thus, it should be discoverable by the ordering service because once a block is cut, the Kafka-based ordering service broadcasts this block to all the leaders in the organization.

- Dissemination of the block. Once the leader receives the block from the orderer, its next job is to send it to all the peers within the organization, and it does so with the help of the gossip protocol.

So, the basic use of this protocol is to keep all the peer ledgers in sync and also to propagate any new incoming blocks.

You might be wondering how a leader is different from an anchor peer, and how the gossip protocol is different from Kafka message service.

Well, first of all, the leader is for communication with the orderer peer, whereas the anchor peer is specific to the channel.

So when you create a channel with multiple organizations, the peers in the channel from each organization communicate with each other using the anchor peer.

Figure 3.11 shows the role of an anchor peer and a leader in channels and block propagation, respectively.

There are various configuration hooks available for managing these in the network, e.g., for the selection of leader in gossip protocol.

```
CORE_PEER_GOSSIP_USELEADERELECTION=true
```

```
CORE_PEER_GOSSIP_ORGLEADER=true
```

This will enable dynamic leader election in an organization from a set of peers available for communicating with the orderer.

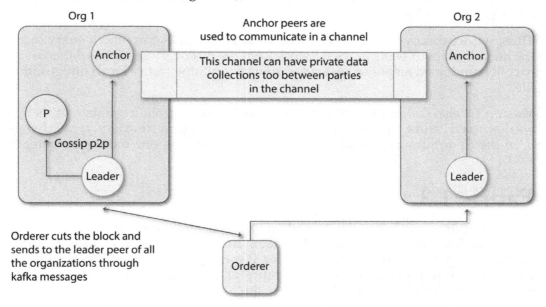

Figure 3.11

Another major feature released along with version 1.2 was the discovery service, which was absent in the previous versions. As seen in previous versions, in the connection profile for static, we had to define everything on the YAML file about the organization structure, channel structure, and so on. This did not allow flexibility like adding new peers or organization without having to redeploy the application.

Also, because the client SDK does not have any metadata about the network state like peer information, writing the proper endorsement policy became difficult.

Endorsement policies are required to be fulfilled for any transaction to be considered valid. Endorsement policies are defined by a logical statement. An example of the same is given in the following code:

```
AND ("org1.msp.member","org2.msp.member")
```

This implies that for a transaction to be valid, it has to be endorsed by at least one member from each organization.

Instead, we can use the following endorsement policy:

```
OR ("org1.msp.admin"," org1.msp.admin" )
```

It states that endorsed response from at least one admin from any organization is enough.

For such configurations, the client has to know about the peers and their state in the channel. Also, it should know about any new addition of peer, removal of peer, and so on in the channel.

Thus, service discovery was introduced where client SDK can send a query to get the metadata about peers in the network from the discovery service and then use it to collect endorsed response, instead of doing everything from a local configuration file.

Version 1.2 also had improved features in the access control mechanism. It also, as we discussed before, made endorsement policies pluggable; that is, you can change it on the fly for any chaincode in a channel, e.g., adding one more parameter in *AND*.

Fabric 1.3

A major upgrade in Fabric 1.3 was identity mixer integration with Fabric CA to enable attribute-based credentials to enable the Fabric CA server to issue these credentials apart from the x.509 certificates. It was a necessary upgrade for enabling zero-knowledge proof (zkp) on the identity of any participants in the network. So using this, anyone can verify whether the given information t is true without knowing it is coming from you. Thus, your identity is not compromised.

Let's consider a case in point. Many agencies will require you to submit your ID proof for various reasons. Once they have the ID proof, they have all crucial details about you like your number, address, etc., which is not ideal. The ideal situation would be for the verifier to only check whether it is valid or not, without having access to all the other details. This is the core idea behind zkp when implemented in public or permissioned blockchains. Such implementations are necessary at identity management level to preserve the anonymity of the participants in the network.

The existing Fabric CA server, which is the current issuer of certificate, has been enhanced to support the Idemix capability. To interact with this CA server, a Java-based SDK is also made available, and implementation in other languages is currently work in progress.

In coming sections, when we talk about certificate management, we will see an example of how you can generate such identity attributes and use them to do a transaction with any verifier.

Moreover, as part of this release, Fabric also started supporting Java for chaincode development, which was an important leap given the enormous number of applications built on Java. We will use Node.js for writing our chaincode and use the Node.js SDK for implementing a client for the network.

CouchDB has been optimized in this release to handle large requests and provide them in a structured manner, which will be used for building front-end application modules like pagination, tables, and so on.

Also, the event hub, which was present in releases before 1.1, was deprecated from this version onwards, so the peer channel-based event service became the only and default event service in this version.

Another important upgrade was the introduction of the per key endorsement policies, which can override the chaincode-level endorsement policies.

So now, we can define an endorsing policy for any particular chaincode at instantiate level as follows:

```
peer chaincode instantiate -C <someChannelId> -n somecc -P "AND('Org1.member', 'Org2.member')"

peer chaincode upgrade -C <someChannelId> -n somecc -P "AND('Org1.member', 'Org2.member','Org3.member')"
```

So, as you can see, we can provide endorsement policies like these from the CLI for a particular chaincode.

But consider the scenario where you need a separate endorser policy for some state, e.g., **OwnerOfCompany** at real time. Endorsement policy is not the right solution for such use cases at state key level.

Thus, there was a need for creating endorsing policies at the key level which can be modified from within the chaincode, without having to depend on lifecycle of chaincode to modify these.

Fabric 1.4 LTS

This year (2019), on January 10, Fabric released the first long-term support version with pledged support for at least one year. The official Fabric announcement encourages the community to use this version for production applications.

You can read the full release information by following the link below from Hyperledger organization:

https://www.hyperledger.org/blog/2019/01/10/introducing-hyperledger-fabric-1-4-lts

One of the major announcements was moving away from the Hyperledger Fabric Composer-based development and providing a richer environment for native development of Fabric applications.

There was a difference in opinion in the community about the use of such tools, which abstracted the important parts of Fabric that needed to be configurable. So Hyperledger Fabric announced that they will stop providing compatibility for Composer after 1.3:

https://lists.hyperledger.org/g/composer/message/125

So, it is important that before moving ahead with the development of a Fabric application, you must choose wisely the tools to ensure that you are not using something that is not native. Dependencies on any tool should be avoided, especially when the core team has put a pause on it.

Composer was great for building some real quick POCs with a few clicks from available templates, but at production level, things have been more robustly implemented.

But it is also true that development setup for chaincode development is a bit complicated and not that easy as in Ethereum where we have Truffle Suite and Ganache available to rapidly test, develop, and deploy smart contracts.

Such tools are a necessity for industry-wide adoption of Hyperledger Fabric. So, a visual studio code extension was introduced: https://marketplace.visualstudio.com/items?itemName=IBMBlockchain.ibm-blockchain-platform

Feel free to try this tool if you are familiar with the VS code. We will be using this extension when we build a sample application.

Fabric 1.4 is definitely a major release from all perspectives. Starting from 0.6, the evolution of Fabric until 1.4 has been truly phenomenal and should be appreciated for building scalable, secure, and modularized blockchain solutions.

The next major release will be 2.0 where some pathbreaking features are planned. However, until the release of 2.0, all minor updates will be provided for 1.4, which will make 1.4 a base version for all production applications in the interim.

We will be building a full end-to-end application based on a use case on Fabric 1.4.

Some of the key updates in this version were as follows:

- Improved logging, as logging is one of the key components of any application that aims to build production-ready version.

- Improved programming model for Node.js SDK. A number of NPM modules were added to make it easy to develop chaincodes and client applications.

World state and states

In this section, we will understand the world state in Hyperledger Fabric.

Prior to understanding world state in Hyperledger Fabric, let's review the idea of blockchain ledger where we will use the concept of world state.

Blockchain ledger: It can be regarded as a storage or file system, where you can store data in an encrypted manner. This encrypted data is available on all the peer nodes of the network. To check the real information stored in a ledger, you have to decrypt it. You can decrypt this information by using a reversal mechanism of encryption (public key of the user for which this information is stored).

You can think of a ledger as a credit or debit memo of your bank transaction, where you want to check your current balance or review the credit and debit trail of your account.

Hyperledger Fabric revolves around the following two concepts:

- Current value in a set of ledger states
- History of transactions that determines these states

Let's have a look at the Hyperledger Fabric structure!

World state: It is defined as a storage (database) that holds the current value of a set of ledger states.

The reason behind keeping the world state is to ensure that you don't have to traverse the whole trail chain (transaction log) as it will increase the time complexity (searching) for fetching the current value in a program (transaction). The default ledger state is represented as a key-value pair. The world state can be created, updated, and deleted frequently, and hence it's mutable.

History of transaction (blockchain): It is a transaction log, a recorder that holds the changes that have happened in the world state. All transactions are collected and stored in a block, and keep on adding dynamically like a **linked list**, termed as blockchain. In a blockchain, you will have the history of the current world state. Blockchain data structure is **immutable**.

Thus, world state is a current value of all the ledger states. Let's take an example to see how the world state is represented as a key-value pair:

```
{key = Book1, value = "The habit loop"} version 0
{key= Book2, value = {name: "Zero to one", author: "Peter thiel",
age:"51" }} version 0
```

You can have simple values corresponding to a key, or you can have more complex data structures corresponding to a key. Both keys (Book1, Book2) have the version 0.

Ledger states are used to hold the necessary information, and this is to be shared via the blockchain. You can access the states using APIs like get, put, and delete. These APIs are available in your chaincode program. World state is implemented as a database, because a database provides various operations for storage, search, and retrieval of the state.

Since every transaction has a life cycle associated with it, transaction hold changes to world states. It is invoked by the application and gets added to the ledger blockchain. Only transactions that are signed by a set of **endorsing organizations** will result in an update to the world state. The transactions that are not signed by a minimum number of endorsers fails and does not get updated to the world state.

Above we have seen that version number is associated with world state. An increment in the version happens when the state changes. It is also checked when the state is updated, to make sure the state matches the version when a transaction is created. This check gives surety that the value change before and after the transaction is expected and no random complex value is assigned.

World state as database:

World state is an implementation of the database. Currently CouchDb and LevelDb are supported by Hyperledger world state database. These are pluggable components. As we have seen, world state is represented by a key-value pair—thus, a NoSQL database can be used for this storage. But world state database can be a relation data store, graph, or other. LevelDb is co-located and embedded in the network node with the same operating system.

CouchDb can be used provided ledger states are described as JSON, because the database supports various queries on get and set and can handle various data types as well. CouchDb runs on a separate OS process instance, but there is a relation between network node and CouchDb instance. This relation and Db are invisible to the chaincode.

Membership service provider (MSP)

Business needs trust, and if there are two different organizations participating in that business, you definitely need to build trust and identify/verify users who are participating in transactions. By using cryptography (digital certificates), this can be achieved.

In this section, we will understand MSP. This is one of the core components in Hyperledger Fabric. We will try to answer three fundamental questions—what, why, and how?

Note: MSP is both a module in Fabric's node (peer and orderer)—they validate identities and classify them into principals (rules)—and an instance of such modules. By this analogy, we can say there can be multiple MSPs in each peer and orderer, and they can belong to the node itself or a channel.

Fabric policy/Access control: These describe who can do and

what can be done by instance of an MSP.

If a node (peer/orderer) uses access control check or any policy defined with it in a channel, we say that the node uses MSP for that channel.

What?

It's a set of cryptographic materials (certificates) that define the organization itself. Every peer and orderer needs this type of certificate.

Note: We are not talking about certificates for user from Fabric CA.

This certificate has some common property by which we can determine whether the peer and the orderer belong to the same organization or not.

Peers, which are a part of the same MSP, can communicate with each other. Peers with other organizations cannot be allowed to communicate with each other.

Below we will be discussing more on MSP, certificates, and setup. Please go through the document for more details.

Membership service provider:

- It is a component that serves as an abstraction over membership operation architecture.

- The abstraction is on cryptography mechanism and protocol, validation certificates, and user authentication.

- MSPs may define their own notion of identities and the rules that govern these identities (identity validation) authentication (signature generation and verification).

- A Fabric network can have one or more MSPs.

Configuration:

- Instance setup of MSP can be configured locally on peers, orderer, and channel (to enable peer, orderer signing, and in the channel to enable client identity validation and signature verification).

- Each MSP described above should have a name for referencing in the network. Let's take a simple name for example, Organization 1_name. The rules of MSP represent a consortium and an organization is to be referenced in a channel referred to as **MSPID** (**MSP identifier**). MSP identifier should be unique for every instance of the node.

Note: Avoid giving two MSP instances with the same identifier as it will throw an error while setting up an orderer.

Going further from this point, we will dive a little deeper into cryptography and PKI (public key infrastructure).

PKI is a structure/framework of encrypting the communication between server (terminal) and client (website/mobile). This structure involves two keys— cryptographic keys and public-private keys. The public key is open and accessible to users that connect with the client (web/mobile). The private key should be a unique key and is generated when a connection is made. This private key should be kept secretly. If data exchange or any communication is happening between a client and the server, the client uses the public key for encryption and decryption of data, while the server uses the private key only.

Key management:

Security of any system (in our case cryptosystem) is dependent on how uniquely you can identify your users. In a cryptosystem, each user is associated with a public key for the client and a private key for the server. If these keys are secure enough, the cryptosystem is also secure. In *Figure 3.12*, you can see the key management and its lifecycle:

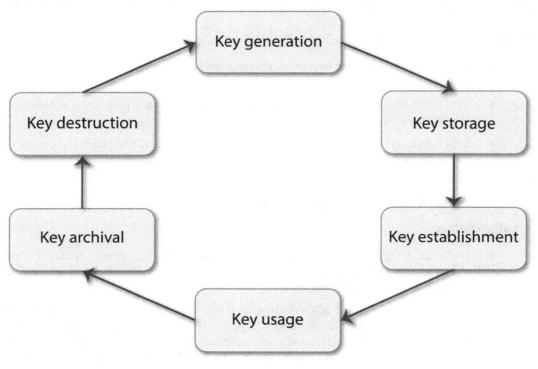

Figure 3.12

PKI framework provides assurance, identification, and distribution of the public key. The PKI framework has the following components:

- Public key certificate AKA digital certificate (ITU standard X.509)
- Private key tokens
- Certification authority
- Registration authority
- Certificate management system

Figure 3.13 depicts the process of obtaining a digital certificate by a person/entity:

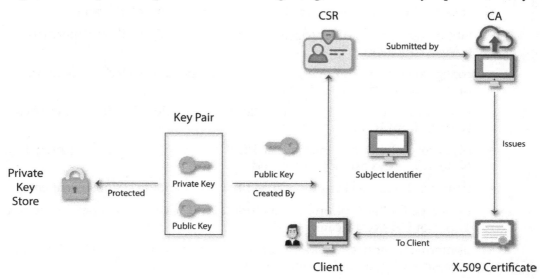

Figure 3.13

Generate MSP certificates and their signing keys

X.509 certificates:

It is a standard defining the format of public key certificates. X.509 certificates are used in IP (internet protocol), including **TLS/SSL (Transport Layer Security/ Secure Socket Layer)**, which is the basis for HTTPS—the secure protocol for browsing the web. An X.509 certificate is addressed with a public key and an identity (a hostname, or an organization, or an individual), and is either signed by a **CA** or is self-signed:

- To get such X.509 certificates to pass to its MSP configuration, the application leverages an open source tool called **OpenSSL**.

- Alternately, one can also use a cryptogen tool, which may not be ideal for production.

MSP setup on the peer and orderer side:

One important point for setting an MSP is to set it up locally (for each peer and orderer). This is important because it enables peers and orderers, which sign the administrator, and should create a folder (for example, $my_path/mspconfig) that contains subfolders and files:

- admincerts: Folder that includes **PEM (Privacy Enhanced Mail**, Base64 encoded) files of admin certificates.

- cacerts: Folder that includes PEM files of root CA's certificates.

- intermediatecerts: Folder (optional) that includes PEM file for intermediate CA's certificates.

- config.yaml: File (optional) to configure the supported organizational units and identity classifications.

- crls: Folder (optional) to include the considered **CRLs (Certificate Revocation Lists)**.

- keystore: Folder that includes a PEM file with the node's signing key. Note: RSA keys are not supported.

- signcerts: Folder to include a PEM file with the node's X.509 certificate.

- tlscacerts: Folder (optional) to include PEM files, each corresponding to a TLS root CA's certificate.

- tlsintermediatecerts: Folder (optional) to include PEM files each corresponding to an intermediate TLS CA's certificate.

In the configuration file of the node (core.yaml file for the peer, and orderer.yaml for the orderer) you need to specify the path to mspconfig folder and the MSP identifier of the node's MSP. The path to the mspconfig folder is expected to be relative to FABRIC_CFG_PATH and is provided as the value of parameter mspConfigPath for the peer and LocalMspDir for the orderer. The node's MSP is provided as a value of the environment parameter LocalMspID and LocalMSPID for peers and orderers, respectively.

How MSP differs from Fabric CA:

As seen previously, MSP is an interface that you can plug for providing various credential architectures. Fundamentally, it's an abstraction layer for membership orchestration architecture.

It provides the following:

- Concrete identity format

- Validation of user credential

- Revocation of user credential when required

- Signature generation and verification

Fabric CA: It helps generate certificates and keys to initialize the MSP. Fabric CA is a default implementation in MSP that you can use in other ways to replace Fabric CA (OpenSSL).

Node.js SDK for Hyperledger Fabric

To enable the interaction programmatically with the Hyperledger Fabric network, there are currently two SDKs. Many others based on different languages are being planned for future release. The current ones include Node.js and Java-based SDKs.

First, let's understand Node.js, SDK which is the most popular one out there amongst the two.

The APIs available in the SDK are used for the following:

- **Install chaincodes in the peers**: This is probably the most important step as it involves deploying smart contracts remotely. Later we will see how this comes bundled with the extension of visual studio code for you to perform these using few clicks.

- **Instantiate the chaincodes in peers**: This is another very important functionality available.

- Channel-related tasks like creating and managing channels and fetching channel meta data.

- Query the ledger.

- Carrying out transactions.

The functionality is not limited to these but these are the most important ones. We will be using these mostly in the upcoming sections.

The Node.js SDK provides the following npm modules to work with the Hyperledger Fabric network:

- **Fabric network**: https://www.npmjs.com/package/fabric-network.

- **Fabric client**: https://www.npmjs.com/package/fabric-client.

- **Fabric CA client**: https://www.npmjs.com/package/fabric-ca-client.

The Fabric network module is basically an encapsulation of both the Fabric client and Fabric CA client module, so it provides high-level APIs, whereas the Fabric client and Fabric CA client are preferred for more fine-grained control of the operations to be performed over the network.

The Fabric CA client provides APIs to work with enrolment service. Fabric CA is used to perform lifecycle operations over certificates. Fabric client modules provide high-level APIs to interact with the peers and orderers to perform lifecycle operations on a chaincode, that is, its instantiation, upgradations, sending transactions, query chaincode, and so on.

It also performs operations related to channels, e.g., adding organizations, installing a chaincode on an organization, and more.

The module uses the connection profile YAML file to know about the Fabric network profile and channel details, which we briefly saw in the connection profile YAML in previous sub modules. We will see it in detail when we build our first network.

We can get standalone scripts or reusable modules in Node.js for performing these operations using SDKs. Thus, these can be called from anywhere in your application, e.g., from within a route in your existing web application built on Express.

Here is how the process looks like from the Node.js SDK. We will take a scenario to explain how we can use the Node.js SDK to interact with the network.

Getting required certificates from CA server using admin for user context:

Before we can interact with the network, we need to be registered and enrolled in the network to get the required certificates from a CA server.

So, for any type of user, there are two steps to be followed: first register them in the CA server with credentials, and then enroll them to get the required certificates, which will be stored in a specific location. These certificates can then be used to interact with the network.

For registering, we use the register (config) method available in CA client, and for enrolling, we use the setUserContext (config) method.

An admin identity is already registered with the CA server so we can use those credentials to first enrol the admin in the CA service:

```
client.setUserContext({username:'org1peeradmin',
password:'org1PWD'})

    .then((adminDetails)
```

This will enroll the admin in the CA server and return the admin details, which we will use to register and enroll new users.

But practically, we have multiple organizations and multiple CAs for them, so we have to first build the Fabric client CA for a particular CA server on the basis of the network profile provided earlier.

To do that enter the following command:

```
let  ca_client = client.getCertificateAuthority();
```

This will configure the Fabric CA client, and then we can register and enrol new users in the CA server.

So once we have a CA client set up and admin object available, we can register a new user by providing an ID, an organization to add the user to, and admin details.

Once we have the user registered, we will get user details that we can use to enroll users to get certificates and use them to sign transactions that we build:

```
ca_client.register({enrollmentID: 'org1user1', affiliation:
'org1'}, adminDetails)

    .then((secret) => {

        return client.setUserContext({username:'user1',
password:secret});

    }).then((user)=> {
```

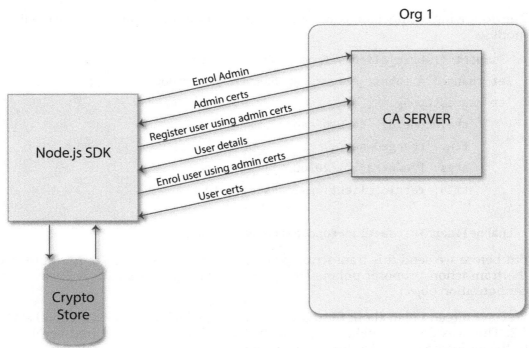

Figure 3.14

To make it easy for you to understand the process, a flow diagram is shown in *Figure 3.14*.

Hyperledger Fabric sending transactions from Node.js SDK:

Once we have the required certificates, we can proceed with writing the logic for executing transactions on chaincodes or do lifecycle operations for chaincodes, channels, and so on.

We will take a simple example of sending a transaction for a particular function in a chaincode using Fabric SDK.

To execute a method in the deployed chaincode, we will need the following information:

```
Chaincode name,
Function name,
Arguments for the function,
A generated transaction id
```

We also need a channel name so we can send a transaction proposal to that channel.

The following snippet of code shows how it is done using the Fabric client module:

```
    import {fabric_client} from 'fabric-client';
  let channel = fabric_client.newChannel('carTradeChannel');
  let requestConfig = {
        chaincodeId: 'carOwnershipCC',
        fcn: 'changeOwner',
        args: ['owner2' , '2030031'] ,
        txId: fabric_client.newTransactionId
  }
  channel.sendTransactionProposal(requestConfig)
```

But before we send this transaction proposal to the peers, we have to figure out the transaction proposal policy. This policy is passed in a structured way as a configuration object.

We have already read about the discovery service, which was introduced in Fabric 1.2. This was done to make it easy to discover all the peers required according to the endorsement policy. So under the hood, Fabric client sends all transaction proposals to the respective peers according to the policy with the help of discovery service.

Peers returning transaction proposal

Once the client sends the transaction proposals to the required peers according to the chaincode endorsement policy, any peer on receiving the transaction proposal does the following:

Check that the signature is valid and signed from a valid CA server.

Check for any duplicity of the transaction proposal and ensure it is well structured.

Run some more validation:

Once done, arguments and function names from the request object are executed in the deployed chaincode. Then the peer generates a transaction response, that is, the read-write set, and returns and signs it, and then returns the proposed transaction response back to the SDK.

Sending signed transaction proposals from client SDK to the orderer:

So once we have enough proposed transaction results from the peers, we can club them together and send them to the orderer. The orderer in turn will order them in a chronological order, based on channels, into a block and return the status to the client SDK:

```
}).then((proposalResults) =>{
    let proposalResponse = proposalResults[0];
    let proposalArray = proposalResults[1];
    var AreAllproposalsCorrect = true;
    proposalArray.forEach((response)=>{
        if(response.status === 200) {
            AreAllproposalsCorrect = false;
            if(response) {
                AreAllproposalsCorrect =                channel.ve
rifyProposalResponse(response);
            }
            // check whether all read write sets are same from all
peers
            // .......
            //Then set an event listener for this transaction
        }
    })
    requestObjForOrderer = {
```

```
        proposalResponses: proposalArray,
        proposal: proposalResponse
    };
    return Promise.all(channel.sendTransaction(requestObjForOrdere
r));
```

Let's briefly explain what's happening here. First, we get the proposed responses from peers as proposalResponse. We then retrieve all the response array from this returned object and also the proposed response.

We iterate through these arrays of transaction proposals and check whether they are valid.

Then, we take all these responses and send them to the orderer using the sendTransaction function.

Now, the SDK's job is done, and the leader peers of the organizations will propagate the received blocks to all the peers through the gossip protocol. Then, all the peers will execute these transactions in order and update the ledger.

This defines the entire process. Without the use of client SDK, everything has to be done from CLI, which is only meant for operation purposes.

So this brings us to the end of our primer about the Node.js SDK, where we have explained, with the help of a simple scenario, how it can be used to interact with the network. This may not be a complete example, but these code snippets can help you understand how to use the SDK.

Chaincode in Node.Js

For writing chaincodes or smart contracts, Hyperledger provides support in many languages like Golang, Node.js, and Java. This section provides an overview of the process of writing a chaincode using Node.js. We will be using typescript to write the chaincode, which is one of the standard and better ways to write JavaScript, similar to es6. To develop chaincodes in Node.js, the Fabric team has provided two npm modules. These packages are analogous to the Go and Java packages used to write chaincodes. One of them provides high-level API for contract development, while the other provides a low-level API for chaincode development.

Prior to introducing you to the process of writing a chaincode in Node.js, let us understand the structure of a chaincode. Fabric has defined an interface for writing chaincodes. All contracts, whether in Go, Node.js, or Java, should implement this interface.

This interface is available in Fabric shim package for all the three programming languages.

It has two methods that each chaincode has to implement if it is extending this package.

Init(stub) Asynchronous

This method is called when the chaincode is instantiated or upgraded. This is the correct place to initialize some states.

It also has the stub parameter that provides a number of methods to interact with the peer. It can also be used for invoking identities, target channels, argument, and so on.

Some of the important methods are as follows:

- Stub,getArgs(): This method will provide all the arguments passed while instantiating a chaincode from CLI. It returns an array of strings. This will be used in all the chaincode implementations.

- Stub.getFunctionAndParameters(): This is another method that provides the function names that need to be invoked from the chaincode and all parameters related to it.

To manage or query state data, following functions are provided:

- Stub.getState (key): This method takes the name of the key of the state whose state has to be retrieved from the peer, e.g., stub.getState (ownerOfCar).

- Stub.putState (key, value): This method takes the name of the key of the state and its value that has to be put in the peer ledger, e.g., stub.putState (ownerOfCar, Rob).

- Stub.deleteState (key): This method deletes the state from the state store, e.g., stub.deleteState (ownerOfCar).

- Stub.getHistoryForKey (key): This method returns an iterator object containing the history of the state, e.g., stub.getHistory (ownerOfCar).

This will return all the previous owners of the cars.

There are other useful methods available in the stub modules of shim package that can be used to work with the chaincode state and also to get other information like client identity information. Please review the link (https://fabric-shim.github.io/release-1.3/fabric-shim.ChaincodeStub.html) for all the method definitions available for various use cases.

Invoke(stub) Asynchronous

This is the main method that can be called throughout the lifecycle of the chaincode to carry out business logic and update the states in the process.

Most of the logic shown here goes for almost all use cases.

This method also has a parameter of stub, ChaincodeStub, to work with peer states.

Now, let's review one of the development setup methods for smart contract creation.

To develop smart contract written using VSCode extension:

- Install the VSCode and IBM Blockchain Platform called VSCode extension.
- Use the keyboard shortcut *Shift + CMD + P* to bring up the command palette and select IBM Blockchain Platform: Create Smart Contract Project from the dropdown.
- Click JavaScript from the dropdown.
- Create a new folder and name it whatever you want, e.g., TestContract.
- Start by creating a new folder and open it. Next, from the dropdown on left top, click Add to Workspace.
- Check the smart contract lib/my-contract.js in this location.

Modify smart contract:

Replace this contract with an existing contract written in lib/my-contract.js:

```
'use strict';
const { Contract } = require('fabric-contract-api');
class MyDemoContract extends Contract {
```

This instantiate method is from Fabric contract API and takes an argument. Here we have set a state in the ledger (updating the ledger) with "Hello World" and shown that the function is called.

```
  */
  async instantiate(ctx) {
    let temp = { text: 'Instantiate Method from was called!' };
    await ctx.stub.putState('Hello',
    Buffer.from(JSON.stringify(temp)));
  }
```

```
/*
```

A custom build method to take an argument and create a temp object that can be updated to the ledger:

```
*/
  async transaction1(ctx, arg1) {
    console.info('transaction1', arg1);
    let temp = { text: arg1 };
await ctx.stub.putState('Hello', Buffer.from(JSON.stringify(temp)));
    return JSON.stringify(temp);
  }
}
module.exports = MyDemoContract;
```

Let's examine the function MyDemoContract that we just defined. The instantiate function creates a temp (any pseudo name) object and then stores that on the ledger with the key Hello. The transaction1 function takes the Hyperledger Fabric context (contract-api) and one argument, arg1, which is used to store a temp object as defined by the user. The ctx.stub.putState method is used to hold the temp object on the ledger and then return that object back.

Packaging: Packaging smart contract means you can install it on peers:

- Open the command palette with the command *Shift + CMD +P*, and select Package smart contract.
- Check the left sidebar. Then click on the IBM Blockchain Platform icon (square symbol). In the top-left corner, you can see all of your smart contract packages. You can see TestContract @0.0.1 if everything has gone well so far.

Smart contract installation on peer:

To install smart contracts on peer nodes, you have to first connect with the Hyperledger Fabric network. A default network that comes with VSCode extension is fine for this play (test and development).

It requires minimal resources to test and develop your smart contract.

The following Docker containers start on your local machine with different roles in the network:

- Orderer
- CA
- CouchDb

- Peer

To start your network, select the IBM Blockchain Platform extension at the bottom-right corner, where you get the popup: Blockchain Connections.

You should see local_fabric. Click it, and it should automatically run a script. You can see the following output:

```
Starting fabricvscodelocalfabric_orderer.example.com_1          ... done
Starting fabricvscodelocalfabric_ca.example.com_1               ... done
Starting fabricvscodelocalfabric_couchdb_1                      ... done
Starting fabricvscodelocalfabric_peer0.org1.example.com_1       ... done
```

Click the local_fabric connection again. Now that it's up and running, it should take you to your channel view. There would be a default channel named mychannel. Click that.

This expands your default channel mychannel and shows the peers and smart contracts. Click on Peers, and you should see peer0.org1.example.com that you defined in the cryptoconfig file (for this example, it's default setting with some peers and organization). Right-click on that peer and click on Install Smart Contract.

The extension asks you which package to install. Choose TestContract@0.0.1.

Instantiate the smart contract:

In the bottom-left corner of the IBM Blockchain extension, go to Blockchain Connections and right-click on mychannel. Then, click on instantiate smart contract, or you can use the shortcut *Shift + CMD + P* by going through the command palette and choose the IBM-Blockchain Platform. Then instantiate the smart contract from the dropdown list.

The IBM Blockchain extension will ask you which contract and version to instantiate. Choose TestContract @0.0.1, because there could be one or many contracts with different versions.

The IBM Blockchain extension will ask you which function to call. Type in instantiate.

The next process chain will ask you for the arguments. For this example, there are no arguments, so just hit Enter to bypass this check.

After some time (seconds/minutes), in the bottom-right corner you can see the contract successfully instantiated.

This is enough for us to understand the basics of chaincodes in Hyperledger. We will be looking into them in more detail when we start developing these chaincodes for real use cases.

Summary

In this chapter, we first explored the current blockchain landscape and how a permissioned blockchain, like Hyperledger, is the way forward. We also understood the subtle differences between public and permissioned blockchain networks. We then looked into various blockchain projects hosted by the Linux foundation and the various tools used to aid to these solutions. We also learnt how Hyperledger Fabric differs from other permissioned blockchain networks and traditional distributed databases.

We then learnt how Fabric has evolved in the past three years, starting as a POC-based blockchain network to becoming a production-ready permissioned network. This giant leap for Hyperledger Fabric was phenomenal and has laid the foundation for its industry-wide adoption.

We then understood the key details about the network itself and the role of various nodes like orderer, peer, MSP, and so on. We also followed the journey of a transaction in the network and tried to understand its process.

Finally, we looked briefly into the details of chaincodes and Node.js-based chaincodes in Fabric. Here, we also looked into the Node.js SDK available for interaction with the network.

References

- https://www.hyperledger.org/
- https://hyperledger-fabric.readthedocs.io/en/release-1.4/
- https://hyperledger-fabric-ca.readthedocs.io
- https://fabric-SDK-node.github.io/
- https://github.com/hyperledger/fabric
- https://www.tutorialspoint.com/cryptography/
- https://www.npmjs.com/package/fabric-network
- https://developer.ibm.com/technologies/blockchain/

## CHAPTER 4

Frameworks, Network Topologies, and Modeling

In this chapter, we will review how Fabric network modeling is executed, along with the implementation process of such a network topology. But before we dive into the details, it would be good to explain a use case on Hyperledger that we will gradually build in order to understand the pieces of a Hyperledger network and programming model.

Unlisted company network in Hyperledger

Traditionally, unlisted companies face efficiency and business continuity challenges because of a lack of access to formalized credit structures and public stock exchanges. Blockchain and Hyperledger technologies can aid unlisted companies to build a trusted digital platform to manage shareholder data and increase their credit access. The blockchain platform will replace paper trading certificates that are issued by the unlisted entities in many countries.

Primarily, there will be three main parties in this platform: issuers (companies), regulators, and investors. The blockchain platform will provide a more digitized, efficient, and transparent system to have greater insight into the company's detailed information:

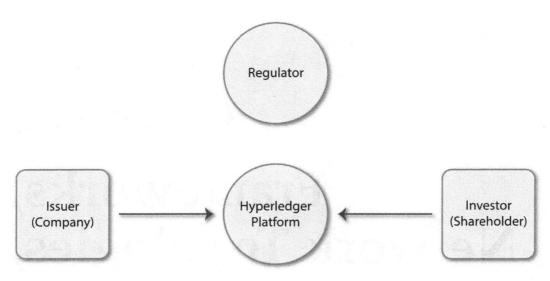

Figure 4.1

By implementing this solution, companies can join a matured and broader investor ecosystem and enhance their ability to obtain funding. With this, a company can set up new trading networks and access credit by sharing financial information in a highly secure and transparent public arena. Moreover, the unlisted entities will get an opportunity to take the lead over their rivals in transforming how the companies can exchange shareholder data, thereby bringing transparency and expanding credit reach.

The blockchain solution will be developed on a security-rich infrastructure technology. The system is designed to enable gated and secured sharing of highly sensitive securities data amongst permissioned network participants.

Hyperledger network and application model

Here we will try to understand the Hyperledger blockchain network from a conceptual standpoint. This topic is useful for those who have a technical background and work as a developer, an architect, or an administrator. This topic will give you a deep understanding of the Hyperledger Fabric network and the major components involved in this process. You might have some basic idea about policies from the last few chapters. In this section, we will deep dive into those policies, network evolution and its management (declarative policies), and decisions that consortiums need to take while establishing and controlling such networks. So, let's *go with the flow*.

Blockchain network

Blockchain network is a technical infrastructure where you (client/application) store data (transaction records) by means of some logical smart contract (chaincode in Hyperledger terminology) services. Smart contracts are a way to generate transactions in an application, and the output of these transactions is stored in every peer node as a ledger. This ledger is immutable by nature.

For businesses, a consortium of organizations forms a network and their permissions, rules, and validations are all decided by policies. These policies should be mutually accepted by each member of the network. Over a period of time, the administrator of a consortium network has the power to change the policies of the network using a concept called policy modification.

Build a sample network

Problem statement:

Org1, Org2, Org3, Org4: Organizations

C1, C2: Channels

Pr1, Pr2, Pr3: Peers

O: Orderer

L1, L2: Ledgers

NC4: Network configuration

CC1: Channel configuration

CA1, CA2, CA3, CA4: Certificate authorities

Let's say there are four organizations.

They have decided to form a consortium and have written an agreement that states they will form a network. Org4 is not a part of any transaction. Org1 and Org2 want to have a private communication, as well as Org2 and Org3. Org1 is running a client application as well and doing business transactions within channel C1. Org2 is also running a client application and is doing business transactions in both channels C1 and C2. Similarly, Org3 is also running a client application and doing business transactions in channel C2.

Peer nodes are attached by channels. Peer nodes only maintain a copy of the ledger, so they are connected with a client application as well. Let's check which peer is connected among which channels.

Peer node Pr1 stores a copy of ledger L1 and is connected to channel C1. Peer node Pr2 stores and maintains a copy of ledgers L1 and L2 and is connected to channels C1 and C2. Another peer node Pr3 stores and maintains a copy of ledger L2 and is connected to channel C2.

This network should follow the rules specified by a common agreement of consortium members. Policies are defined at the time of network configuration, i.e., NC4. This configuration is in control of Org1 and Org4. Channel configuration CC1 defines the policy rule of C1. Channel configuration CC2 defines the policy rule of C2 and is under control of Org2 and Org3.

In between these nodes, there is an ordering node O that is responsible for network administration. It uses the system channel. Ordering service is connected with channels C1 and C2 for ordering of transactions into a block of distribution. All four organizations have a certificate authority.

Finally, the overall network should look as shown in *Figure 4.2*:

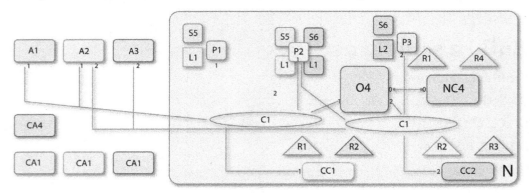

Figure 4.2

Creating network from scratch

The first thing we will setup is the *mind* of the network, i.e., the orderer. Ordering service is configured according to NC4 (network configuration) and gives administrative right to Org4. CA4 is used to generate and dispense the certificate for Org4:

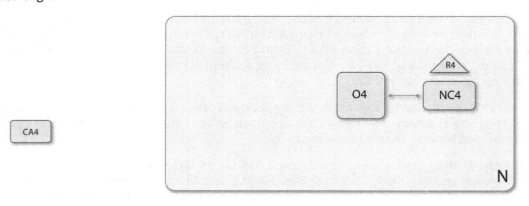

Figure 4.3

Certificate authority

In the previous figure, you saw that CA4 is used to issue certificate to the network node and administrator. CA4 has a primary role in this network because it issues X.509 certificate that is used to identify the functionality owned by organization Org4. Transaction can be signed by a CA, which indicates that an organization can endorse the transaction results.

The first step is for all the nodes, peers, orderers, and channels to identify themselves to each other in the network. More than one CA can support a blockchain network, and it is a good practice to have this kind of separation. In this network setup, we will use four CAs, one for each organization. The role of a CA is very important in a Hyperledger Fabric network. There is a default and built-in CA provider in Hyperledger Fabric network (Fabric CA).

A membership services provider (MSP) maps the certificate to member organizations. Network configuration NC4 uses a given *MSP*. It identifies the properties in the certificate issued by CA4. The CA4 configuration associates the certificate holder with organization Org4. NC4 uses the MSP name in policies to give rights to Org4.

Later in this section, we will see how a CA plays an important role in transaction generation and its validation process. We will also see how this certificate plays a very important role. The X.509 certificate is used by the transaction generated from client application to digitally sign the transaction for smart contract responses. The network node responsible for hosting the copy of ledger will verify the transaction signature's validity before accepting transactions to append to the ledger.

Network administration node

See *Figure 4.4*:

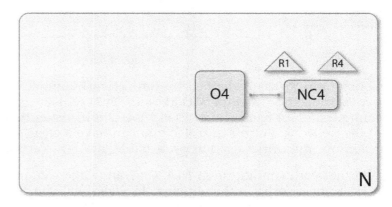

Figure 4.4

Initially NC4 was configured to only accept Org4 as the administrator in the network. Now we will extend this structure and add another organization, Org1, as an administrator in the network. Both Org1 and Org4 are acting as administrators and are configured with NC4 network configuration. With the addition of the new administrator Org1, we can see the addition of a new certificate authority, CA1, for Org1 for issuing and validating certificates. With this, we can identify users in the network from Org1. The orderer node O is running on Org4 platform. Org1 has shared administrator power on it. Org1 and Org4 both have rights to update the network configuration NC4 that allows Org2 to be a part of the network operation. Thus, Org4 is running the ordering service and Org1 has full administrative power similar to Org4. Org2 has limited powers to create/change new policies of the consortium. Ordering service is a single node in a Fabric network. Ideally, ordering service should be multi-node, which means that the configuration should be on different nodes on different organizations. For example, we can run orderer O4 in Org4 and connect it to orderer O2, which will be a separate orderer in organization Org1. We will discuss ordering service in further detail later.

Consortium definition

A consortium is a *group of companies with the same goal.*

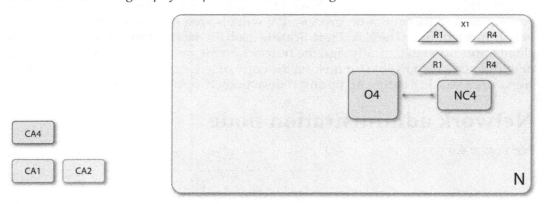

Figure 4.5

Consortium $$(X1) is defined by the network admin. This consortium contains two organization members Org1 and Org2. NC4 is used to store the network configuration of consortium $$(X1). We will be using this to build the next stage of the network. From *Figure 4.5*, you can have a clear idea that CA1 and CA2 are certificate authorities used to issue and identify the certificate in the network.

With network configuration NC4, Org1 and Org4 can append/create/modify new rules and consortia in the network. In *Figure 4.5*, you can see we are adding this new consortium $$(X1) to the network and it takes Org1 and Org2 as its constitution organization. CA2 is added, and its role is to identify users from Org2. Admin can add any number of organizations to the network.

We have seen from *Figure 4.5* and explanation that a consortium is formed between organizations who want to transact with one another. These organizations have a common goal to conduct business activities with each other. In the preceding example, Org1 and Org2 want to transact and are part of the network. We started the preceding network with a single organization Org4 and is joined by a larger set of participating organizations. Now, let's take a look at the concept of a *channel*.

Channel for consortium

See *Figure 4.6*:

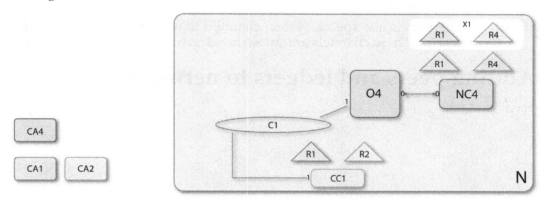

Figure 4.6

A channel is a mechanism by which the members of a consortium communicate with each other.

Figure 4.6 shows channel C1 created for organizations Org1 and Org2 by using the consortium definition $$(X1). The channel is handled by channel configuration CC1. This channel configuration is totally separate from the network configuration. It's important to note that channel configuration CC1 is managed by Org1 and Org2. Both these organizations have equal rights on channel C1. However, Org4 has no rights on CC1.

Points to note:

1. In consortium $$(X1), channel C1 provides a private communication.

2. Channel C1 is attached to the ordering service node O4.

3. Channel C1 is used to privately transact between Org1 and Org2.

4. We started with Org4, which has the admin rights and is controlling the network. Later, we have granted these same permissions to organization Org1 as well, with the power to create a new consortium and channel in the Fabric network.

5. Any number of organizations can be connected in the same channel.

6. For channel C1, we have channel configuration settings, and that is separate from network configuration NC4.

7. Channel configuration CC1 has a policy that drives the rights for organization Org1 and Org2 in channel C1.

8. Only authorized organizations, Org1 and Org2, can add a new organization to channel C1.

9. One channel is completely disconnected from the other, thus making each channel a private one.

10. There are some special system channels that are used by the ordering service. These channels are sometimes known as application channels.

Adding peers and ledgers to network

See *Figure 4.7*:

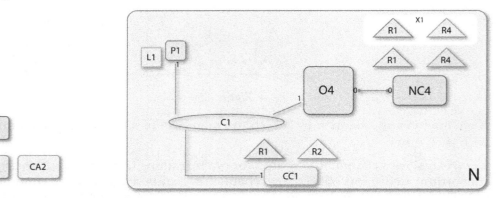

Figure 4.7

The next step in network evolution is to add peer nodes and ledgers to the channel.

Peer Pr1 can join channel C1. This peer node can communicate with orderer node O4 using channel C1. Peer node Pr1 also hosts a copy of the ledger.

Points to note:

1. A peer node is a part of the network (network component) where copies of the ledger are hosted.

2. Peer Pr1 can communicate with orderer node O4 using channel specification C1.

An important part in Pr1 configuration is an X.509 identity issued by certificate authority CA1. This CA1 associates Pr1 with organization Org1. At the onset, peer node Pr1 can join channel C1 and can communicate with orderer O4. When O4 receives the request to join, it uses channel configuration CC1 to help find Pr1's permission on channel C1.

For example, channel configuration CC1 helps determine if Pr1 can read/write information to ledger L1 or not.

The next step in Hyperledger Blockchain network setup is to run the client application and chaincode.

Client/application and chaincode

See *Figure 4.8*:

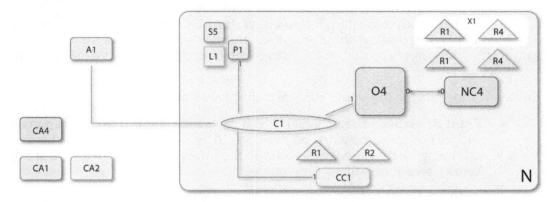

Figure 4.8

As the network evolves, we can see that node A1 (client/application) is added to network N, which is a new node.

Here you can see that smart contract S5 is installed on peer node Pr1. Client/application A1 in organization Org1 uses smart contract (chaincode) S5 to access the ledger via peer node Pr1. Pr1, O4, and A1 are all connected by channel C1. Like peer and orderer services, the client/application also has an identity in the network. This identity is associated with an organization. Here client/application A1 is associated with organization Org1, though it is outside of the Hyperledger Fabric network.

Exploring Hyperledger frameworks

Hyperledger has mainly provided us with five major frameworks:

1. Sawtooth

2. Fabric

3. Indy

4. Burrow

5. Iroha

Hyperledger Sawtooth

Hyperledger Sawtooth is a blockchain platform built for enterprise use. Its design focuses on maintaining the safety of smart contracts and ledgers by keeping it distributed. Sawtooth offers a simplified platform for blockchain application development by separating the application domain and the core system level. Application developers could opt for a language of their choice to write the smart contract logic.

Sawtooth supports the following consensus implementations:

- **Proof of elapsed time (PoET)**: It is a consensus algorithm that can give support to large network populations. It relies on secure execution on achieving scaling benefits without the drawbacks of **PoW** (**Proof of Work**), which consumes high power.

- **PoET simulator**: It provides a PoET consensus on any type of hardware.

- **Dev mode**: It is a simple random-ledger algorithm used for development and testing.

Sawtooth allows a native business logic or smart contract VM application to be made in a transaction-processing layer that could exist in the same instance of a blockchain network. Sawtooth brings in the separation between application level and core system. Sawtooth offers several transaction families to be models for low-level functions, especially for applications such as performance analysis and block information storage.

Sawtooth is mainly designed to ease the challenges of a private network. Sawtooth Clusters could easily be deployed with separated permissioning. There is no service that is centralized and could leak confidential information or transaction patterns. The blockchain stores common settings such as roles and permissions so that all participants are accessible to the network.

Sawtooth also includes an advanced parallel scheduler that splits up the transactions into parallel flows. It isolates the execution of transactions from each other on the basis of the locations accessed by the transaction and maintains contextual changes.

Transactions are executed in parallel whenever possible, thus preventing double spending even after having multiple transactions in the same state. This feature of parallel scheduling provides a potential increase in the performance over serial execution.

Hyperledger Sawtooth also offers the creation and broadcasting of events. It allows us to subscribe to events, e.g., when committing a new block or switching to a new fork. It subscribes to application-specific events and relays information about the execution of a transaction back to the clients. The subscriptions are serviced over a ZMQ socket.

Hyperledger Fabric

Hyperledger Fabric is the most widely used private blockchain. It is primarily used within enterprise settings for efficient transactions between multiple businesses. Fabric has a modular design, i.e., businesses can plug in different functionalities to suit their particular needs. Like all blockchains, Fabric records a history of transactions in a chronological ledger.

In Bitcoin, for example, the ledger holds the record of bitcoins as they transfer from one party to another. In Fabric, the definition of what gets transferred is a bit loose and it is defined as an asset. An asset could be anything that has some monetary value. Hyperledger Fabric allows the businesses to set their asset types and values autonomously. Assets are nothing but a collection of key-value pair, with state changes recorded as transactions on the ledger system. Hyperledger Fabric enables assets to be modified by use of a chaincode. A chaincode is a software that defines an asset and corresponding transaction instructions required to modify the assets. In other words, it's the business logic. Smart contracts that are deployed to Fabric ledger execute the chaincode. Instead of each business having its own business logic, which changes its own database, the businesses share the business logic along with all the sign-off required on making changes to the database. Members of each permissioned network of Hyperledger Fabric can use the chaincode to interact with the ledger. This can be done by either deploying new contracts that add new business logic or by invoking transactions that have been codified in past contracts.

To enable these permissioned networks, Hyperledger Fabric provides a membership identity service that manages user IDs used to authenticate all participants on the network.

Access control lists can be utilized to provide extra layers of permission through authorization of specific network operations. For example, a specific user ID could be permitted to invoke a chaincode application but be blocked from deploying a new chaincode. This permission network also assigns network roles by node types. There are two node types within the Hyperledger Fabric network:

- Peer nodes
- Ordering nodes

Peer nodes are responsible for executing and verifying transactions. Ordering nodes are responsible for ordering transactions and propagating the correct history of events to the network. By allowing peer nodes to batch and process multiple transactions simultaneously, the efficiency and scalability of the network are increased. The network consensus protocol, which could be customized by the business and the network, is then implemented by the ordering nodes to create a single true record of transactions.

Fabric ledger is comprised of two components: a blockchain log to store the immutable sequenced record of transactions in blocks, and a state database to maintain the blockchain's current state. In the Bitcoin blockchain, there is no database and the current state of the chain is always calculated by going through all the transactions in the ledger. For speed and efficiency sake, Hyperledger Fabric stores the current state as well and allows the members of the network to query it in the form of sequel-like transactions. The purpose of the blockchain log here is to trap an assets providence or place of origin as it is exchanged amongst multiple parties. To track an assets providence means to track where and when it was created, along with a history of its exchange. In a typical database, where only the current state of an asset is kept and not a log of all transactions, tracking an assets providence becomes very difficult. Hyperledger Fabric solves this problem by using private channels, which are restricted messaging pods, that can be used to provide transaction privacy and confidentiality for specific subsets of the network members. All data including transactions are invisible to members who are not granted access.

Hyperledger Fabric has a modular design that enables five core functionalities:

1. Asset types and consensus protocol can be defined.
2. Permissions on who can join the network can be set.
3. Two types of nodes are present: peer and orderer.
4. Ledger consists of a database of the current state and a log of transactions.
5. Assets are added, updated, and transferred using the chaincode.

Hyperledger Indy

Hyperledger Indy is also a distributed ledger that provides tools for creating and using independent and decentralized digital identities, where individuals would not have to rely on any organization to store their personal data. The individuals could be owners of their own data and decide whom they should provide the data and for how long. This provides a decentralized identity to the user, rooted on blockchains, guaranteeing utmost privacy. This is also an added advantage for the companies, where they need not spend money and resources to store user data and deal with privacy concerns. This enables meaningful transactions for individuals. It is basically a software ecosystem that provides a powerful identity for its users.

Now let's put theory aside and understand the concept through a use case. Suppose an employee, Bob, needs to get his experience certificate from a company, Sate, and the company offers a website where Bob could get his certificate digitally. He logs into the website and requests for his certificate by clicking on **Get Certificate**.

Sate, on the ledger, already has a trust anchor, which is basically implemented on the code base of Indy. A trust anchor is not actually a *trusted third party*. Instead, it is a person or an organization that is well known to the ledger. Bob would need a new stype of identity that is a portable one and independent of any past relationship with Sate that nobody could co-relate without his permission. This is the core feature of the ledger: self-sovereign identity.

Sate would have understood the requirements and given Bob an Indy app that leverages a third-party service provider, which could be considered as an agency. This app would get installed as a part of the **Get Certificate** workflow.

When Bob clicks the **Get Certificate** button, he will download a file that will send an Indy connection request. The connection request file would contain a .indy extension that would allow him to establish a secure channel of communication with Sate, which is another party in the ledger. Thus, when Bob clicks the **Get Certificate** button, the app will be installed automatically and it will ask him whether he wants to accept the request to connect with Sate.

Hyperledger Burrow

Hyperledger Burrow is a project by the Linux Foundation. It offers a modular blockchain client along with a permissioned smart contract interpreter partially developed to the specification of the **Ethereum virtual machine** (**EVM**). It is a permissioned blockchain node that executes smart-contract codes following the specifications of Ethereum.

Burrow is constructed using three main components:

1. Consensus engine
2. Permissioned EVM
3. RPC gateway

In the consensus engine, transactions are ordered using to the Byzantine fault-tolerant Tendermint protocol.

The **application blockchain interface** (**ABCI**) enables the transactions to be processed in the language you prefer.

The smart contract application assists in the integration of complex business logic.

Permissioned EVM ensures that the required permissions are provided, and the VM is built to Ethereum's specifications.

API gateway provides an interface for user and system integration.

Hyperledger Iroha

Hyperledger Iroha is another Hyperledger project by the Linux Foundation. It is a simple C++-domain-driven design that basically emphasizes on mobile application development. It is designed in such a way that it could be easily incorporated into any distributed ledger technology. It is designed to create a library of reusable modular components that would enhance the existing distributed ledger frameworks and also comprises a YAC consensus algorithm.

Hyperledger Iroha aims for the following three goals:

1. It should provide an infrastructure for mobile and web application support.

2. It should provide an environment for C++ developers to contribute to Hyperledger.

3. It should provide a framework to bring in APIs and new consensus algorithm that could be potentially plugged into other frameworks in future.

Iroha architecture

The main architecture was inspired by Hyperledger Fabric. Its basic goal is to fulfil the need of user-friendly interfaces. They have developed a framework that has a modular C++ design and a new chain-based Byzantine fault-tolerant consensus algorithm named Sumeragi. Iroha is capable of freely interoperating with other Hyperledger projects. The open source allows developers to easily build functions for performing common operations:

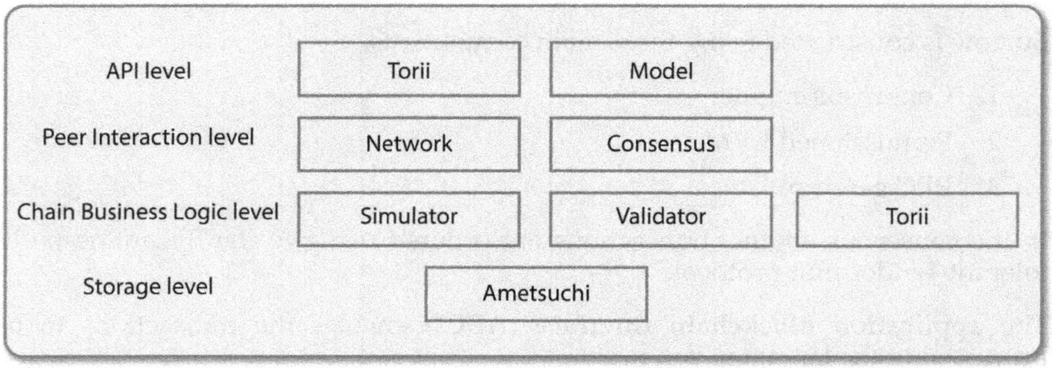

Figure 4.9

The four main layers are **API level, peer interaction level, chain business logic level**, and **storage level**.

Model classes are plainly system entities. **Torii**, i.e., the gate, provides the input and output interfaces for the clients. A single gRPC server is used by clients to interact with the peers of the network. The RPC call made by the clients is non-blocking, which makes Torii an asynchronous server. Through this interface, both command and queries are performed.

Network consists of interaction with the network of peers.

- **Consensus** is required for peers agreeing on chain content in the network. **YAC (yet another consensus)** is used by Iroha, which is a Byzantine fault-tolerant algorithm based on voting for block hash.

- **Simulator** gives a temporary snapshot of storage. Transactions are validated by executing them against this snapshot to form a verified proposal, which consists of only valid transactions.

- **Validator** classes scan the transactions and check the business rules and validity of transactions or queries.

There are two types of validations that happen in Hyperledger Iroha:

- **Stateless validation** is a quicker form of validation. It performs signature and schema checks of the transaction.

- **Stateful validation** is slower compared to stateless and checks the permissions and the current world state view (which is the latest and most actual state of the chain) to see if the desired business rules and policies are feasible.

A synchronizer helps in synchronizing new peers in the system or temporarily disconnecting peers.

Ametsuchi is the ledger block storage consisting of a block index, block store, and world state view component.

Transaction flow in Iroha happens as follows:

1. The client creates and sends a transaction to the Torii gate, which routes the transaction to a peer responsible for stateless validation.

2. After the peer has performed a stateless validation, the transaction is sent to the ordering gate. The ordering gate is responsible for choosing the correct strategy to connect to the ordering service.

3. The ordering service orders the transactions and sends them to the peers in the consensus network in the form of proposals. A proposal is an unsigned block that is shared by the ordering service and consists of a batch of

ordered transactions. Proposals are only sent when the ordering service has enough transactions, or a certain amount of time has elapsed since the last proposal. This prevents the ordering service from forwarding empty proposals.

4. Each peer verifies the proposal's contents in the simulator and creates a block that consists of only the transactions that are verified. This block is then forwarded to the consensus gate, which carries out the YAC consensus logic.

5. An ordered list of peers is generated, and a leader is elected on the basis of the YAC consensus algorithm logic. Each peer casts a vote by signing and sending its proposed block back to the leader.

6. If the leader gets enough signed proposed, i.e., more than 2/3 of the peers, then it starts to send a commit message, indicating that this block should be applied to the chain of each peer who is participating in the consensus. Once the commit message has been forwarded, the proposed block becomes the next block in the chain of every peer through the synchronizer.

YAC consensus algorithm

Hyperledger Iroha currently gears the YAC consensus algorithm logic, which is implemented on the basis the votes for the block hash. The YAC performs two functions: ordering and consensus.

Ordering is accountable for ordering all transactions, wrapping them into proposals, and forwarding them to the peers in the network. The ordering service is an endpoint to set an order of transactions and their broadcast in the form of a proposal. Ordering is not accountable for carrying out stateful validation of transactions.

Consensus comprises taking blocks after they have been verified, collaborating with the other blocks to agree on a commit, and broadcasting commits between peers. Consensus is accountable for an agreement on blocks based on the same proposal.

Validation is an essential part of the transaction flow; however, it is isolated from the consensus process.

Transaction privacy and security

One of the core advantages of a permissioned network like Hyperledger is transaction privacy and security. It's vital that the information is not visible to all the entities and only the entities involved in it should be able to see it rather than everyone else in the network.

Hyperledger provides the following solution for enabling the above:

- Channels: They are at the heart of a Hyperledger network and facilitate sub-networking among the network participants for doing such transactions. They are controlled and governed according to channel policies. We will be working with channels a lot in our examples and solutions.

- Private data collection: Channels are resource-intensive entities of the network. If we assume you have a channel with four organizations and two of these organizations want to have a private transaction without letting the other organizations know, instead of creating another two channels we can use a functionality known as private data collection. They are not governed by channel policies. Instead, their policies are defined at chaincode level itself.

- Encryption: It's common paradigm to hash the transaction details and store it in the ledger. This is employed heavily in the blockchain space, especially public chains, but we also do it in permissioned blockchains like Hyperledger. We will see how Fabric chaincode packages provide such utility functions to facilitate it.

- **ZKP, ZKAT**: Using the power of cryptography, we can enable zero-knowledge proofs, zero-knowledge asset transfer, and so on. Many public blockchains are investing time and money to enable such powerful technologies. In Hyperledger, providing it as an out-of-the-box feature is still work in progress.

Understanding pre-requisites

Now that we have some understanding of how the Fabric blockchain network functions and its vital parts, it is time to get some hands-on experience. But before we start, let's understand some of the prerequisites that will be helpful in understanding the network.

Fabric uses a very powerful and modern stack of technology that makes it robust. Some of these technologies include the following:

1. Docker as a containerization technology

2. Node.js for chaincode and client application

3. Golang for chaincode and for Fabric itself

Now, let's take them one by one and gain some level of understanding through examples. We will start with Docker!

Docker

First, let's understand how Docker came into picture.

In good old days when there were physical machines for deploying applications, there existed a need for a better technology as such deployment was a tragic waste of resources. Just imagine the entire physical machine running a single application, which was also prone to faults.

Then came VMWare with hypervisor solution where on a single host machine or an **operating system (OS)** there can be multiple virtual machines installed with each having its own operating system, CPU, memory, and more. These soon became industry standard, and even today virtual machines are used heavily for deployment.

However, they still were not even close to an ideal solution.

Let's think like this. Assume you have a Linux Ubuntu virtual machine and you want to have two backend applications, one built on Node.js 8 and other one on Node.js 9. How will you deploy these two applications together? Obviously, you will have to spin up another VM, but there are a number of issues with that. For each VM you deploy, the operating system and other important resources are deployed again. VMs can be costly based on the usage. If you use any of the cloud providers like Azure and AWS you know it's not feasible to spin up a lot of VMs for complex applications, which may have a lot of microservices.

Then came the concept of containers, and they have revolutionized the way microservices-based complex applications are built and deployed. They still share the same OS but do not use a guest OS like VMs. Instead, they just use the binaries and libs required to run the applications. Thus, you can run as many containers as you want on your virtual machine with each having its own application.

The most popular container technology is from Docker, which is an open source GitHub project built on OCI standards.

Think of containers as VMs.

To install a Docker based on your OS, go to https://docs.docker.com/install/. Make sure Docker is up and running once you have installed. You can also use https://labs.play-with-docker.com/, which is a web-based option for quick and temporary deployments. You can use it to quickly run through these.

There are some important terminologies related with Docker:

1. **Images**: They are like templates for your VM or like classes if you know object-oriented concepts. It is just a text file where you provide instructions on how your VM will look like. Let's take an example of building an image of an Angular application. Angular is a popular front-end framework to build complex front-end applications. Don't worry if you are not familiar

with Angular. This hands-on is not about Angular. Let's quickly have a front-end application that we can Dockerize. You can use https://cli.angular.io/ to create a new application. If you don't want to, just clone this repo https://github.com/SateDev/Angular-seed in your application:

```
git clone https://github.com/SateDev/angular-seed_
cd angular-seed
```

Now open your favorite editor and create a new file named Dockerfile (no extension).

This is the instruction file used to build your image.

Below are the steps to run your Angular application:

      a.   First of all, you need Node.js installed in the machine you want to run Angular apps on.

      b.   Then, you should ensure all dependencies using npm are specified in package.json for it to run.

      c.   Lastly, you run ng serve for serving the bundle.

These are some basic steps in a development environment. In production, these steps may change.

So, now that you know how to run an Angular application, let's write it in a Dockerfile. Follow the below instructions:

```
# first chose the node image https://hub.docker.com/_/node
#install it in the container
FROM node:8.15.0-alpine
# then copy the package.json
COPY package.json package-lock.json ./
## this will install all dependencies, make a dir in the container and
copy the node_modules from last few steps
```

RUN npm install && mkdir /sample-app && cp -R ./node_modules ./sample-app && npm install -g @angular/cli.

```
# this will make the sample-app directory the base directory for running
any command
WORKDIR /sample-app
#now copy the code
COPY . .
## serve the application on 4200 port
```

```
ENTRYPOINT ["ng" , "serve"]
```

Next, to build this image from instructions above do the following:

```
docker build -t angular-app:latest .
```

Here –t specifies a tag, i.e., how you want to tag the image and . specifies the context to be used, i.e., the current directory. If everything goes right, you will see an output similar to *Figure 4.10* below:

```
Step 6/6 : ENTRYPOINT ["ng" , "serve"]
 ---> Running in 8d7f1e34d381
Removing intermediate container 8d7f1e34d381
 ---> 273db7b13e15
Successfully built 273db7b13e15
Successfully tagged angular-app:latest
```

Figure 4.10

Congratulations! You have built the first image. But this image does nothing. It is just the template that has everything stored in it to run the application.

To check the images, type the following command on command prompt:

```
docker images
```

For all the supported instructions and references, please visit https://docs.docker.com/engine/reference/builder/.

Also, to have a look at how images of the Fabric network look, check out the folder https://github.com/hyperledger/fabric/tree/release-1.4/images where we have a Dockerfile for creating images of peers, orderers, and so on. This is not necessary, but looking at it can help you understand Fabric better.

2. **Containers**: There are actual instances of those images. Just like an object, they are created from a class in the OOPS world or just like the real VMs created from the template.

To run the container for the above image, just type the following command in CMD:

```
docker run -p 4200:4200 -v ./src:./src  angular-app:latest
```

This will start the application on localhost:4200, and if you open it in a browser, you should be able to view it.

Here, -p specifies the port to map from the local to the host machine. The last argument is the image name to create the container from, and –v specifies the volume mapping, where the src in your local machine is mapped to src in the host machine. Thus, any changes you make in the local machine will automatically appear inside the container folder src.

There are other parameters you can specify, like network, secrets, environment variables, and so on. To have a look at all the options, feel free to visit https://docs. docker.com/engine/reference/run/.

3. **Docker Compose, Docker Swarm, Kubernetes**: Now that you understand what are images and containers in Docker, it's important to take a look at the real-world scenario, which will not have just one container. Instead, a lot of containers will be present and it will be necessary for them to interact with each other. For example, in e-commerce portal there might be a cart container, a Postgres database, an ordering container, an API gateway, and so on. We need a mechanism for these to work together in a more declarative way. This is where tools like Docker Compose, Kubernetes, and so on come handy.

For development purpose, Docker Compose is used, whereas for production deployment, Docker Swarm or Kubernetes is used. We will discuss Docker Swarm in detail in the upcoming section where we will deploy the Fabric network in production spread across multiple VMs!

You can install the Docker Compose tool from this link based on your OS: https:// docs.docker.com/compose/install/.

Running docker-compose –v should output the latest version.

Let's understand Docker Compose from a real Fabric network example.

We will be looking at building your first network in the next session. However, for now, let's have a look at a Docker Compose file to understand how declaratively the fabric network is created.

Let's clone the Fabric sample repo of Hyperledger Fabric.

git clone https://github.com/hyperledger/fabric-samples.git

Once cloned, open it in the code and open the file /samples/ first-network/docker-compose-cli.yaml.

Few points to note about this YAML:

a. It declares volume for hosting the data of orderer and peers.

b. Secondly, it declares the network BYFN. Network in Docker helps to create a sub network for services declared in the YAML file, such that each of them can identify each other on this sub network.

c. It then defines services required for running the Hyperledger network, e.g., orderer, peers, etc. It also declares the network section BYFN, which we declared before. They also reference other base Docker Compose files for definition using extends.

    d. Notice that in the CLI service, there is a section on passing the environment variables that your CLI uses inside the containers to do some tasks.

There is also a section named as *depends upon*, which basically means start this service once all the services are up and running.

To start these declarative services do the following:

```
Docker-compose -f docker-compose-cli.yaml  -d up
```

This will pull all the other images specified and start the containers. To list the container's running type, use the command:

```
docker ps
```

This will list all the running containers, but you will notice only one container running, i.e., the CLI container. But wait, there are other containers as well, defined in that Docker Compose file under services. Your obvious question would be, where are they? To view them, run:

```
docker ps -a
```

This will show all the containers (including the ones that stopped owing to some error). But why are the other containers in an exited state? To find out, let's find what went wrong with the peer1.org1.example.com container, i.e., peer1 of Org1. To retrieve the information, type the following:

```
docker logs peer1.org1.example.com
```

Logs should show that the MSP certificates were not available for this peer, and so they failed to start. This is obvious as we started the network directly from the Docker Compose file, but before that, we should have generated the crypto material.

But there is one container running, i.e., the CLI container, as it does not require MSP certificates to start during the development phase. Let's get inside this container by running the following command:

```
docker exec -it cli bash
```

You will see something like this:

root@281291eaf7f4:/opt/gopath/src/github.com/hyperledger/fabric/peer#

Now, run env, which is a standard Linux command to show environment variables in the VM. This will show all the variables including the ones we declared in the docker-compose-cli.yaml file. So now you might have understood to a certain degree how Docker Compose helps in designing our Hyperledger network.

Please keep in mind these handy commands to work with Docker: https://www. docker.com/sites/default/files/Docker_CheatSheet_08.09.2016_0.pdf.

Docker is a very powerful technology. Thus, mastering it will help you immensely even if you are not a developer. Having basic knowledge of Docker is enough to get started.

4. Node.js

Node.js, developed by Ryan Dahl (in 2009), is a server-side JavaScript framework that enables us to write the back end in JavaScript using Google Chrome's v8 engine. This programming language is asynchronous, non-blocking, and event-driven. It is different from traditional backend technology as it can handle multiple requests on a single thread.

Let's first understand how the Node.js project is created, and then we will understand how this project can be extended to work with a Fabric network using the npm modules that Fabric provides.

In order to begin, you have to install Node.js in your machine. This will also install npm that is a useful command-line utility for working with a Node.js project.

Once Node.js is installed, check the same by running the following commands:

```
node -v

npm -v
```

Now, to create the Node.js project, start by typing the following command:

```
npm init
```

This will ask you a series of questions like what is the name of the project, and so on.

Once done, we can see it generate some files for you. The most important one among them is package.json.

This is the file you will declare your project's dependencies in, along with the commands to run.

You will see a dependencies section in package.json.

Node.js has many built-in packages for developing applications. Some of the important packages are as follows:

- http
- net
- fs
- os

Now create a JS file in the repo you just built, named app.js, and put the following code inside it. This is just to create a plain server:

    a.   Create a file named hello.js:

```
var http = require('http');
http.createServer (function (req, res) {
 res.writeHead (200, {'Content-Type': 'text/html'});
  res.end ('Hello World!');
}).listen (8080);
```

    b.   To run the file, open the Node.js command prompt and type node hello.js.

    c.   Then, open the browser and hit localhost:8080 to see the response sent.

This is a very basic Node.js project that serves the web pages. We suggest you build a command of this programming language by learning various patterns.

We suggest you get experience in functional programming, which is very useful as Node.js is JavaScript that enables such programming paradigm. Here the functions are first class objects.

We suggest you write Node.js in typescript or es6 language for writing more standard code rather than writing an error-prone code.

You can also look into this repo https://github.com/Microsoft/TypeScript-Node-Starter for examples on how to write Node.js code in typescript.

In the following repository, you can find a curated list of all the important Node.js modules for different use cases https://github.com/SateDev/awesome-nodejs.git.

You can find ample of resources on the Internet to learn and master Node.js, but make sure you follow the right resources and learn it as thoroughly as possible.

    5. **Golang**: You can also write chaincodes in Golang, but we will be writing in Node.js and also the client will be built on Node.js.

You can install Golang from here: https://golang.org/.

Golang is a fast and statically typed programming language like C. Its data structure includes structures, slices, map, and so on. It was developed by Google and has a great garbage collection in place.

It is a great programming language to master.

Process of creating Hyperledger network

These steps will guide you to install the required binaries and Fabric images needed to run the network.

The typical process to work with Hyperledger Fabric can be divided into the following steps.

Note: We suggest working with Ubuntu or Mac OS for Hyperledger Fabric.

1. **Installing all pre-requisites**:

    a. Docker and Docker Compose (for running network):

    Install Docker from https://docs.docker.com/install/linux/docker-ce/.

    For Ubuntu, make sure you follow the steps given in the official site properly and do not end up with an older version.

    Install Docker Compose from the link below and make sure it is the latest one https://docs.docker.com/compose/install/.

    b. Install Git: https://git-scm.com/book/en/v2/Getting-Started-Installing-Git.

    If you are using a private GitHub repo, make sure you have generated the ssh keys and added them in your GitHub account.

    c. Golang (for Fabric and chaincode):

    Install Golang from here, based on your operating system: https://golang.org/doc/install.

    Make sure you set the path in the environment variables: https://github.com/golang/go/wiki/SettingGOPATH.

    d. Node.js (for Node.js SDK and chaincode):

    Install Node.js from here: https://nodejs.org/en/download/.

    e. Curl (for pulling binaries):

    It's a command line utility to pull resources from the web: https://curl.haxx.se/download.html.

    f. Java (if writing chaincode or client application in it).

    g. Pull the Fabric samples from https://github.com/hyperledger/fabric-samples.git.

Note that some of these are only required for development purposes.

Writing the configuration files based on your network design and other requirements includes writing three configuration files:

a. configtx.yml

b. crypto-config.yml

c. docker-compose files

Configtx.yml:

This config file defines the organization structure, channel details, profile details, and so on.

It also consists of organization definition, profile definition, and so on.

2. **Pulling all required binaries**:

Hyperledger Fabric makes it easy for you to perform some of the important operations like generating certificates, generating channel artifacts, and so on by providing a number of binaries.

a. **Configtxgen**: This tool is required to handle channel-related operations and inspection. It basically depends on a file named configtx.yaml that includes channel definition and network profile.

You can find more information here: https://hyperledger-fabric.readthedocs.io/en/release-1.4/commands/configtxgen.html?highlight=configtx.yaml.

b. **Configtxlator**: Most of the configuration is stored as Protobuf in the ledger like the block or the, genesis block and can be used to decode/encode to the JSON format.

This comes in two flavors, one as Rest http server and the other as CLI.

c. **Cryptogen**: It is the utility available to generate key materials for easily setting up and testing the network for development purposes. However, this is not used in production.

d. **Idemixgen**: Like we discussed in the previous chapter, this was introduced in version 1.3 for generating configuration-based MSP.

e. Peer Fabric CA and orderer binaries to perform certain common operations.

3. **Generating crypto files**:

Using the Docker Compose file, all but one container failed to start because of the missing MSP certificates.

So, the first step is to generate these certificates using a cryptogen tool by providing a configuration file named crypto-config.yml. These configuration files will have information like we discussed in the crypto config yaml file. This tool will generate certificates in separate folders.

4. **Pulling all required Docker images**:

Once the crypto material is generated, the next step is to start the network. Based on your design for these containers that are part of the network, we will have to pull images from the Hyperledger Docker hub repo https://hub.docker.com/u/hyperledger/.

Fabric-network-related images:

- Peer (for peers in the organization)
- Orderer (for orderer in the organization)
- Ccenv (for chaincode environment)
- CLI (for network-related operation)

CA-related image:

- Fabric CA (for certificate authority server)

External images required in the network:

- CouchDB (as state DB)
- Kafka (for consensus)
- Zookeeper (for consensus)

They are tagged in such a way that they will be pulled on the basis of the Fabric version required.

5. **Starting the network**:

This is the final step required to bootstrap the network. Based on your service definition and other configuration declaration in Docker Compose, the network is started. All the containers should be up and running at this point, and they can be identified by the names given in Docker Compose. Also, mapping of the exposed ports can be controlled in the Docker Compose YML file.

Hands-on with network

In this section, we will get a taste of Hyperledger network setup. We will also create a channel, install a chaincode, instantiate the chaincode, and query the chaincode.

In the next section when we work with Fabric Node.js SDK we will learn how this all can be done from SDK, but the first network setup in this section is ideal for someone looking to understand how to interact and do common operations in a Hyperledger network.

Prior to proceeding, make sure you have followed and installed all the prerequisites stated in the previous section. You will most likely see errors if you haven't followed it properly. Here are the important things to make sure before we move forward:

- Make sure you have the latest Docker and Docker Compose.

- Make sure you have Golang installed.

- Make sure you have cloned the repository https://github.com/hyperledger/fabric-samples and opened the same in your favorite editor (visual studio code preferred) for reference.

You can verify the above prerequisites by using the following commands. This would also provide you with the information on their versions:

```
docker -v
docker-compose -v
go version
```

And they should all print some reasonable version details and not something like **Command not found**. If they do, go back and ensure that you install them properly before moving forward.

Let's start the process.

First, start the network and do some common operation with it.

It might be good to make a directory and start working with it.

So, start a terminal or Git Bash and type the command mentioned below:

```
mkdir fabric-tutorial
cd fabric-tutorial
```

Now, follow the steps below from the same terminal. However, keep an eye on the visual studio code as well, as we will come back to it for reference and further explanation.

1. Pull the latest Docker images and binaries.

The most important step is to have all the images and binaries required, locally.

There are two ways to get them: the first one is to use a shell script to do it, and the second one is to build the Git repos. We strongly suggest you follow the first approach, which is easier and conserves time.

a. Using bootstrap shell file:

Run the following in your terminal. If cURL does not exist, please install it from https://curl.haxx.se/download.html:

```
curl -sSL http://bit.ly/2ysbOFE | bash -s 1.4.0
```

What does this script do?

a. It clones the Fabric sample repo we discussed earlier, the same you have in your editor.

b. Then it pulls the binaries that we discussed, like confitxgen, cryptogen, and so on, and puts them in the bin folder inside the fabric-sample folder cloned in the last step.

c. It then pulls all the images and tags them with the version that we provided, i.e., 1.4.0.

Upon successful execution of this script, you shall see a friendly output on your terminal.

Thus, we have all the images and binaries pulled successfully. If you type the following command in the command prompt, the images should be seen:

```
docker images
```

```
bash-4.4# docker images
REPOSITORY                        TAG          IMAGE ID        CREATED         SIZE
hyperledger/fabric-javaenv        1.4.0        3d91b3bf7118    2 weeks ago     1.75GB
hyperledger/fabric-javaenv        latest       3d91b3bf7118    2 weeks ago     1.75GB
hyperledger/fabric-tools          1.4.0        0a44f4261a55    3 weeks ago     1.56GB
hyperledger/fabric-tools          latest       0a44f4261a55    3 weeks ago     1.56GB
hyperledger/fabric-ccenv          1.4.0        5b31d55f5f3a    3 weeks ago     1.43GB
hyperledger/fabric-ccenv          latest       5b31d55f5f3a    3 weeks ago     1.43GB
hyperledger/fabric-orderer        1.4.0        54f372205580    3 weeks ago     150MB
hyperledger/fabric-orderer        latest       54f372205580    3 weeks ago     150MB
hyperledger/fabric-peer           1.4.0        304fac59b501    3 weeks ago     157MB
hyperledger/fabric-peer           latest       304fac59b501    3 weeks ago     157MB
hyperledger/fabric-ca             1.4.0        1a804ab74f58    3 weeks ago     244MB
hyperledger/fabric-ca             latest       1a804ab74f58    3 weeks ago     244MB
hyperledger/fabric-zookeeper      0.4.14       d36da0db87a4    3 months ago    1.43GB
hyperledger/fabric-zookeeper      latest       d36da0db87a4    3 months ago    1.43GB
hyperledger/fabric-kafka          0.4.14       a3b095201c66    3 months ago    1.44GB
hyperledger/fabric-kafka          latest       a3b095201c66    3 months ago    1.44GB
hyperledger/fabric-couchdb        0.4.14       f14f97292b4c    3 months ago    1.5GB
hyperledger/fabric-couchdb        latest       f14f97292b4c    3 months ago    1.5GB
bash-4.4#
```

Figure 4.11

And if you look into the terminal inside the fabric-samples folder, this cloned script will be the bin folder:

```
cd fabric-samples/bin && ls
```

It will show that the following binaries are available:

```
bash-4.4# cd fabric-samples/bin && ls
configtxgen        cryptogen        fabric-ca-client    idemixgen        peer
configtxlator      discover         get-docker-images.sh orderer
bash-4.4#
```

Figure 4.12

Now these tools will be used to generate a certificate, channel transaction, and so on. So let's add them in the path. Depending upon which OS you are using, the steps to add an entry in the path variable differs. We will show how to do in Ubuntu.

First, find out the current directory path from bin by typing the following command in the command prompt:

```
pwd
```

Copy the output directory path now:

```
export PATH=<copied pwd from above>:$PATH
```

This is how it should look:

```
export PATH=/root/fabric-samples/bin/:$PATH
```

That's it. You can verify it it's added in the path by running the following command:

```
cryptogen --help
```

This will show the following output, but if you see one-line error like **cryptogen is not recognized** it's probably not added to your path.

```
bash-4.4# cryptogen --help
usage: cryptogen [<flags>] <command> [<args> ...]

Utility for generating Hyperledger Fabric key material

Flags:
  --help  Show context-sensitive help (also try --help-long and --help-man).

Commands:
  help [<command>...]
    Show help.

  generate [<flags>]
    Generate key material

  showtemplate
    Show the default configuration template
```

Figure 4.13

Also, if you are running this on https://labs.play-with-docker.com/, note that this lacks packages to run these binaries, so follow the steps here https://github.com/sgerrand/alpine-pkg-glibc#installing to install these. But if you are running locally or in a VM, this is not an issue.

2. Generate crypto material and channel configuration files.

Note: From here on a script is available as byfn.sh in the first-network folder to do all the tasks, but we will be doing each step manually to get a feel of the network.

Now we have all binaries available to use. Let's move to the next part.

Here on, please focus on the repo first-network in your code editor where you have cloned the repo. We will use this repo as reference for now, while we will be using our repo for use case in the next section.

Next, we have to generate the crypto materials that are certificates for all the entities in the network. For this, as discussed before, we need to write crypto-config.yaml.

You can see crypto-config.yml in the first-network folder as shown below:

```
# ---------------------------------------------------------------------
------
# "OrdererOrgs" - Definition of organizations managing orderer nodes
# ---------------------------------------------------------------------
------
OrdererOrgs:
  # -------------------------------------------------------------------
--------
  # Orderer
  # -------------------------------------------------------------------
--------
  - Name: Orderer
    Domain: example.com
    # -----------------------------------------------------------------
----------
    # "Specs" - See PeerOrgs below for complete description
    # -----------------------------------------------------------------
----------
    Specs:
      - Hostname: orderer
# ---------------------------------------------------------------------
------
```

```
# "PeerOrgs" - Definition of organizations managing peer nodes
# ---------------------------------------------------------------------
------
PeerOrgs:
  # ---------------------------------------------------------------------
--------
  # Org1
  # ---------------------------------------------------------------------
--------
  - Name: Org1
    Domain: org1.example.com
    EnableNodeOUs: true
    # -------------------------------------------------------------------
----------
    # "Specs"
    # -------------------------------------------------------------------
----------
    # Uncomment this section to enable the explicit definition of hosts
in your
    # configuration.  Most users will want to use Template, below
    #
    # Specs is an array of Spec entries.  Each Spec entry consists of
two fields:
    #   - Hostname:   (Required) The desired hostname, sans the domain.
    #   - CommonName: (Optional) Specifies the template or explicit
override for
    #               the CN.  By default, this is the template:
    #
    #                        "{{.Hostname}}.{{.Domain}}"
    #
    #               which obtains its values from the Spec.Hostname
and
    #               Org.Domain, respectively.
    # -------------------------------------------------------------------
----------
    # Specs:
    #   - Hostname: foo # implicitly "foo.org1.example.com"
```

```
    #      CommonName: foo27.org5.example.com # overrides Hostname-based
FQDN set above

    #    - Hostname: bar

    #    - Hostname: baz

    # -------------------------------------------------------------------
----------

    # "Template"

    # -------------------------------------------------------------------
----------

    # Allows for the definition of 1 or more hosts that are created
sequentially

    # from a template. By default, this looks like "peer%d" from 0 to
Count-1.

    # You may override the number of nodes (Count), the starting index
(Start)

    # or the template used to construct the name (Hostname).

    #

    # Note: Template and Specs are not mutually exclusive.  You may
define both

    # sections and the aggregate nodes will be created for you.  Take
care with

    # name collisions

    # -------------------------------------------------------------------
----------

    Template:

      Count: 2

      # Start: 5

      # Hostname: {{.Prefix}}{{.Index}} # default

    # -------------------------------------------------------------------
----------

    # "Users"

    # -------------------------------------------------------------------
----------

    # Count: The number of user accounts _in addition_ to Admin

    # -------------------------------------------------------------------
----------

    Users:

      Count: 1
```

```
# ----------------------------------------------------------------
--------
# Org2: See "Org1" for full specification
# ----------------------------------------------------------------
--------
  - Name: Org2
    Domain: org2.example.com
    EnableNodeOUs: true
    Template:
      Count: 2
    Users:
      Count: 1
```

As you can see above, the OrdererOrgs section defines information related to the orderer in our organization.

The next section PeerOrgs has two organizations defined, Org1 and Org2.

In the template section, we can define how many peers we want crypto material for.

Alright, now that we have crypto-config.yaml already available in the first-network folder, let's use this along with the cryptogen tool to generate certificates.

Run the following command to do so:

```
cryptogen generate --config=./crypto-config.yaml
```

Now you should see a folder crypto-config generated in the first-network directory. Its content should look as shown below. Two directories were generated for the orderer and peers that we specified in the YAML file. For our network example. com you can scan through the folders for generated PEM (privacy enhanced mail) certificates that will be used by the network to validate the peers.

```
bash-4.4# ls
ordererOrganizations    peerOrganizations
```

Figure 4.14

This is the folder that gets mounted in the volume of Docker containers for peers and orderer to make it available inside the container for verification.

    3.   Start the network using Docker Compose YAML.

Next, we need to write configtx.yaml to generate the channel-related artefacts in YAML. We already have it available in the first-network repo. Open it for reference, in your editor.

It defines three sections. The first organization section defines settings related to OrdererOrg, Org1, and Org2. It defines attributes like name, ID, MSP directory path, policies, anchor peers in the organization, and more.

Notice that there is an "&" in front of each definition, e.g., &OrdererOrg. This syntax is YAML specific. It is like pointers. We can reference this orderer definition in other places in the YAML file by using *, e.g., *OrdererOrg.

Another important section is the profile. You will see how these definitions in this profile section are used by the configtxgen tool to generate channel-related artefacts like genesis block, and so on:

```
####################################################################
#########
#
#   Profile
#
#   - Different configuration profiles may be encoded here to be specified
#     as parameters to the configtxgen tool
#
####################################################################
#########
Profiles:


    TwoOrgsOrdererGenesis:
        <<: *ChannelDefaults
        Orderer:
            <<: *OrdererDefaults
            Organizations:
                - *OrdererOrg
            Capabilities:
                <<: *OrdererCapabilities
        Consortiums:
            SampleConsortium:
                Organizations:
                    - *Org1
                    - *Org2
    TwoOrgsChannel:
```

```
Consortium: SampleConsortium
Application:
    <<: *ApplicationDefaults
    Organizations:
        - *Org1
        - *Org2
    Capabilities:
        <<: *ApplicationCapabilities

SampleDevModeKafka:
    <<: *ChannelDefaults
    Capabilities:
        <<: *ChannelCapabilities
    Orderer:
        <<: *OrdererDefaults
        OrdererType: kafka
        Kafka:
            Brokers:
            - kafka.example.com:9092

        Organizations:
        - *OrdererOrg
        Capabilities:
            <<: *OrdererCapabilities
    Application:
        <<: *ApplicationDefaults
        Organizations:
        - <<: *OrdererOrg
    Consortiums:
        SampleConsortium:
            Organizations:
            - *Org1
            - *Org2
```

Let's move forward and generate some artefacts for our channel named testchannel.

But first we need to generate the artefacts for the orderer system channel, which is required for the orderer to work properly:

```
configtxgen -profile TwoOrgsOrdererGenesis -channelID byfn-sys-channel
-outputBlock ./channel-artifacts/genesis.block
```

In the preceding command, we are passing configtxgen profile name defined in the configtxgen.yaml, which is a predefined channel ID, and an output folder name to write artifacts to.

If you look in your channel-artifacts folder now, there should be genesis.block file created.

Next, run the following command to generate channel.tx file using the configuration defined in twoOrgsChannel:

```
configtxgen -profile TwoOrgsChannel -outputCreateChannelTx ./channel-
artifacts/channel.tx -channelID testchannel
```

Then, we have to generate a TX file for the anchor peers in the channel. So, let's create this by running the following command:

```
configtxgen -profile TwoOrgsChannel -outputAnchorPeersUpdate ./channel-
artifacts/Org1MSPanchors.tx -channelID testchannel -asOrg Org1MSP
```

Now run the preceding command again for org2:

```
configtxgen -profile TwoOrgsChannel -outputAnchorPeersUpdate ./channel-
artifacts/Org2MSPanchors.tx -channelID testchannel -asOrg Org2MSP
```

Thus, all the files generated for the channel are in the folder channel-artifacts.

Figure 4.15

4. Start the network using Docker Compose files.

Now that we have crypto-config and channel artefacts generated, it's time to start the network by writing the Docker Compose YAML files. We already have a number of them written for us in the first-network folder that we can use depending on our requirements, i.e., if you are using Solo, Kafka, CouchDB, and so on.

We will be using docker-compose-cli.yml available in the folder for starting the network. Open this Compose file and read its content to understand how the service definition is provided in it. Note it also uses the Docker Compose files available in the base folder. Enough said. Now let's get started:

```
IMAGE_TAG=latest docker-compose -f docker-compose-cli.yaml up -d
```

First, we pass IMAGE_TAG=latest that is used in the image section and then use the up command to start the network:

Run docker ps in terminal to see the following output:

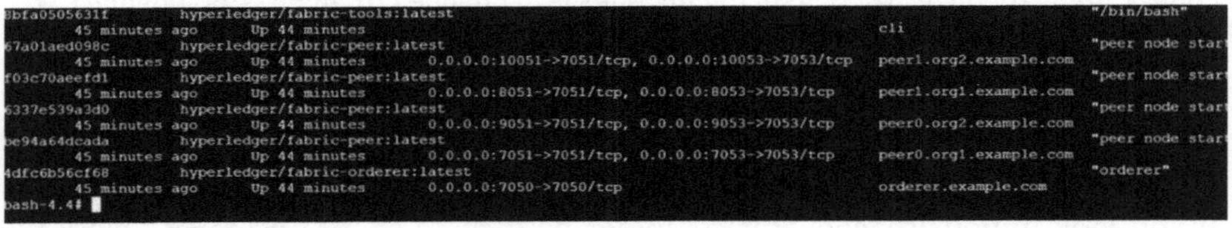

Figure 4.16

5. Create channels and install, instantiate, and query chaincode.

Let's understand the API provided by the CLI container.

Run the following command:

```
docker exec -it cli bash
```

This will take you inside the CLI container.

Now enter the following command:

```
peer channel –help
```

This will show all the available commands for channel-related operations, as shown in *Figure 4.17*:

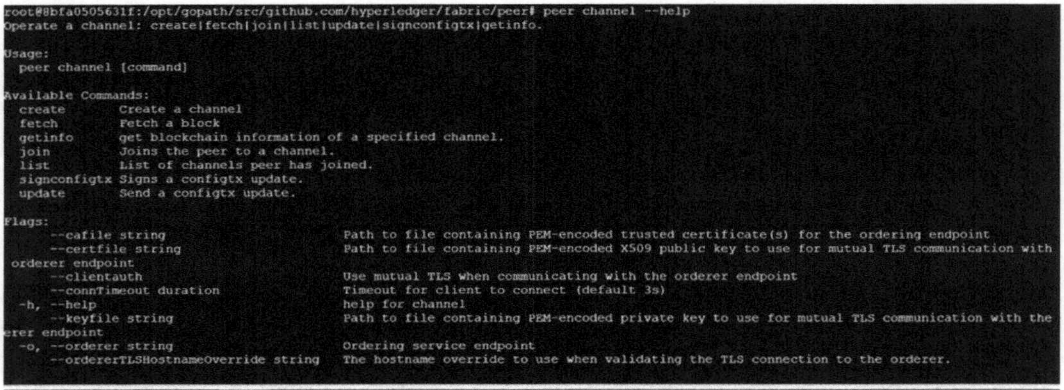

Figure 4.17

For example, to create a channel, we can run the following command:

```
peer channel create -o orderer.example.com:7050 -c dummyChannel-f ./
channel-artifacts/channel.tx
```

This takes the orderer service info channel name and artifacts file name.

Next, to know the common operations available for the chaincode from CLI, do the following inside the CLI container:

```
peer chaincode –help
```

```
root@8bfa0505631f:/opt/gopath/src/github.com/hyperledger/fabric/peer# peer chaincode --help
Operate a chaincode: install|instantiate|invoke|package|query|signpackage|upgrade|list.

Usage:
  peer chaincode [command]

Available Commands:
  install     Package the specified chaincode into a deployment spec and save it on the peer's path.
  instantiate Deploy the specified chaincode to the network.
  invoke      Invoke the specified chaincode.
  list        Get the instantiated chaincodes on a channel or installed chaincodes on a peer.
  package     Package the specified chaincode into a deployment spec.
  query       Query using the specified chaincode.
  signpackage Sign the specified chaincode package
  upgrade     Upgrade chaincode.

Flags:
      --cafile string                Path to file containing PEM-encoded trusted certificate(s) for the orderi
      --certfile string              Path to file containing PEM-encoded X509 public key to use for mutual TLS
  orderer endpoint
      --clientauth                   Use mutual TLS when communicating with the orderer endpoint
      --connTimeout duration         Timeout for client to connect (default 3s)
  -h, --help                         help for chaincode
      --keyfile string               Path to file containing PEM-encoded private key to use for mutual TLS com
erer endpoint
  -o, --orderer string               Ordering service endpoint
```

Figure 4.18

For example, to install a chaincode, we can run the following command:

```
peer chaincode install -n [chaincodename] -v [1.1] -l[ Golang/nodejs]
-p[ chaincodePath]
```

It takes parameters like chaincode name, version, language it is written in, and chaincode path.

```
peer –help
```

This will show all the other available operations in CLI, like logging, version, and so on.

Now let's do the following:

1. Create a channel named testchannel.
2. Add all peers to it.
3. Update anchor peer in org1.
4. Update anchor peer in org2.
5. Install chaincode in peer0 node of both org1 and org2.
6. Instantiate chaincode in peer0.
7. Query chaincode from peer0.

Notice there is a script available for all these in the folder called **scripts**. Open it in the terminal, and if you are aware of Shell or any programming language, you will be able to read the same.

Let's run this script from outside the CLI container. Here we pass channel name testchannel timeout params, programming language, log verbose, and so on:

```
docker exec cli scripts/script.sh testchannel 3 golang 10 true
```

This script will execute all the steps defined above. After successfully running this script, we will see a proper ending message.

This will install the chaincode from the chaincode_example02/go folder that can be found in the fabric-sample repo.

Now let's try to run install chaincode from the Node.js chaincode available in chaincode_example02/node. Note that in your editor, you can review this chaincode contract within the chaincode folder:

1. **Install Node.js chaincode from chaincode_example02/node:**

Again, get inside the CLI container using the following command:

```
docker exec -it cli bash
```

Then do the following:

```
cd /opt/gopath/src/github.com/chaincode
```

You can see all the chaincodes available inside it for you to play with. These are the same as in your chaincode folder.

Now let's install this using the peer chaincode install command:

```
peer chaincode install -n testcc -v 1.1 -l node -p /opt/gopath/src/
github.com/chaincode/chaincode_example02/node/
```

We have named our chaincode testcc and chosen version 1.1. We specified the language as Node.js, and path is the path of the chaincode inside this container.

This should show output as shown below. Note that this is installed in the same channel testchannel that was created using script:

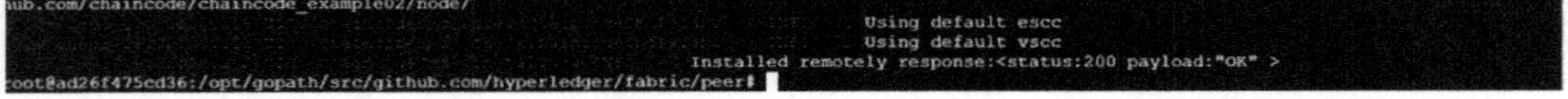

Figure 4.19

This peer has been installed in the peer0 node of org1. Now, we need to install the same in peer1 of the same organization.

We have not specified the peer address and MSP details to be used in the last command that we run because they were already pointing to the peer0 address.

Let's change these environment variables to point to peer1 of org1 before installing the chaincode. To do so, run the following command:

```
export CORE_PEER_ADDRESS=peer1.org1.example.com:7051
```

And once again run the same chaincode install command used above:

```
peer chaincode install -n testcc -v 1.1 -l node -p /opt/gopath/src/
github.com/chaincode/chaincode_example02/node/
```

We have to rerun the same steps for org2. Here we have to change the MSP dir path and cert details before we can install in peer0 and peer1 of org2.

Let's change the env variables.

```
CORE_PEER_LOCALMSPID="Org2MSP"   CORE_PEER_MSPCONFIGPATH=/opt/gopath/
src/github.com/hyperledger/fabric/peer/crypto/peerOrganizations/org2.
example.com/users/Admin@org2.example.com/msp

   CORE_PEER_TLS_ROOTCERT_FILE=/opt/gopath/src/github.com/hyperledger/
fabric/peer/crypto/peerOrganizations/org2.example.com/peers/peer0.org2.
example.com/tls/ca.crt
```

Now change the address of the peer that was pointing to peer0 of org2:

```
CORE_PEER_ADDRESS=peer0.org2.example.com:7051
```

That's it. Run the above command again to install the chaincode in peer0.

Similarly, do it for peer1.

Now, we have the chaincode installed in all peers. Let's instantiate this chaincode.

2. **Instantiate the chaincode**:

First, let's come out of the CLI to the default env settings.

Next, run the command docker exec -it cli bash:

```
peer chaincode instantiate -o orderer.example.com:7050 --tls true
--cafile /opt/gopath/src/github.com/hyperledger/fabric/peer/crypto/
ordererOrganizations/example.com/orderers/orderer.example.com/msp/
tlscacerts/tlsca.example.com-cert.pem  -C mychannel -n testcc -l node
-v 1.1 -c '{"Args":["init","a","100","b","200"]}' -P "AND ('Org1MSP.
peer','Org2MSP.peer')"
```

Again, follow the process of changing env variables and update them accordingly. Then, run this command again for all the peers.

3. **Query the chaincode**:

Now let's query the chaincode for the value of a.

Run the following command:

```
peer chaincode query -C mychannel -n testcc -c '{"Args":["query","a"]}'
```

This should give output as 100.

4. **Upgrade the chaincode**:

Let's install a new version before we can upgrade. Let's name this version 1.3:

```
peer chaincode install -n testcc -v 1.3 -l node -p /opt/gopath/src/
github.com/chaincode/chaincode_example02/node/
```

For testing instead of installing in all the nodes, we will upgrade only in peer0 by using the below command:

```
peer chaincode upgrade -o orderer.example.com:7050 --tls true
--cafile /opt/gopath/src/github.com/hyperledger/fabric/peer/crypto/
ordererOrganizations/example.com/orderers/orderer.example.com/msp/
tlscacerts/tlsca.example.com-cert.pem  -C mychannel -n testcc -l node
-v 1.3 -c '{"Args":["init","a","90","b","200"]}' -P "AND ('Org1MSP.
peer','Org2MSP.peer')"
```

Finally, we can query the chaincode:

```
peer chaincode query -C mychannel -n testcc --c '{" a"]}'
```

This will now show 90.

Thus, you have learnt how to upgrade the chaincode once deployed.

As an exercise, you could run the invoke command similar to instantiate. You can look into the reference file scripts/util.sh to understand how it is run.

You should also create your own chaincode, put it inside the chaincode folder, and run the same steps to get a grasp of how things are done.

Just for practice, you can do the following exercises:

a. Create a new channel marbles_trade_channel and add a new organization to it. The artifacts for the same can be generated from the folder org3-artifacts.

b. Install the marbles chaincode available in the chaincode/marbles02 folder.

c. Instantiate the same.

d. Invoke the chaincode.

e. Query the chaincode for latest value.

Always take help from the available scripts in scripts folders.

Summary

In this chapter, we extended our knowledge of the Hyperledger Fabric network. First, we understood the network topologies and modeling using an example. We also explained how a network evolves in such a trusted ecosystem. We then reviewed different frameworks and tools hosted by the Linux foundation. Then we moved on to understand prerequisites like Docker, Node.js, and more. We understood how vital the knowledge of Docker can be while technically understanding how to build one. We also created the first network by using the Fabric GitHub example. Post creation of the same, as a good hands-on experience to get to know the network deeply, we performed some common operations on the chaincode, like installing, invoking, and instantiating it. Although we did all these operations from CLI, such knowledge is vital while working with the network. In the next chapter, we will see how we can use the client SDK to do such operations. We will build a client for doing such operations.

References

- https://hyperledger-fabric.readthedocs.io/
- https://en.wikipedia.org/wiki/Zero-knowledge_proof

CHAPTER 5

Chaincode in Hyperledger Fabric

In this chapter, we will intricately learn about chaincode development. We will understand chaincodes from two perspectives—developers and operators. This chapter will also cover the various concepts of writing and developing chaincodes and the different patterns involved. We will also develop a basic chaincode and learn to interact with it. We will also learn chaincode development in further detail by implementing an ERC-20 token. We shall see how an operator can perform different lifecycle operations on a chaincode using the tools available within the Fabric network.

In this chapter, we will cover the following topics:

- Chaincodes for developers
- Chaincodes for operators

After perusing this chapter, you will have a clear understanding on how to write, deploy, and test chaincodes on Hyperledger Fabric.

Demystifying chaincodes

Before we get started, let's first understand what a chaincode is.

Chaincodes are also known as smart contracts in public networks. They are simply programs containing business logic that is written in languages like Golang, Node. js, Solidity, and so on. These are deployed inside the blockchain network, and once they are executed, either explicitly or implicitly, they have the ability to change the ledger state. This is one of the most powerful features of blockchain networks that was first popularized by Ethereum's co-founder Vitalik Buterin. Vitalik had introduced a similar capability in Ethereum blockchain.

In Hyperledger, this functionality is referred to as chaincode and can be written in programming languages like Node.js, Golang, and Java. They run inside an isolated container having an ecosystem of the programming languages it is written in.

With that being said, let's understand chaincodes from two different perspectives:

- Chaincode for developers
- Chaincode for operators

Chaincode for developers

Let us understand the process of chaincode development using a simple use case named **Property registry and management in real estate**.

The requirements are simple—we need to write a smart contract that will register the property details, change the ownership, query the property details, and execute a few other operations on the properties. We can extend the functionalities to make it more production-like, but for now, these basic functionalities are enough to understand the process.

We will be writing the chaincode in Node.js, in TypeScript language, which is a more standard JavaScript than native JavaScript, as the latter is more prone to bugs.

Follow the below steps to understand how a chaincode is built:

1. Create a new project.
2. Create a new node project using npm by giving the following commands:

```
mkdir asset-registry
cd asset registry
npm init -y
```

We have created a new Node.js project to develop a chaincode in TypeScript. Now let's open this in Visual Studio Code.

We need two npm modules to help us write the chaincode in Node.js on the Hyperledger Fabric network. These are explained in https://fabric-shim.github. io/release-1.4/index.html. These include interfaces that we need to implement in our project when writing a chaincode. So let's include these as dependencies in package.json or then run the following commands:

```
npm i --save fabric-contract-api
npm i --save fabric-shim
```

Besides these, let us also add other packages as developer dependencies to perform actions like compiling, testing, and more.

These include traditional TypeScript and JavaScript test dependencies like Chai, Mocha, ts-node, TypeScript, and so on.

After adding all the developer and devDependencies objects in the package.json file, it should look as follows:

```
"dependencies": {
        "fabric-contract-api": "~1.4.0",
        "fabric-shim": "~1.4.0"
},
"devDependencies": {
        "@types/chai": "^4.1.7",
        "@types/mocha": "^5.2.5",
        "@types/node": "^10.12.10",
        "@types/sinon": "^5.0.7",
        "@types/sinon-chai": "^3.2.1",
        "chai": "^4.2.0",
        "mocha": "^5.2.0",
        "nyc": "^13.1.0",
        "sinon": "^7.1.1",
        "sinon-chai": "^3.3.0",
        "ts-node": "^7.0.1",
        "tslint": "^5.11.0",
        "typescript": "^3.1.6"
    }
```

After adding these, run the following from the asset-registry repository:

```
npm i
```

This command will take some time to complete execution as it pulls the dependencies from npm. Once done, all your dependencies will be installed inside the node_modules folder created.

Note: TypeScript is a programming language built on top of JavaScript to provide developers a better programming method (object oriented programming, OOP) to avoid any pitfalls due to weird problems in JavaScript.

Once we have written the code, we need to convert this to JavaScript using TypeScript Compiler so it is better to install this as a global dependency. To do so, run the following command:

```
npm i -g typescript
```

Now let us add some scripts in package.json to perform some common tasks like run, build, and test using npm. Copy the following content and put it inside the scripts object in package.json:

```
"scripts": {
    "lint": "tslint -c tslint.json 'src/**/*.ts'",
    "pretest": "npm run lint",
    "test": "nyc mocha -r ts-node/register src/**/*.spec.ts",
    "start": "fabric-chaincode-node start",
    "build": "tsc",
    "build:watch": "tsc -w",
    "prepublishOnly": "npm run build"
},
```

Notice that the build script uses TypeScript Compiler to build it into JavaScript.

The complete package.json looks as follows:

```
{
    "name": "asset-registry",
    "version": "1.0.0",
    "description": "",
    "main": "dist/index.js",
    "scripts": {
      "lint": "tslint -c tslint.json 'src/**/*.ts'",
      "pretest": "npm run lint",
      "test": "nyc mocha -r ts-node/register src/**/*.spec.ts",
      "start": "fabric-chaincode-node start",
      "build": "tsc",
      "build:watch": "tsc -w",
      "prepublishOnly": "npm run build"
    },
      "keywords": [],
      "author": "",
```

```
      "license": "ISC",
      "dependencies": {
        "fabric-contract-api": "~1.4.0",
        "fabric-shim": "~1.4.0"
    },
    "devDependencies": {
        "@types/chai": "^4.1.7",
        "@types/mocha": "^5.2.5",
        "@types/node": "^10.12.10",
        "@types/sinon": "^5.0.7",
        "@types/sinon-chai": "^3.2.1",
        "chai": "^4.2.0",
        "mocha": "^5.2.0",
        "nyc": "^13.1.0",
        "sinon": "^7.1.1",
        "sinon-chai": "^3.3.0",
        "ts-node": "^7.0.1",
        "tslint": "^5.11.0",
        "typescript": "^3.1.6"
    }
  }
```

Now we have the Node.js project set up for writing the chaincode.

Before we start writing the chaincode, let's understand the use case.

We are going to build an asset registry chaincode application that has the following common attributes linked to a property:

- Value of the property
- Owner of the property
- Property area
- Location of the property
- Type of property

Now we know the common attributes associated with a property. Let's write a model file to model this property.

Create a folder src inside the folder asset-registry. Inside src, create another folder named models. It is a popular paradigm in software development to model the asset before writing the business logic for it.

In order to create models for a property, you can create a class and define all the properties as we discussed previously. So, create a file named Asset.model.ts inside models, and write the class AssetDetails with properties discussed previously. This should look as follows:

```
export class AssetDetails {
    public propertyArea?: string;
    public location: string;
    public propertyNumber: string;
    public type: string;
    public ownerName: string;
    public value: number;
}
```

Note: We are using export before the keyword class so that we can use it inside our chaincode contract.

Now that we have the models sorted out, let's start writing the chaincode.

Create a file named property-contract.ts.

Let's first import the required files from the node modules fabric-contract-api and Asset.model:

```
import { Context, Contract } from 'fabric-contract-api';

import { AssetDetails } from './models/Asset.model';
```

Then, create a class named PropertiesContract that extends Contract that we exported earlier:

```
export class PropertiesContract extends Contract {
}
```

Thus, we have our skeleton ready to write the business logic.

Now, let's understand what we want this chaincode to do:

1. Create an initial ledger with some initial property details.
2. Provide functionality to create more properties using the "Create a Property" function.
3. Query the ledger for a property on the basis of property ID.

4. Allow querying all the properties on the basis of indexes.

5. Allow changing the owner of a property.

We can add more functionalities like leasing, shared ownership of property, and so on, but let's accomplish the following for this use case:

1. Create an initial ledger with some basic property details.

    - Let's create an initLedger function that will be called at the time of instantiating the chaincode:

    ```
    public async initLedger(ctx: Context) {

    }
    ```

    - To create the initial ledger data, we need some initial property data. Let's try to create this inside initLedger:

    ```
    const assets: AssetDetails[] = [
        {
            propertyArea: '1400 sqft.',
            ownerName: 'sam dave',
            value: 12332,
                location : '12 avenue,richar street ,
    california',
            type: 'single',
            propertyNumber: 'P100001'
        },
        {
            propertyArea: '12400 sqft.',
            ownerName: 'john dave',
            value: 22330,
                location : '13 avenue,richar street ,
    california',
            type: 'multiplex',
            propertyNumber: 'P100002'
        }
    ];
    ```

Note: This is a dummy data of type AssetDetails having two registry details.

We now have to put this data one by one in the ledger. Note that we have a parameter named ctx of type Context. If you Ctrl click on Context, it will take you inside the module fabric-contract-api that looks as follows:

```
declare module 'fabric-contract-api' {
    import { ChaincodeStub, ClientIdentity } from 'fabric-shim';
    export class Context {
        stub: ChaincodeStub;
        clientIdentity: ClientIdentity;
    }
    export class Contract {
        constructor(name?: string);
        beforeTransaction(ctx : Context): Promise<void>;
        afterTransaction(ctx : Context,result: any): Promise<void>;
        unknownTransaction(ctx : Context): Promise<void>;
        createContext(): Context;
        getName(): string;
    }
    export function Transaction(commit?: boolean): (target: any,
propertyKey: string | symbol) => void;
    export function Returns(returnType?: string): (target: any,
propertyKey: string | symbol) => void;
    export function Object(type?: string): (target: any) => void;
    export function Info(info?: object): (target: any) => void;
    export function Property(name?: string, type?: string): (target:
any, propertyKey: string | symbol) => void;
}
```

So, as you can see, class Context that is passed as a parameter in our initLedger function has two exported members ClientIdentity and ChaincodeStub. This has a number of functions available as documented here https://fabric-shim.github.io/release-1.4/fabric-shim.ChaincodeStub.html for interacting with the ledger.

One of the key methods available in this object is putState. Let's use this method to put all the property objects inside the ledger one by one using traditional loops:

```
        for (let i = 0; i < assets.length; i++) {
                await ctx.stub.putState(assets[i].propertyNumber, Buffer.
from(JSON.stringify(assets[i])));
            console.info('Added <--> ', assets[i]);
        }
```

Using the preceding code, we are using property number as a unique identifier and putting the information related to that property number in the ledger.

Thus, we have written a method to add initial data to the ledger. This is how the finished function should look like:

```
public async initLedger(ctx: Context) {
    const assets: AssetDetails[] = [
        {
            propertyArea: '1400 sqft.',
            ownerName: 'sam dave',
            value: 12332,
            location : '12 avenue,richar street , california',
            type: 'single',
            propertyNumber: 'P100001'
        },
        {
            propertyArea: '1400 sqft.',
            ownerName: 'sam dave',
            value: 12332,
            location : '12 avenue,richar street , california',
            type: 'single',
            propertyNumber: 'P100002'
        }
    ];
    for (let i = 0; i < assets.length; i++) {
        await ctx.stub.putState('Properties' + i, Buffer.from(JSON.
stringify(assets[i])));
        console.info('Added <--> ', assets[i]);
    }
    console.info('============== END : Initialize Ledger
===========');
}
```

2. Provide functionality to create more properties using create a property.

Now we should write a method in the contract to allow the user/admin to add/register a new property by passing all the required information associated with it, as described in the model file.

We have to now accept more arguments apart from the context like initLedger method.

Then, we deserialize the object of type AssetDetails as shown below.

Once deserialized, we can again use the putstate command to put entries in the ledger by property number.

```
    public async createProperty(ctx: Context,
propertyNumber: string, propertyArea: string, cost: number,
type: string, location: string,value: number, ownerName:
string) {

        const asset: AssetDetails = {

        propertyArea,

        location,

        propertyNumber,

        type,

        value,

        ownerName,

    };

        await ctx.stub.putState(propertyNumber, Buffer.
from(JSON.stringify(asset)));

    }
```

Please note that we have not added any validations and checks before putting it into the ledger. However, in the real world, it's advisable to check if any of the values passed is invalid or the property number sent is already registered, to avoid any collision or corruption.

A simple validation to check if the property number already exists could be written using another function, which Shim provides. This function is getState:

```
    public async createProperty(ctx: Context,
propertyNumber: string, propertyArea: string, cost: number,
type: string, location: string,value: number, ownerName:
string) {
```

```
          const assetDetailsAsBytes = await ctx.stub.
getState(propertyNumber); // get the car from chaincode
state

     if (assetDetailsAsBytes || assetDetailsAsBytes.
length !== 0) {

          throw new Error(`${propertyNumber} already
exists`);

     }

     const asset: AssetDetails = {

          propertyArea,

          location,

          propertyNumber,

          type,

          value,

          ownerName,

     };

     await ctx.stub.putState(propertyNumber, Buffer.
from(JSON.stringify(asset)));

   }
```

3. Query the ledger for a property on the basis of property number.

   This is a straightforward command that uses context.stub.getState to get the property by number passed in the argument stringify, and then returns the result. Let's write this function called queryAsset:

```
     public async queryAsset(ctx: Context, assetNumber:
string): Promise<string> {

          const assetAsBytes = await ctx.stub.
getState(assetNumber); // get the car from chaincode state

          if (!assetAsBytes || assetAsBytes.length === 0) {

               throw new Error(`${assetNumber} does not
exist`);

          }

          console.log(assetAsBytes.toString());

          return assetAsBytes.toString();

     }
```

4. Allow querying all the properties on the basis of indexes.

There might be a requirement from the admin to fetch a lot of property details on the basis of a range of property numbers, or indexes, instead of querying them one at a time. We can do that by using another method available in the stub for querying in between a range. This function is getStateByRange, and it returns an iterator. So, we have to iterate one by one, build the result object and stringify, and return it as shown in the following code:

```
public async queryAllAssets(ctx: Context,startKey:
number,endKey: number): Promise<string> {
    const iterator = await ctx.stub.
getStateByRange(startKey, endKey);
    const allResults = [];
    while (true) {
        const res = await iterator.next();
        if (res.value && res.value.value.toString()) {
            console.log(res.value.value.
toString('utf8'));
            const Key = res.value.key;
            let Record;
            try {
                Record = JSON.parse(res.value.value.
toString('utf8'));
            } catch (err) {
                console.log(err);
                Record = res.value.value.
toString('utf8');
            }
            allResults.push({ Key, Record });
        }
        if (res.done) {
            console.log('end of data');
            await iterator.close();
            console.info(allResults);
            return JSON.stringify(allResults);
        }
    }
}
```

```
        }
```

5. Allow changing the owner of a property.

   Follow the below steps to perform this action.

   First, find the property details on the basis of the property number passed.

   If it doesn't exist, throw an error.

   If it exists, change the owner details and put it in the ledger, indexed to the same property number once again.

   Following is the code for the same:

```
public async changePropertyOwner(ctx: Context,
propertyNumber: string, newOwner: string) {
        console.info('============= START :
changeOwner ===========');


        const assetDetailsAsBytes = await ctx.
stub.getState(propertyNumber); // get the car from
chaincode state
        if (!assetDetailsAsBytes ||
assetDetailsAsBytes.length === 0) {
            throw new Error(`${propertyNumber}
does not exist`);
        }
        const asset: AssetDetails = JSON.
parse(assetDetailsAsBytes.toString());
        asset.ownerName = newOwner;


        await ctx.stub.putState(propertyNumber,
Buffer.from(JSON.stringify(asset)));
        console.info('============= END :
changeCarOwner ===========');
    }
```

Alright, now we have finished writing the chaincode for property registry and transfer. Now, let's expose this contract by writing an index.ts file in the src folder. It is a good paradigm to write an index.ts file and expose the contract as an API. So, create index.ts and enter the following:

```
import { PropertiesContract } from './property-contract';

export const contracts: any[] = [ PropertiesContract ];
```

Now, add tsconfig.json inside the asset-registry folder:

```
{
        "compilerOptions": {
            "outDir": "dist",
              "target": "es2017",
              "moduleResolution": "node",
              "module": "commonjs",
              "declaration": true,
              "sourceMap": true
        },
        "include": [
            "./src/**/*"
        ],
        "exclude": [
            "./src/**/*.spec.ts"
        ]
    }
```

This informs TypeScript about the config instructions and where to compile.

Thus, we have completed the chaincode development.

Now let's go ahead and build this, i.e., build it into JavaScript by executing the following command:

```
npm run build
```

This should generate a dist folder for you and not give you any errors, hopefully.

Deploying and testing the chaincode

Pulling images and binaries and putting a project inside chaincode:

Now that we have created the chaincode setup, let's deploy and test it in the dev network.

We will be running a development network for deploying this, which will have all the preconfigured material for us to start deployment and invoke the code.

There are two ways test it. You can test everything locally and check if it works, or you can use Docker labs' web-based setup. Let's get started.

Open your terminal and run the following commands:

```
mkdir chaincode-dev
cd chaincode-dev
```

Fabric samples https://github.com/hyperledger/fabric-samples/ has a folder set up for this purpose to allow us to manually deploy and test chaincodes.

Before we get started, let's remove all containers and images to avoid any bugs.

Note: If you are using Docker labs, these steps are not needed. Just get an instance and run sudo su.

To stop containers and remove them, run the following commands:

```
docker stop $(docker ps -aq)
docker rm $(docker ps -aq)
```

Now clear Docker of images:

```
docker system prune -a
```

This will prompt you for a Yes/No response. Type Y to proceed.

It will take some time, but once done, our system is ready.

Now let's pull the images, binaries, and Fabric samples repo:

```
curl -sSL http://bit.ly/2ysbOFE | bash -s 1.2.1
```

Once installed, run the following command:

```
docker images
```

And the output should be similar to the one shown as follows:

Figure 5.1

Also, there will be a repo pulled with the name fabric-samples. Enter that folder using the following command:

`cd fabric-samples`

There will be a repo named chaincode-docker-devmode. This repo is useful in development mode. It also has another repo named chaincode in the same fabric-samples folder, which gets mounted as volume inside the peers, CLI, and chaincode containers. This repo has some chaincode projects already available; however, we need to put our own project that we developed in the previous step inside it. To do so, run the following commands:

`cd chaincode`

Then copy the asset-registry folder manually or using `cp` command inside this chaincode folder.

If you are using Docker labs, clone this repo inside the chaincode folder by using the Git clone command.

Starting the containers and running our chaincode project:

Now enter the chaincode-docker-devmode folder inside fabric-samples.

There will be a docker-compose-simple.yaml file. Also note that crypto material is available inside the msp folder. Use the YAML file to start the network:

`docker-compose -f docker-compose-simple.yaml up`

Open a separate terminal.

Note: If you are using Docker labs, you can copy the SSH URL from the icon shown below and paste it into the terminal or Git Bash in your local machine.

Figure 5.2

Now run the following command:

```
docker ps
```

You should have the following containers up and running:

```
bash-4.4# docker ps
CONTAINER ID    IMAGE                          COMMAND                CREATED        STATUS           PORTS
a0e8a0006bca    hyperledger/fabric-ccenv       "/bin/bash -c 'sleep."  3 hours ago    Up 28 seconds
ca473152c1d4    hyperledger/fabric-peer        "peer node start --p." 3 hours ago    Up 28 seconds    0.0.0.0:7051
6ab42e04570d    hyperledger/fabric-orderer     "orderer"              3 hours ago    Up 28 seconds    0.0.0.0:7050
bash-4.4#
```

Figure 5.3

Now let's run our project. To test it, we will need to get inside the chaincode container, which is a special container that contains the chaincode environment already set up for us to run the chaincode project—either in Node.js or Golang.

So, let's get inside this container using docker exec:

```
docker exec -it chaincode bash
```

You should be able to see the asset-registry available inside:

```
cd asset-registry
```

Now we need to install node_modules that are required for this project to run inside this chaincode container. To do so, run the following command:

```
npm i
```

This will install all node_modules required. Now, let's build this project to generate a build folder using TypeScript:

```
npm run build
```

Wait for some time. If no errors are thrown, you are good to go.

Next, inside package.json, we have a start command for fabric-chaincode-node. This fabric-chaincode-node expects two arguments: one is the peer address to connect and install this chaincode project, and other is the chaincode name and version. So, provide the following information:

```
npm run start -- --peer.address "peer:7052" "--chaincode-id-name"
"asset-cc:0.1"
```

Here we are specifying the peer address as peer (which points to the running peer container) on port 7052 and we are giving a name asset-cc and version 0.1. This name and version are important for the upcoming steps.

Wait for some time, and it will start the stream with a ready message in the end.

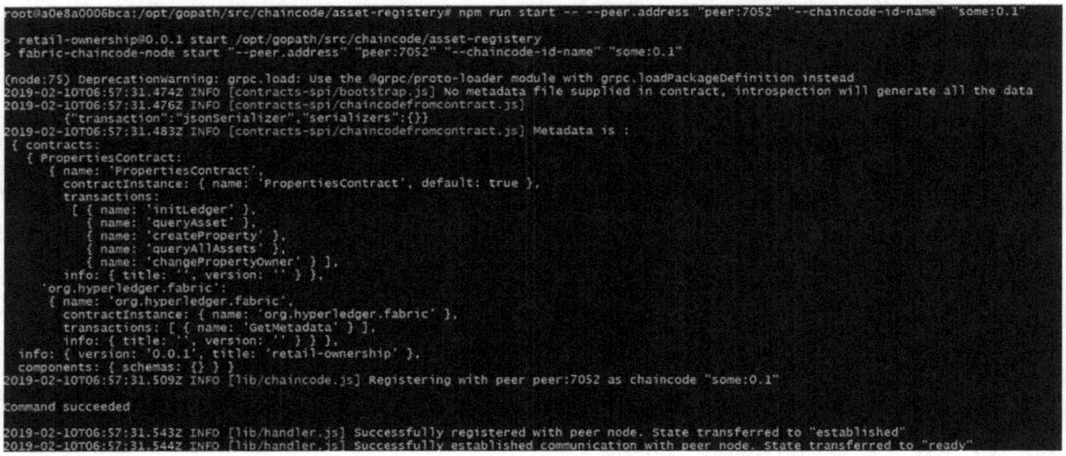

Figure 5.4

Our chaincode is now listening for any requests for peers and bash containers in order to run operations.

Installing, instantiating, and invoking the chaincode:

Once we have started the server, the next step is to start interacting with it using the CLI container.

Next, get inside the CLI container:

```
docker exec -it cli bash
```

First install the chaincode using peer command. This might look like a redundant step, but it is needed to keep up with the lifecycle. Thus, run the following to install the chaincode:

```
peer chaincode install -p chaincode/asset-registery/ -n asset-cc -l node
-v 0.1
```

Once done, you will see a success response as shown in the following screenshot:

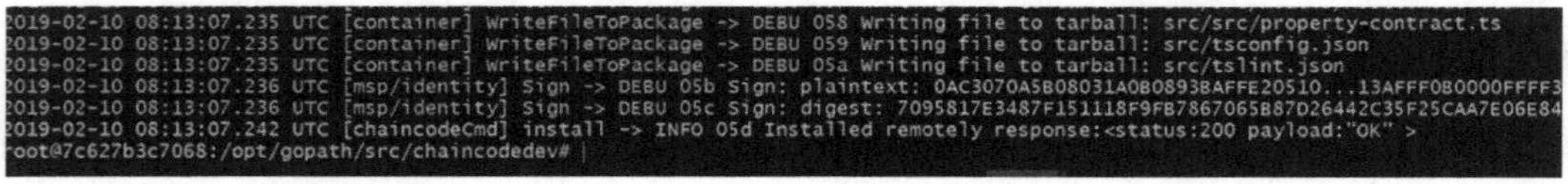

Figure 5.5

Now let's instantiate this. We will use the default channel created as myc:

```
peer chaincode instantiate -n asset-cc -v 0.1 -l node -c
'{"Args":["initLedger"]}' -C myc
```

This will give us the following response in the chaincode container terminal:

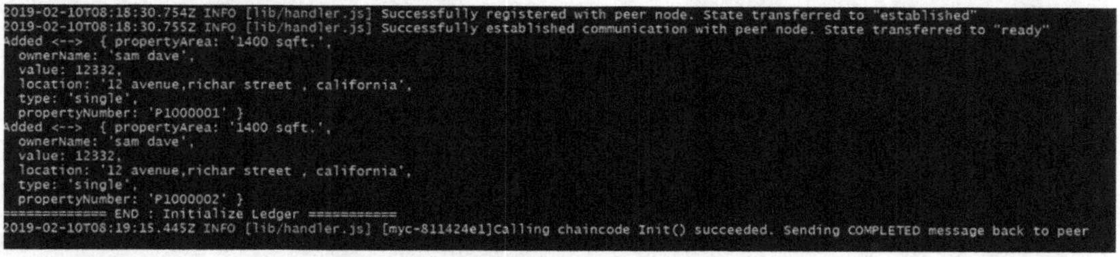

2019-02-10T08:18:30.754Z INFO [lib/handler.js] Successfully registered with peer node. State transferred to "established"
2019-02-10T08:18:30.755Z INFO [lib/handler.js] Successfully established communication with peer node. State transferred to "ready"
Added <--> { propertyArea: '1400 sqft.',
  ownerName: 'sam dave',
  value: 12332,
  location: '12 avenue,richar street , california',
  type: 'single',
  propertyNumber: 'P1000001' }
Added <--> { propertyArea: '1400 sqft.',
  ownerName: 'sam dave',
  value: 12332,
  location: '12 avenue,richar street , california',
  type: 'single',
  propertyNumber: 'P1000002' }
=========== END : Initialize Ledger ===========
2019-02-10T08:19:15.445Z INFO [lib/handler.js] [myc-811424e1]Calling chaincode Init() succeeded. Sending COMPLETED message back to peer

Figure 5.6

Now that we have instantiated, let's query the details of a property using property number P1000001:

```
peer chaincode query -n asset-cc  -c '{"Args":["queryAsset","P1000001"]
}' -C myc
```

This should give the following output on the screen:

2019-02-10 08:31:28.618 UTC [chaincodeCmd] getChaincodeSpec -> DEBU 043 java chaincode disabled
2019-02-10 08:31:28.619 UTC [msp/identity] Sign -> DEBU 044 Sign: plaintext: 0ACE070A6608031A0CC08E0C2FFE20510...7941737365740A085031303030303031
2019-02-10 08:31:28.619 UTC [msp/identity] Sign -> DEBU 045 Sign: digest: 87F114F8AAA2D23838B21CB185916304E6EEA4212EF7493889ECE080858853FD
{"propertyArea":".\"1400 sqft.\",\"ownerName\":\"sam dave\",\"value\":12332,\"location\":\"12 avenue,richar street , california\",\"type\":\"single\",\"propertyNumber\":\"
P1000001\"}
root@7c627b3c7068:/opt/gopath/src/chaincodedev#

Figure 5.7

Let's test another function, createProperty:

```
peer chaincode invoke -n asset-cc -c '{"Args":["createProperty","P100000
3","howbe","2838","somehg","asdf","2323","someowner"]}' -C myc
```

We are passing the createProperty function name and set of parameters needed for creating the property. We shall see the following output:

2019-02-10 08:33:19.712 UTC [chaincodeCmd] chaincodeInvokeOrQuery -> DEBU 047 ESCC invoke result: version:1 response:<status:200 > payload:"\n B\004024B2\353\256\347\035U\
53\007\376\270A\243D+\177\137\373S\361\352\232\006G\r\325\331\217\235\304\215\022\336\001\n\304\001\022\246\001\n\tasset-cc2\221\230\001\n\n\n\010P1000003\032\211\001\n\010P100
003\032}{\"propertyArea\":\"howbe\",\"location\":\"asdf\",\"propertyNumber\":\"P1000003\",\"type\":\"somehg\",\"value\":\"2323\",\"ownerName\":\"someowner\"}\022\031\n\004
lscc\021\n\017\n\tasset-cc2\002\010\003\032\003\010\310\001\"\020\002\022\002\021\n\005DEF0030.1" endorsement:<endorser:"\n\007DEFAULT\022\272\006-----BEGIN CERTIFICATE
-----\nMIICNjCCAdIgAwIBAgIRAMnf9;dmV9RvCCVw9p2QUfUwCgYIKoZIzj0EAwIwgvEk\nCzAJBgNvBAYTA1VTMRMwEQYDVQQIEwpDYWxpp2m9ybm1hMRYwFAYDVQQHEwlTYW4g\nRnJhbmppc2NvMRkwFwYDVQQKExBvcmcxLm
V4YW1wbGUuY29tMRwwGgYDVQQLEwND\nTlAxHDAaBgNVBAMTE2NhLm9yZzEuZXhhbXBsZS5jb20wHhcNMTcxMTEyMTM0MTE1\nWhcNMjcxMTEwMTM0MTE1WjBpMQswCQYDVQQGEwJVUzETMBEGA1UECBMKQ2FsaWZv\ncm5pYTEW
MBQGA1UEBxMNU2FuIEZyYW5jaXNjbzEMMAoGA1UECxMDQ09QMRwwGgYD\nVQQDExZwZWVyMC5vcmcxLmV4YW1wbGUuY29tMFkwEwYHKoZIzj0CAQYIKoZIzj0D\nAQcDQgAEZ8S4V7loBJpyMIVZdwYdFXAckIItrpvSrCfOHQg40
Ww9XSo0OO7GI+Umf\nEkmTIJJXP7/AyRRSRU38oI8Ivtu4M6NNMEswDgYDVROPAQH/BAQDAgeAMAwGA1Ud\nEwEB/wQCMAAwKwYDVR0jBCQwIoAgin0RIhnPEFZUhXm6ewBkm7k72c8R4/z7Lw4H\nnossDICswCgYIKoZIzj0EAw
IDRwAwRAIgvikIUZzgfuFsGLQHwJUVJCU7pOaETkaz\nPzFgsCiLxUACICgzJYlw7nv2xP7b6tbeu3t8mrhMXQs956mD4+BoKuNI\n-----END CERTIFICATE-----\n" signature:"0D\002 u\342\004d\254\223k\306
Js\275D#+G\020\010\261j\204\246\304\366\364\037\354,\304\250&\325\002\027M\"v\0364\350{\201\256},b\370\353\000\001\002}\242\231h\346\363\334k_\317M\003\360U" >
2019-02-10 08:33:19.712 UTC [chaincodeCmd] chaincodeInvokeOrQuery -> INFO 0a8 Chaincode invoke successful. result: status:200

Figure 5.7

Now let's test the last function that allows you to change the owner. This needs function name, property ID, and new owner name as the parameters:

```
PEER CHAINCODE INVOKE -N ASSET-CC -C '{"ARGS":["CHANGEPROPERTYOWNER","P1
000003","CRAZY"]}' -C MYC
```

Now we have to check the owner of this property again to ensure the change has been made. Let's run the query again for property P1000003 that we just changed:

```
peer chaincode query -n asset-cc  -c '{"Args":["queryAsset","P1000003"]
}' -C myc
```

```
2019-02-10 08:36:47.263 UTC [msp/identity] Sign -> DEBU 044 Sign: plaintext: 0ACD070A6508031A08089FC5FFE20510...79417373657404085031303030303033
2019-02-10 08:36:47.263 UTC [msp/identity] Sign -> DEBU 045 Sign: digest: A9BADADA8C6E141871127CB77F5D799165FC0C35E831A5CCD1A78E93DFB94DDA
{\"propertyArea\":\"howbe\",\"location\":\"asdf\",\"propertyNumber\":\"P1000003\",\"type\":\"somehg\",\"value\":\"2323\",\"ownerName\":\"crazy\")"
root@7c627b3c7068:/opt/gopath/src/chaincodedev#
```

Figure 5.8

You can see that the new owner name is updated in the ledger.

Also, in the chaincode terminal, we see the following logs. This confirms that the interaction is happening:

```
2019-02-10T08:32:21.369Z INFO [lib/handler.js] [myc-f4e5f0ad]Calling chaincode Invoke() succeeded. Sending COMPLETED message back to peer
{ type: 'Buffer', data: [] }
2019-02-10T08:33:19.706Z INFO [lib/handler.js] [myc-97c4f1c7]Calling chaincode Invoke() succeeded. Sending COMPLETED message back to peer
============ START : changeOwner ============
============ END : changeCarOwner ============
2019-02-10T08:34:56.651Z INFO [lib/handler.js] [myc-833ce8b8]Calling chaincode Invoke() succeeded. Sending COMPLETED message back to peer
============ START : changeOwner ============
============ END : changeCarOwner ============
2019-02-10T08:36:18.309Z INFO [lib/handler.js] [myc-0908e5b9]Calling chaincode Invoke() succeeded. Sending COMPLETED message back to peer
{"propertyArea":"howbe","location":"asdf","propertyNumber":"P1000003","type":"somehg","value":"2323","ownerName":"crazy"}
2019-02-10T08:36:47.270Z INFO [lib/handler.js] [myc-df69fb64]Calling chaincode Invoke() succeeded. Sending COMPLETED message back to peer
```

Figure 5.9

Chaincode best practices

Let us understand some of the important considerations while writing chaincodes. Chaincodes are valuable and important pieces of the code running inside the peers. So, they need to be performant, secure, turing complete, and efficient. Here are some of the best practices to follow while writing chaincodes:

1. Avoid initializing global variables in Init phase.

   Chaincodes aren't just another Node.js program. They run in a very isolated and constrained environment, so doing something like this can prove to be very bad for your ledger data:

   ```
   export class PropertiesContract extends Contract {

       let assetGlobal:AssetDetails = {

           propertyArea: '1400 sqft.',

           ownerName: 'sam dave',

           value: 12332,

           location : '12 avenue,richar street , california',

           type: 'single',

           propertyNumber: 'P1000001'

       }

       public async initLedger(ctx: Context) {
   ```

```
        assetGlobal.ownerName = test;  // may not work
    properly
```

```
    ....continue
```

Using putstate is the only reliable way of confirming whether the data will be available in such a condition, like when the container restarts. So never rely on global variables. As the init function is only called once, when the container restarts, the invoke function will only be called and the global initialization inside init may not work.

2. Don't work with raw interfaces.

   Like we have seen before, with all the programming languages supported for writing chaincodes, the interface is provided with the init and invoke methods.

   These are not reliable, and working with them natively is not a great thing to do. Therefore, tools like Composer are really great but it is not in active development, so it's better to use some other tools to develop the chaincode.

   From Fabric 1.4 onwards, a proposal was implemented to provide a framework over the existing native package to improve the programming model.

   https://jira.hyperledger.org/browse/FAB-11246

   We also have Fabric Chaintool (https://github.com/hyperledger/fabric-chaintool) to convert our model's schema into client and chaincode applications.

   There is another great tool from Convector that we will use in the next section to create a token.

3. Avoid testing the chaincode in Fabric environment.

   For speedy development, it is suggested to develop the chaincode locally and unit test it locally before finally deploying it.

   This saves a lot of time. Also, it is suggested to use the Fabric development setup to perform integration testing on the chaincode.

4. Avoid common pitfalls.

   Avoid using duplicate keys, as there might be a chance of a collision and simultaneous read-and-write updates, causing problems in storage.

   It's better to use a UTXO format like bitcoin.

   Avoid doing non-deterministic transactions. There are other improvements coming up in Fabric to tackle these.

Creating a token using Convector tool

We created a chaincode project using models, but that is not truly the enterprise requirement. Controller is where the common logic can go.

If you have heard of ERC token implementations, you might be aware of certain parameters related to it. Check this link on ERC-20 token: https://en.wikipedia.org/wiki/ERC-20.

Also, please feel free to review the interface of ERC-20 token from this proposal: https://github.com/ethereum/EIPS/issues/20.

- Create a new folder named token.
- Clone this repo https://github.com/worldsibu/convector.git.
- git clone https://github.com/worldsibu/convector.git.
- In it, move into the examples/token folder.
- Open it in the code.

First, in package.json, we can see a number of extra dependencies that have been created to help us write the chaincode:

```
"@worldsibu/convector-core-storage": "^1.2.0",
"@worldsibu/convector-core-chaincode": "^1.2.0",
"@worldsibu/convector-core-adapter": "^1.2.0",
"@worldsibu/convector-core-controller": "^1.2.0",
"@worldsibu/convector-core-model": "^1.2.0",
"@worldsibu/convector-storage-stub": "^1.2.0",
"reflect-metadata": "^0.1.12",
"tslib": "^1.9.0",
"yup": "^0.24.1"
```

Notice we have Yup package https://www.npmjs.com/package/yup included, which is a popular schema parser package to help run validations. Note this is not a must and you can use other libraries as well, like joi.

Now look inside the src folder, where we have a model and controller. It is great to have this kind of separation where the modelling and logic are in different modules.

Look at the model file token.model.ts:

```
import * as yup from 'yup';
import {
```

```
    ConvectorModel,

    ReadOnly,

    Required,

    Validate
} from '@worldsibu/convector-core-model';
export class Token extends ConvectorModel<Token> {
    @ReadOnly()
    public readonly type = 'io.worldsibu.examples.token';
    @ReadOnly()
    @Required()
    @Validate(yup.object())
    public balances: { [key: string]: number };
    @ReadOnly()
    @Required()
    @Validate(yup.number().moreThan(0))
    public totalSupply: number;
    @ReadOnly()
    @Required()
    @Validate(yup.string())
    public name: string;
    @ReadOnly()
    @Required()
    @Validate(yup.string())
    public symbol: string;
}
```

Note that it extends the ConvectorModel, which will make all the base methods accessible. This is somewhat similar to Mongoose schema modelling related to mongodb for Node.js.

Once this is extended, we can now use methods like getOne() instead of getState, which is unreliable and native.

It also has a set of decorators attached to the properties of this model class. These are useful for writing a robust, error-free chaincode. Recall when we wrote a property's chaincode model. What if the property number, area, etc. was not passed properly? A validation is thus required.

Constraint on balances is defined as ReadOnly, Required and Validate decorators. So, this property is required and has to be an object.

Similarly, the total supply is defined with ReadOnly, Required and Validate decorators. Here a Yum instance is passed with the condition that it should be a number more than 0.

Thus, if someone tries to send a negative supply value in init, it will throw a validation error. Similarly, the decorators on name and symbol are defined.

We can write a similar file for our properties model file. In fact, you can convert the whole project using Convector and try to learn from this example, if you like.

Now let's see the controller file.

Notice that the imports Controller and ConvectorController act as a wrapper over the package and help us write the logic while taking care of all the other things:

```
import * as yup from 'yup';
import {
  Controller,
  ConvectorController,
  Invokable,
  Param
} from '@worldsibu/convector-core-controller';
import { Token } from './token.model';
@Controller('token')
export class TokenController extends ConvectorController {
  private initialized = false;
  @Invokable()
  public async init(
    @Param(Token)
    token: Token
  ) {
    if (this.initialized) {
      throw new Error('Token has already been initialized');
    }
    const totalSupply = Object.keys(token.balances)
      .reduce((total, fingerprint) => total + token.balances[fingerprint],
0);
```

```
    if (totalSupply !== token.totalSupply) {
        throw new Error('The total supply does not match with the initial
balances');
    }
    await token.save();
  }
  @Invokable()
  public async transfer(
    @Param(yup.string())
    tokenId: string,
    @Param(yup.string())
    to: string,
    @Param(yup.number().moreThan(0))
    amount: number
  ) {
    const token = await Token.getOne(tokenId);
    if (!token.id) {
      throw new Error(`No token found with id ${tokenId}`);
    }
    console.log('Using token id', token.id);
    if (token.balances[this.sender] < amount) {
      throw new Error('The sender does not have enough founds');
    }
    token.balances[to] += amount;
    token.balances[this.sender] -= amount;

    await token.save();
  }

  @Invokable()
  public async whoAmI(): Promise<string> {
    return this.sender;
  }
```

```
}
```

We have three functions, all of which are of invokable type.

Let's see the init function where the user can set important properties of token like name, totalSupply, and so on. The input is deserialized and validated, and if any of the conditions are met, then an error is thrown.

Note that this init function is only called once, similar to the Shim API, so all the details regarding the token are set here and cannot be changed as they are ReadOnly. Also, please make a note that we have a save function available instead of a put function.

Next, we have the transfer function where we expect fields like tokenId, to and amount. First, input validation is done for these. Then we can retrieve the information about that token from tokenId using the getOne(id) function.

If the function is not available, an error is thrown. It is also checked to see if the balance of the user is less than the requested amount. If it is, an error is thrown.

Finally, the balance is increased by the amount and then the save function is called again to save the token details.

A simple function is provided to return the user info. This is a TypeScript project like ours, so first test and build this as follows:

```
npm i
```

Then enter the following command:

```
npm run build
```

If everything goes fine, move ahead and test the deployment in chaincode dev setup.

Follow the same steps as we did for the chaincode.

This is a nice paradigm to follow in order to write standard chaincodes. You can know more about this suite by going through https://worldsibu.tech/convector/.

Writing unit tests for chaincode

Testing chaincodes has always been a pain, especially with the kind of setup it has. We can use traditional JavaScript tools like Mocha and Chai to test the chaincode. The official chaincode library fabric-shim provides the ChaincodeStub package to do so.

First, import the following dependencies related to the chaincode:

```
import { Context } from 'fabric-contract-api';
```

```
import { ChaincodeStub, ClientIdentity } from 'fabric-shim';
import { PropertiesContract } from '../src/property-contract';
import { AssetDetails } from '../src/models/Asset.model';
```

Then import other packages related to unit testing:

```
import * as chai from 'chai';
import * as sinon from 'sinon';
import * as sinonChai from 'sinon-chai';
chai.should();
chai.use(sinonChai);
```

Then write a class that implements the Context class to create mock instances:

```
class PropertyContratTest implements Context {
    public stub: ChaincodeStub = sinon.createStubInstance(ChaincodeStub
);
    public clientIdentity: ClientIdentity = sinon.createStubInstance(Cli
entIdentity);
}
```

Then write a basic test for initializing the contract.

First, we take an instance of the contract and then an instance of the context. We can then call the initLedger function to initialize the ledger.

```
describe(Properties contract testing, () => {
    describe('init ledger', () => {


        it('should initialize the ledger', async () => {
            const contract = new PropertiesContract();
            const ctx = new TestContext();
            await contract.initLedger(ctx);
        });
    });
});
```

Similarly, you can write more tests for your chaincode.

There are also some third-party libraries to test the chaincode: https://github.com/wearetheledger/fabric-mock-stub.

This mock stub is also very useful to test some key functionalities and also to do e2e testing.

Chaincode development using IBM blockchain platform

Note: This works only with the Fabric 1.4 LTS version.

In this section, we will learn to use the IBM blockchain platform extension to create, package, install, instantiate, and test the chaincode using Visual Studio Code.

Create an empty directory test and open it in Visual Studio Code with the IBM blockchain platform extension installed.

Hit *Ctrl + Shift + p* to open the terminal as shown below, and type Create smart contract. Then select the highlighted option that reads IBM Blockchain Platform: Create Smart Contract Project.

Figure 5.10

It will prompt you for the type of programming language. You can choose TypeScript:

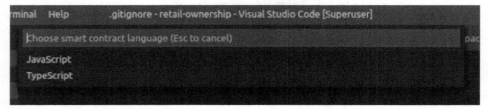

Figure 5.11

The structure shown in *Figure 5.12* will be generated by the tool:

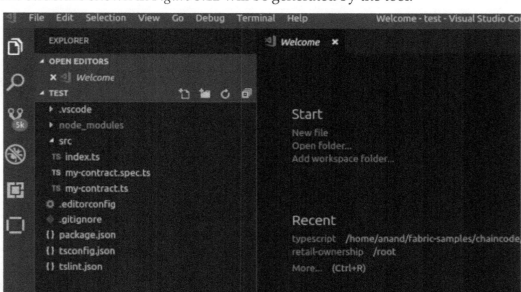

Figure 5.12

Now let us run our asset registry project using this tool. First, remove the content of src and copy the content of **asset-registry/src** inside this project src/.

Also, in package.json, change the lint line, mentioned below, inside scripts

```
"lint": "tslint -c tslint.json src/**/*.ts'",
```

to

```
"lint": "tslint -c tslint.json 'dummy/**/*.ts'",
```

Now we are all set up. Also, add all the missing dependencies inside package.json from asset-registry package.json.

Then run the following command:

```
npm i
```

We are all ready now.

Now move to the extension by clicking on the extension icon.

You will see a **+** icon as shown in *Figure 5.13*, which is provided to package and add a new smart contract project.

Click on this icon, and let the extension run.

It will compile using TypeScript and package our project:

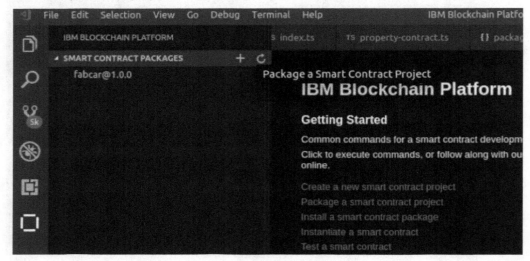

Figure 5.13

Once it is packaged, you can see it in the list of smart contracts packages available:

Figure 5.14

Notice test@0.0.1 shown here.

Now that we have packaged our smart contract, let's interact with the blockchain network, i.e., the Hyperledger network.

Notice that at the bottom of this extension panel there will be a connection available by the name local_fabric. Click on this connection **fabric_local** to start the containers, create a channel, and get all the meta data.

If you are doing it for the first time, it will probably take a while as this will install all images and binaries related to Fabric.

Once connected, it will show the channel information and all installed chaincodes in it as shown in *Figure 5.15*.

Notice it shows one channel named **mychannel**, an organization named **peer0. org1.example.com**, and an installed chaincode:

Figure 5.15

Now select this organization, right-click, and choose Install chaincode in it. It will then prompt you to choose the smart contract package. Choose the one we installed, i.e., the test package:

Figure 5.16

Once selected, it will take some time and you will get a notification that it was successfully installed on the peer.

Next, you have to instantiate it. To do so, choose the channel and select the Instantiate chaincode option. You will be prompted for some arguments. Pass initLedger, as this is the function we need to call for instantiation. You should now see the test appearing as follows:

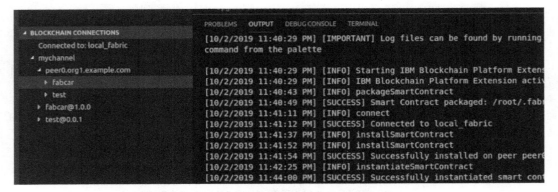

Figure 5.17

You now have a number of operations available related to the functions we wrote inside our chaincode:

Figure 5.18

These functions can be called to test. Let's start by calling queryAsset.

Select **queryAsset**, right-click, and choose **submit transaction**. This will ask for parameters. Pass property ID **P1000001** created at the time of init.

To see this output, you should see the logs of the chaincode container that were installed.

Run the Docker ps command to find out the test chaincode container ID. This should look as shown in *Figure 5.19*:

Figure 5.19

```
docker logs <containerid>
```

This will show the logs, and you will see the query function return the asset details on the basis of the property ID:

Figure 5.20

Let's execute one more transaction, i.e., change the owner of the property

Choose **changePropertyOwner** and hit the **submit transaction** button. It will ask you for arguments and type.

```
P1000001,somenewowner
```

Press *Enter*. This will submit the transactions.

Once completed, check the new owner by querying the chaincode again. Submit queryAsset again and pass the property ID **P1000001**. It should give you the new owner name as follows:

Figure 5.21

We have just learnt how easy it becomes to deploy and test our chaincode on a real Fabric network using the extension. It is recommended to use this extension to work with chaincodes as they are a great aid in setting up a complex network.

Chaincode for operators

From the perspective of Hyperledger Fabric, developer is not the only role. Owing to the size and complexity of Fabric, many different roles have evolved and co-exist on this platform. One such important role is that of operators.

Some of the most important functionalities of Fabric include packaging, installing, instantiating, invoking, and upgrading. These roles are explained as follows.

Packaging the chaincode

Packaging comprises three stages:

1. In Fabric, encode specification is provided by **CDS** (**ChaincodeDeploymentSpec**), which refers to the chaincode deployment pack. This typically includes properties such as code name and version.

2. There is an extra policy that can be used at the time of instantiation.

3. Signatures by the owners of the chaincode are included:

   a. To ensure that the owner of the code is known.

   b. To make sure that the contents of the packages are verified.

   c. To ascertain if the current package has been tampered with.

Creating the package

We can package the chaincode by following a couple of approaches. The first one is when you have multiple owners of the chaincode, where we will need this package signed from each of the entities. Here, we first create a signed package by CDS, which is then passed to all, one at a time, to get the signatures. The other approach is to have a signed CDS only from the peer that has issued the install command. This is a simple way as we only need to collect one signature.

Let's understand the first case:

```
peer chaincode package -n mycc -p github.com/hyperledger/fabric/
examples/chaincode/go/example02/cmd -v 0 -s -S -i "AND('OrgA.admin')"
ccpack.out
```

Notice that in this command, we are providing the package command and mentioning -s to specify that it is going to be signed by multiple owners. Without this, it will be a single signed package and won't let the others owners sign.

-i is used to specify the policy for instantiation. In this case, the policy needs to state that only the organization has to instantiate this or sign this. If no such policy is defined, which is normally the case, then a default policy takes over wherein the admin's MSP identity is taken for deployment at the time of instantiation.

Package signing by other owners

The package that was signed before can now be made available for the other owners to sign. The command to sign the existing package by the other owners is given as follows:

```
peer chaincode signpackage ccpack.out signedccpack.out
```

This will sign the package named ccpack.out as signedccpack.out.

Installing package

Installation of peer chaincodes bundles the source code into a prescribed format that is installed in the peers to run the chaincode. The chaincode needs to be installed on all the peers that are part of the channel.

As seen in the asset registry project, we can install a chaincode by sending a signed proposal lifecycle system chaincode (LSCC).

For example, to install asset-registry, we had used the following command:

```
peer chaincode install -n asset-registry-cc -v 1.0 -p asset-registry
```

Here -n specifies the name, which is arbitrary but should be unique, -v specifies the version, and -p specifies the path for the chaincode repo.

Instantiating the chaincode

Similar to installation, the instantiate command calls the LSCC to do an initialization in the channel.

In this instantiation, there is a total isolation among different instances of the chaincode. In other words, this chaincode can be a part of multiple channels but all of these instants created are isolated from each other. Thus, the state is totally isolated. The invoker of this instantiate should specify the instantiate policy.

An important part of instantiation is the endorsement policy, which is specified to ensure that if any invoke operation happens, all the proposals from the specified organization should be gathered before the orderer admits it in the next block.

To instantiate a chaincode, we can use following command:

```
peer chaincode instantiate -n asset-cc -v 0 -c '{"Args":[]}' -C myc -P
"AND ('Org1.admin,'Org2.member')"
```

Here we have specified an endorsement policy as well.

Once it is instantiated properly, it is marked as active state. Also, instantiating creates a new chaincode container as shown in the following screenshot:

Figure 5.22

Upgrading, starting, and stopping the chaincode

One can upgrade a chaincode by changing its version. The new version must be installed and the corresponding version should be used in the upgrade command:

```
peer chaincode upgrade -n asset-cc2 -v 1.1 -c '{"Args":"initLedger"[]}'
-C myc
```

Also, when a chaincode is instantiated, you can see it has started in a separate Docker container that should be stopped and removed manually as no such mechanism is available out of the box.

You can have a look at the entire API available as CLI by logging into your CLI container:

```
docker exec -it cli bash
```

Now type the following:

```
peer chaincode –help
```

```
root@8bfa0505631f:/opt/gopath/src/github.com/hyperledger/fabric/peer# peer chaincode --help
Operate a chaincode: install|instantiate|invoke|package|query|signpackage|upgrade|list.

Usage:
  peer chaincode [command]

Available Commands:
  install      Package the specified chaincode into a deployment spec and save it on the peer's path.
  instantiate  Deploy the specified chaincode to the network.
  invoke       Invoke the specified chaincode.
  list         Get the instantiated chaincodes on a channel or installed chaincodes on a peer.
  package      Package the specified chaincode into a deployment spec.
  query        Query using the specified chaincode.
  signpackage  Sign the specified chaincode package
  upgrade      Upgrade chaincode.

Flags:
      --cafile string          Path to file containing PEM-encoded trusted certificate(s) for the orderi
      --certfile string        Path to file containing PEM-encoded X509 public key to use for mutual TLS
 orderer endpoint
      --clientauth             Use mutual TLS when communicating with the orderer endpoint
      --connTimeout duration   Timeout for client to connect (default 3s)
  -h, --help                   help for chaincode
      --keyfile string         Path to file containing PEM-encoded private key to use for mutual TLS com
erer endpoint
  -o, --orderer string         Ordering service endpoint
```

Figure 5.23

System chaincode

A system chaincode has an equivalent programming model except that it runs among the peer instances instead of an isolated container like the traditional chaincode. Therefore, a system chaincode is installed into the peer and doesn't follow an equivalent lifecycle delineation on top. Specifically, install, instantiate, and upgrade don't apply to system chaincodes.

The purpose of system chaincodes is to crosscut the gRPC communication value between the peer and the chaincode and trade-off the flexibleness in management. For instance, a system chaincode will solely be upgraded with the peer binary. It should additionally register with a set of parameters that are compiled and don't have endorsement policies or endorsement policy practicality.

System chaincodes are employed in Hyperledger material to implement a variety of system behaviors to get replaced or changed, as applicable, by a better system.

Summary

In this chapter, we saw what is chaincode and how we can develop a chaincode in Node.js. We first created a chaincode project based on a simple use case and then learnt to test it in the development setup provided by the Fabric network. We also learnt some of the best practices related to chaincodes. The chapter also covered the different tools available to write a chaincode, like Convector. It also gave us an overview of how we can develop using code extension. Lastly, we saw how operators can work with chaincodes by performing some of the common operations. In the next chapter, we will learn about building an application with Fabric SDK.

References

- https://hyperledger-fabric.readthedocs.io

- https://worldsibu.tech/convector/

- https://medium.com/wearetheledger/how-to-start-testing-your-hyperledger-fabric-nodejs-chaincode-229453c3c214

- https://marketplace.visualstudio.com/items?itemName=IBMBlockchain.ibm-blockchain-platform

## CHAPTER 6

Fabric SDK: Interaction with Fabric Network

In this chapter, we will be looking into Fabric SDKs. This is something external to the network itself but performs a number of important functions. There are different SDKs available based on programming languages, e.g., Node.js SDK, Java SDK, and so on. In this chapter, we will be working with the Node.js SDK; however, the functionality of other Fabric SDKs is similar to that of the Node.js SDK.

In order to understand the concepts in this chapter, we will be extending our asset-registry example defined in *Chapter 3* by using the Node.js SDK in order to interact with it. We will also provide details on the use of chaincodes.

As you can see in *Figure 6.1*, the Fabric SDK client is used to perform operations like managing channels, creating channels, managing chaincodes, installing chaincodes, upgrading channels, and invoking methods from chaincodes, like invoke, query, and more.

Figure 6.1 also shows two modules—fabric-client and fabric-ca-client—inside the Fabric Node.js SDK box, which represents the two npm modules: https://www.npmjs.com/package/fabric-client and https://www.npmjs.com/package/fabric-ca-client.

These are official Node.js modules used to interact with the network.

Also, at any point if you are stuck, please refer to this repository https://github.com/SateDev/asset-registry-sdk. It's better to clone this repository and keep it as a reference.

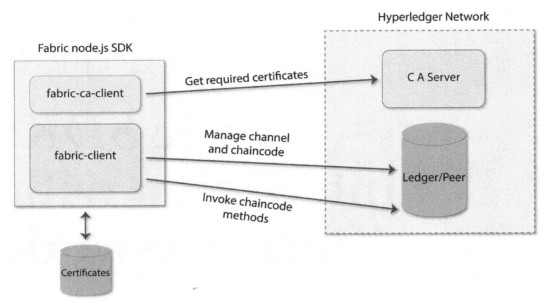

Figure 6.1

Let's get started with the Node.js SDK. The first step is to get all the prerequisites for working with the Fabric SDK.

Prerequisites

Start Fabric network

Before we start interacting with the network, we need to have a network in place.

Let us start a basic network with the chaincode installed in it so we can start interacting with the same. One of the quickest ways to start a basic network is by cloning the Fabric samples repositories again.

Note: If you have any other existing Fabric network running, please remove it before proceeding.

git clone https://github.com/hyperledger/fabric-samples.git

`cd fabric-samples`

The above commands will clone the repository and a new folder will be created, called fabric-samples. You can go inside the basic-network folder within the fabric-samples folder to see the structure and code to start the basic network. *Figure 6.2* depicts the network configuration of this basic network. It is a one-organization network comprising one peer, one orderer, Fabric CA, CouchDB, and CLI container. This is what we require in order to test our Fabric SDK network:

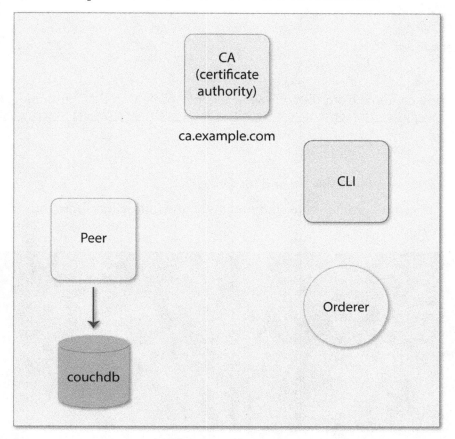

Figure 6.2

We will not be starting this network now. Instead, we will be doing it in the next step when we create a Fabric SDK project.

We will be interacting with our asset-registry chaincode created in *Chapter 3* using the Fabric SDK.

Let's go inside the chaincode folder within fabric-samples and pull the asset registry example in it.

```
git clone https://github.com/SateDev/hyperledger_chaincode_asset_registry
```

We now have our chaincode project inside the chaincode folder that is mounted within the CLI container.

Now, create a shell file to start the basic network. Create a file startup.sh:

```
mkdir startup
cd startup
vi startup.sh
```

Press *i*.

Now, copy contents from the following file and paste it in the command prompt: https://raw.githubusercontent.com/SateDev/asset-registry-sdk/master/scripts/startup.sh.

Click *Esc*.

Press *Shift + ;* and then type wq and hit *Enter*.

In order to grant permission to startup.sh, type the following command:

```
chmod 777 startup.sh
```

```
CODE_OF_CONDUCT.md   basic-network              first-network
CONTRIBUTING.md      chaincode                  high-throughput
Jenkinsfile          chaincode-docker-devmode   interest_rate_swaps
LICENSE              ci.properties              scripts
MAINTAINERS.md       commercial-paper           startup.sh
README.md            docs
balance-transfer     fabcar
[root@UbuntuHyperledger1:/home/nakulshah23/fabric-samples# chmod 777 startup.sh  ]
[root@UbuntuHyperledger1:/home/nakulshah23/fabric-samples# ls                     ]
CODE_OF_CONDUCT.md   basic-network              first-network
CONTRIBUTING.md      chaincode                  high-throughput
Jenkinsfile          chaincode-docker-devmode   interest_rate_swaps
LICENSE              ci.properties              scripts
MAINTAINERS.md       commercial-paper           startup.sh
README.md            docs
balance-transfer     fabcar
root@UbuntuHyperledger1:/home/nakulshah23/fabric-samples#
```

Figure 6.3

This file starts the basic network with components mentioned above, creates a channel, and installs and instantiates our chaincode.

Now, let us start this network. To do so, give the following command:

```
./startup.sh typescript
```

We are providing TypeScript as it is the language we used to write our chaincode.

This will also install node_modules and will also do an npm run build.

Once done, give the command docker ps and you shall see the following output. You should also see the asset chaincode container coming up:

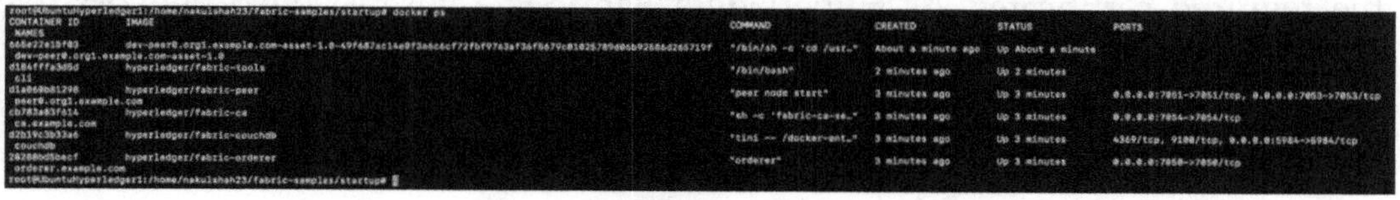

Figure 6.4

Alright, so our network setup is ready. The next step in the process is to start building our node application.

Install Node.js and NPM

You should have Node.js and npm installed in your system. If not, use the link https://nodejs.org/en/download/ and follow the instructions to install Node.js and the npm that matches your operating system.

Create a Node.js SDK project

Make a directory:

```
mkdir property-node-client
```

```
cd property-node-client
```

```
npm init
```

This will ask you a series of general questions related to the project that we are creating. These aren't important for now, so select the default answers. Open this in Visual Studio Code editor or any other JS-based IDE.

Install Fabric npm modules

Two npm modules are required to create a Node.js project that will interact with the Hyperledger network. Let us learn more about these modules.

Fabric client

This is the module used for executing the methods of the chaincode installed in Fabric networks as well as performing other operations like installing chaincodes, creating channels, and so on. Start by installing this module inside your project folder:

```
npm i --save fabric-client
```

Fabric CA client

This is the module that interacts with the CA server of the Fabric network to pull the required certificates. As Hyperledger Fabric is a permissioned network, we need to establish the identity of the user who is interacting with the network by getting certificates from the CA server, which is part of the network itself.

```
npm i --save fabric-ca-client
```

gRPC module

We will need this module to call the endpoints of Fabric components like peers, orderer, and so on, which have gRPC endpoints instead of Rest API.

```
npm i --save grpc
```

Now we have all the dependencies required to run this project.

Process of working with the network

Interacting with the network is a two-step process. In this section, we will be learning about the following two steps in detail:

1. Enrolment and registration of admin and user by using CA server.

2. Interacting with network and chaincode using certificates stored from *Step 1* above.

Let's start with the first part and write the code for the same.

Enrolment and registration of admin and user using CA server

This is a multi-step process and is required to get the appropriate certificates from the CA server. Let us understand the theory behind this step so we can write the logic for the same.

Figure 6.5 will help us understand this process better as we move forward:

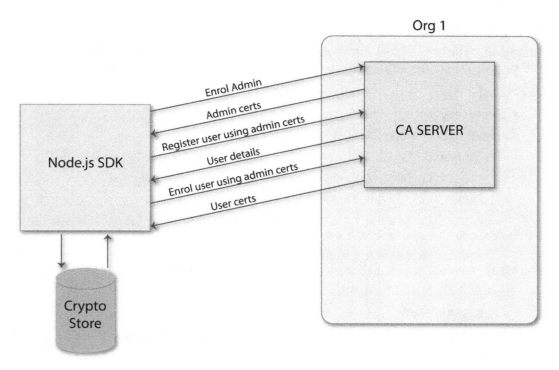

Figure 6.5

In simple language, we need to basically get certificates from the CA server to be able to interact with the network. This process involves the following steps:

1. First, we need to register with the network by providing a username and organization details.

2. Once we have registered with the network, the CA server returns a secret or password. Using this we can get enrolled with the network by providing a username and secret that we received from the server.

3. The CA server accepts the enrolment request if the username and secret are correct and returns the certificates back to the client.

4. The certificate received in the step above is stored in the file system or store, which can be used by the Fabric client to sign and send any transaction.

This is the overall process of getting the certificate. But we need to understand that for the first step, we need admin privilege to be able to send a user registration request to the CA server. So, we first need the certificates of the admin prior to registering a new user and getting their certificate to sign the transactions sent by the Fabric client.

Now, how do we get the admin certificates first?

Just head over to the basic-network folder inside fabric-samples that we cloned in the previous section and look into the following line in docker-compose.yml:

```
services:
  ca.example.com:
    image: hyperledger/fabric-ca
    environment:
      - FABRIC_CA_HOME=/etc/hyperledger/fabric-ca-server
      - FABRIC_CA_SERVER_CA_NAME=ca.example.com
      - FABRIC_CA_SERVER_CA_CERTFILE=/etc/hyperledger/fabric-ca-server-config/ca.org1.example.com-cert.pem
      - FABRIC_CA_SERVER_CA_KEYFILE=/etc/hyperledger/fabric-ca-server-config/4239aa0dcd76daeeb8ba0cda701851d14504d31aad1b2ddddbac6a57365e497c_sk
    ports:
      - "7054:7054"
    command: sh -c 'fabric-ca-server start -b admin:adminpw'
    volumes:
      - ./crypto-config/peerOrganizations/org1.example.com/ca/:/etc/hyperledger/fabric-ca-server-config
    container_name: ca.example.com
    networks:
      - basic
```

This is the YAML used to start the Hyperledger network, and here you can see (highlighted in bold) that we have started fabric-ca-server with credentials admin:adminpw. These are our admin credentials, which means that an admin is already registered with the following credentials in the Fabric CA server.

Now we need to simply enroll this admin to the Fabric CA server in order to get the required certificates that then can be used for registering and enrolling new users.

So, we will have to create a Node.js program file that will be able to enroll an admin using these credentials and get the required certificate and store it in the key store.

To do so, first create a file named enrolAdmin.js inside the new project that you have created in Visual Studio Code. As the name suggests, it will be used to enroll admin and put the required certificates in the store.

Let's import the modules that we will be using here:

```
var Fabric_Client = require('fabric-client');
var Fabric_CA_Client = require('fabric-ca-client');
var path = require('path');
var util = require('util');
var os = require('os');
```

Above, we are importing fabric-client, fabric-ca-client modules. We are also including other built in modules like path, util, os which will be used for some common purposes.

Now let's declare some global variables:

```
var fabric_client = new Fabric_Client();
var fabric_ca_client = null;
var admin_user = null;
var member_user = null;
var store_path = path.join(__dirname, 'hfc-key-store');
```

The fabric_client variable will hold the instance of the Fabric client throughout this program lifecycle.

Also, fabric_ca_client is initialized to null here.

Note: The line "var store_path = path.join(__dirname, 'hfc-key-store');" sets the path for storing certificates. We will be using this to store our certificates in this path once we have them from the CA server.

The next step is to connect to this store path that we specify to our Fabric client and load all the certificates present in this path for the Fabric client to use. To do so, we will be using a method named newDefaultKeyValueStore that can be used to get an instance of the key-value pair store of the certificates stored in the path https:// fabric-sdk-node.github.io/BaseClient.html#.newDefaultKeyValueStore__anchor.

Since this expects a path, we will pass the same path that we created in the last step, store_path:

```
Fabric_Client.newDefaultKeyValueStore({ path: store_path
})
```

So, this will return the state store at the path that we have specified here.

Then, we follow the steps below to proceed further:

1. Set this returned store as the state store for our fabric_client instance that we created at the beginning.

2. Once we have the state store set up, we need to set up the crypto suite for the Fabric client using fabric_client.setCryptoSuite (crypto_suite).

3. This sets up our key store for the Fabric client, which it can use to sign the transaction when sending chaincode invoke operations.

4. Then we need to instantiate our fabric_ca_client that we will use to connect to the CA server in order to get the required certificates as discussed before.

```
fabric_ca_client = new Fabric_CA_Client('http://localhost:7054',
tlsOptions , 'ca.example.com', crypto_suite);
```

As you can see here, it accepts the following parameters:

- url (Fabric CA URL)
- tlsOptions (for secure communication)
- Name of the CA in the network
- Crypto suite that can be used to get certificates

If you run the Docker ps command, you can see that the Fabric CA runs on port 7054 and localhost. Therefore, we have specified this URL here.

After setting this up, we need to check whether the admin user is already enrolled or no. If its certificates are found in the local key store that we have setup in the previous stage, we don't have to go to the CA server to get them. To get the user from the store, we can use the getUserContext function that will load the user from the key store:

```
return fabric_client.getUserContext('admin', true);
```

Below is the code for the process mentioned. Paste it in the previous snippet.

```
.then((state_store) => {
    fabric_client.setStateStore(state_store);
    var crypto_suite = Fabric_Client.newCryptoSuite();
    var crypto_store = Fabric_Client.newCryptoKeyStore({path: store_
path});
    crypto_suite.setCryptoKeyStore(crypto_store);
    fabric_client.setCryptoSuite(crypto_suite);
    var tlsOptions = {
        trustedRoots: [],
        verify: false
    };
    fabric_ca_client = new Fabric_CA_Client('http://localhost:7054',
tlsOptions , 'ca.example.com', crypto_suite);
```

```
        return fabric_client.getUserContext('admin', true);
})
```

Note: This is a standard check that needs to be performed every time to set up the key store for our local instance and check whether the certificate for any user is already existing. Thus, we will not be repeating this explanation going forward.

The function getUserContext will return user_store information from the store, and we can check whether it is enrolled by using the isEnrolled method. If it is enrolled, it means that we already have the certificates generated. Thus, we need not do it again. However, if it is not enrolled, we need to use the credentials admin:adminpw to send a request to the CA server in order to get us the required certificates.

Once we have those, we can put them into the store so we don't have to repeat these steps next time.

Following is the code for the same:

```
.then((user_from_store) => {
    if (user_from_store && user_from_store.isEnrolled()) {
        console.log('Successfully loaded admin from persistence');
        admin_user = user_from_store;
        return null;
    } else {
        // need to enroll it with CA server
        return fabric_ca_client.enroll({
          enrollmentID: 'admin',
          enrollmentSecret: 'adminpw'
        }).then((enrollment) => {
          console.log('Successfully enrolled admin user "admin"');
          return fabric_client.createUser(
              {username: 'admin',
                  mspid: 'Org1MSP',
                  cryptoContent: { privateKeyPEM: enrollment.key.
toBytes(), signedCertPEM: enrollment.certificate }
              });
        }).then((user) => {
          admin_user = user;
          return fabric_client.setUserContext(admin_user);
```

```
        }).catch((err) => {
            console.error('Failed to enroll and persist admin. Error: ' +
err.stack ? err.stack : err);
            throw new Error('Failed to enroll admin');
        });
    }
}).then(() => {
    console.log(admin_user.toString());
}).catch((err) => {
    console.error('Failed to enroll admin: ' + err);
});
```

The final file looks as shown in *Figure 6.6* and *Figure 6.7*:

```
 1   'use strict';
 2   /*
 3   * Copyright IBM Corp All Rights Reserved
 4   *
 5   * SPDX-License-Identifier: Apache-2.0
 6   */
 7   /*
 8   * Enroll the admin user
 9   */
10
11   var Fabric_Client = require('fabric-client');
12   var Fabric_CA_Client = require('fabric-ca-client');
13
14   var path = require('path');
15   var util = require('util');
16   var os = require('os');
17
18   //
19   var fabric_client = new Fabric_Client();
20   var fabric_ca_client = null;
21   var admin_user = null;
22   var member_user = null;
23   var store_path = path.join(__dirname, 'hfc-key-store');
24   console.log(' Store path:'+store_path);
25
26   // create the key value store as defined in the fabric-client/config/default.json 'key-value-store' setting
27   Fabric_Client.newDefaultKeyValueStore({ path: store_path
28   }).then((state_store) => {
29       // assign the store to the fabric client
30       fabric_client.setStateStore(state_store);
31       var crypto_suite = Fabric_Client.newCryptoSuite();
32       // use the same location for the state store (where the users' certificate are kept)
33       // and the crypto store (where the users' keys are kept)
34       var crypto_store = Fabric_Client.newCryptoKeyStore({path: store_path});
35       crypto_suite.setCryptoKeyStore(crypto_store);
36       fabric_client.setCryptoSuite(crypto_suite);
37       var tlsOptions = {
38           trustedRoots: [],
39           verify: false
40       };
```

Figure 6.6

```
41    // be sure to change the http to https when the CA is running TLS enabled
42    fabric_ca_client = new Fabric_CA_Client('http://localhost:7054', tlsOptions , 'ca.example.com', crypto_suite);
43
44    // first check to see if the admin is already enrolled
45    return fabric_client.getUserContext('admin', true);
46  }).then((user_from_store) => {
47    if (user_from_store && user_from_store.isEnrolled()) {
48      console.log('Successfully loaded admin from persistence');
49      admin_user = user_from_store;
50      return null;
51    } else {
52      // need to enroll it with CA server
53      return fabric_ca_client.enroll({
54        enrollmentID: 'admin',
55        enrollmentSecret: 'adminpw'
56      }).then((enrollment) => {
57        console.log('Successfully enrolled admin user "admin"');
58        return fabric_client.createUser(
59          {username: 'admin',
60              mspid: 'Org1MSP',
61              cryptoContent: { privateKeyPEM: enrollment.key.toBytes(), signedCertPEM: enrollment.certificate }
62          });
63      }).then((user) => {
64        admin_user = user;
65        return fabric_client.setUserContext(admin_user);
66      }).catch((err) => {
67        console.error('Failed to enroll and persist admin. Error: ' + err.stack ? err.stack : err);
68        throw new Error('Failed to enroll admin');
69      });
70    }
71  }).then(() => {
72    console.log('Assigned the admin user to the fabric client ::' + admin_user.toString());
73  }).catch((err) => {
74    console.error('Failed to enroll admin: ' + err);
75  });
```

Replace with ip address

Figure 6.7

Note: If you are running your Hyperledger network on a remote VM, please specify the IP address of the remote VM instead of localhost (marked above).

Just to reiterate, we needed to get the admin certificates so that we could put them in the local certificate store and use them to create new user identities. We also did some basic checks here so we do not pull the certificates again once it is already done.

Save this file and run it to generate the key value store and save the certificates.

Now run the file using Node.js.

`node enrolAdmin.js`

This will fetch the certificates from the CA server and put them in the path. You shall see an output similar to the one shown in *Figure 6.8*:

```
Nakuls-MacBook-Pro:property-node-client nakulshah$ node enrolAdmin.js
Successfully enrolled admin user "admin"
{"name":"admin","mspid":"Org1MSP","roles":null,"affiliation":"","enrollmentSecre
t":"","enrollment":{"signingIdentity":"1811bdf255487681e93e749741ed1b0c28265966d
00f0a469c0ac0e4af0613f5","identity":{"certificate":"-----BEGIN CERTIFICATE-----\
nMIICAjCCAaigAwIBAgIUN5tYPdtjdTc3cPUmjYtLsufoEMMwCgYIKoZIzj0EAwIw\nczELMAkGA1UEB
hMCVVMxEzARBgNVBAgTCkNhbGlmb3JuaWExFjAUBgNVBAcTDVNh\nbiBGcmFuY2lzY28xGTAXBgNVBAo
TEG9yZzEuZXhhbXBsZS5jb20xHDAaBgNVBAMT\nE2NhLm9yZzEuZXhhbXBsZS5jb20wHhcNMTkwNDA8M
TkyMTAwWhcNMjAwNDA3MTky\nNjAwWjAhMQ8wDQYDVQQLEwZjbGllbnQxDjAMBgNVBAMTBWFkbWluMFk
wEwYHKoZI\nzj0CAQYIKoZIzj0DAQcDQgAER+ovf5mXZhtW06Eu0oR9phszFSfRAUgw6o95zzeB\n2Yu
7tgI9qU99kW/S6YEPM67TL3gfhMDASFiLSTh4su6y5qNsMGowDgYDVR0PAQH/\nBAQDAgeAMAwGA1UdE
wEB/wQCMAAwHQYDVR0OBBYEFCR4t6p1pzn1+uanXEXSvyoO\nBFdsMCsGA1UdIwQkMCKAIEI5qg3Ndtr
uuLoM2nAYUdFFBNMarRst3dusalc2Xkl8\nMAoGCCqGSM49BAMCA0gAMEUCIQDCqMs0+IEIt529s3ZQt
UctmUXZj1qvi5xNETdS\ntLYzYgIgZDW8g4TxG31NiOsvw4EIRIEhMZLW/sBWydyhdEXwB+A=\n-----
END CERTIFICATE-----\n"}}}
Nakuls-MacBook-Pro:property-node-client nakulshah$ ▮
```

Figure 6.8

Here, we can see the path of the store that was created.

If you run the ls command, you will see a folder titled hfc-key-store created inside your project directory:

```
[Nakuls-MacBook-Pro:property-node-client nakulshah$ ls
enrolAdmin.js          node_modules          package.json
hfc-key-store          package-lock.json
Nakuls-MacBook-Pro:property-node-client nakulshah$ ▮
```

Figure 6.9

If you enter the directory, you can see the files related to the admin user, namely, its public and private keys:

```
[Nakuls-MacBook-Pro:property-node-client nakulshah$ cd hfc-key-store/
[Nakuls-MacBook-Pro:hfc-key-store nakulshah$ ls
1811bdf255487681e93e749741ed1b0c28265966d00f0a469c0ac0e4af0613f5-priv
1811bdf255487681e93e749741ed1b0c28265966d00f0a469c0ac0e4af0613f5-pub
admin
Nakuls-MacBook-Pro:hfc-key-store nakulshah$ ▮
```

Figure 6.10

Registration and enrolment of the user

Next step in the process is to register our new user with Fabric CA using the certificates that we created in the previous step.

Follow the below steps:

1. First, set up the key store and assign it to fabric_client like we did before.

2. Then, check whether the admin user exists in our key store. If it does not finish the program and throws an error saying admin certificates are not there, you cannot proceed.

3. If the admin user exists, use its certificates to register a new user by providing the new enrolmentId and organization details.

4. The step above will return the secret/password that we can then use in enrolAdmin.js to enroll the user with Fabric CA and get the certificates.

5. Once we have the certificates for user1, we can put them in the store and use them to invoke chaincode methods.

So, let's get started!

Create a new file named registerUser.js and set up imports and global variables:

```
'use strict';
var Fabric_Client = require('fabric-client');
var Fabric_CA_Client = require('fabric-ca-client');
var path = require('path');
var util = require('util');
var os = require('os');
//
var fabric_client = new Fabric_Client();
var fabric_ca_client = null;
var admin_user = null;
var member_user = null;
var store_path = path.join(__dirname, 'hfc-key-store');
```

Now, we need to again connect to our key state store and crypto store, and check whether the admin user already exists locally. This is exactly like the previous time. Therefore, paste the following code:

```
Fabric_Client.newDefaultKeyValueStore({ path: store_path
}).then((state_store) => {
    fabric_client.setStateStore(state_store);
    var crypto_suite = Fabric_Client.newCryptoSuite();
    var crypto_store = Fabric_Client.newCryptoKeyStore({path: store_
path});
    crypto_suite.setCryptoKeyStore(crypto_store);
    fabric_client.setCryptoSuite(crypto_suite);
```

```
var tlsOptions = {
    trustedRoots: [],
    verify: false
};
fabric_ca_client = new Fabric_CA_Client('http://localhost:7054',
null , '', crypto_suite);
    return fabric_client.getUserContext('admin', true);
})
```

If the admin user already exists, we can use the register method available in fabric_ca_client to register a new user https://fabric-sdk-node.github.io/release-1.4/ FabricCAClient.html#register.

The method's signature is as follows:

```
Register (enrollmentID, enrollmentSecret, role, affiliation,
maxEnrollments, attrs, signingIdentity)
```

Here enrollmentID and enrollmentSecret are the user name and secret, respectively, that we need to register with CA.

Also, we will use the admin user details for signingIdentity. So, paste the following code:

```
.then((user_from_store) => {
    if (user_from_store && user_from_store.isEnrolled()) {
        console.log('Successfully loaded admin from persistence');
        admin_user = user_from_store;
    } else {
        throw new Error('Failed to get admin.... run enrollAdmin.js');
    }
    return fabric_ca_client.register({enrollmentID: 'user1', affiliation:
'org1.department1',role: 'client'}, admin_user);
})
```

After the registration, the CA server will return the secret. It can be used to generate the certificate and register this user locally, and keep its certificates.

The entire process can be coded as below:

```
.THEN((SECRET) => {
    CONSOLE.LOG('SUCCESSFULLY REGISTERED USER1 - SECRET:'+ SECRET);
    RETURN FABRIC_CA_CLIENT.ENROLL({ENROLLMENTID: 'USER1',
ENROLLMENTSECRET: SECRET});
}).THEN((ENROLLMENT) => {
  CONSOLE.LOG('SUCCESSFULLY ENROLLED MEMBER USER "USER1" ');
  RETURN FABRIC_CLIENT.CREATEUSER(
    {USERNAME: 'USER1',
    MSPID: 'ORG1MSP',
    CRYPTOCONTENT: { PRIVATEKEYPEM: ENROLLMENT.KEY.TOBYTES(),
SIGNEDCERTPEM: ENROLLMENT.CERTIFICATE }
    });
}).THEN((USER) => {
    MEMBER_USER = USER;
    RETURN FABRIC_CLIENT.SETUSERCONTEXT(MEMBER_USER);
}).THEN(()=>{
    CONSOLE.LOG('USER1 WAS SUCCESSFULLY REGISTERED AND ENROLLED AND IS
READY TO INTERACT WITH THE FABRIC NETWORK');
}).CATCH((ERR) => {
    CONSOLE.ERROR('FAILED TO REGISTER: ' + ERR);
    IF(ERR.TOSTRING().INDEXOF('AUTHORIZATION') > -1) {
    }
});
```

The final file looks as shown in *Figure 6.11* and *Figure 6.12*:

```
1    'use strict';
2
3    /*
4     * Register and Enroll a user
5     */
6
7    var Fabric_Client = require('fabric-client');
8    var Fabric_CA_Client = require('fabric-ca-client');
9
10   var path = require('path');
11   var util = require('util');
12   var os = require('os');
13
14   //
15   var fabric_client = new Fabric_Client();
16   var fabric_ca_client = null;
17   var admin_user = null;
18   var member_user = null;
19   var store_path = path.join(__dirname, 'hfc-key-store');
20   console.log(' Store path:'+store_path);
21
22   // create the key value store as defined in the fabric-client/config/default.json 'key-value-store' setting
23   Fabric_Client.newDefaultKeyValueStore({ path: store_path
24   }).then((state_store) => {
25       // assign the store to the fabric client
26       fabric_client.setStateStore(state_store);
27       var crypto_suite = Fabric_Client.newCryptoSuite();
28       // use the same location for the state store (where the users' certificate are kept)
29       // and the crypto store (where the users' keys are kept)
30       var crypto_store = Fabric_Client.newCryptoKeyStore({path: store_path});
31       crypto_suite.setCryptoKeyStore(crypto_store);
32       fabric_client.setCryptoSuite(crypto_suite);
33       var tlsOptions = {
34           trustedRoots: [],
35           verify: false
36       };                                              Replace with ip address
37       // be sure to change the http to https when the CA is running TLS enabled
38       fabric_ca_client = new Fabric_CA_Client('http://localhost:7054', null , '', crypto_suite);
39
40       // first check to see if the admin is already enrolled
```

Figure 6.11

```
41        return fabric_client.getUserContext('admin', true);
42    }).then((user_from_store) => {
43        if (user_from_store && user_from_store.isEnrolled()) {
44            console.log('Successfully loaded admin from persistence');
45            admin_user = user_from_store;
46        } else {
47            throw new Error('Failed to get admin.... run enrollAdmin.js');
48        }
49
50        // at this point we should have the admin user
51        // first need to register the user with the CA server
52        return fabric_ca_client.register({enrollmentID: 'user1', affiliation: 'org1.department1',role: 'client'}, admin_user);
53    }).then((secret) => {
54        // next we need to enroll the user with CA server
55        console.log('Successfully registered user1 - secret:'+ secret);
56
57        return fabric_ca_client.enroll({enrollmentID: 'user1', enrollmentSecret: secret});
58    }).then((enrollment) => {
59        console.log('Successfully enrolled member user "user1" ');
60        return fabric_client.createUser(
61            {username: 'user1',
62            mspid: 'Org1MSP',
63            cryptoContent: { privateKeyPEM: enrollment.key.toBytes(), signedCertPEM: enrollment.certificate }
64            });
65    }).then((user) => {
66        member_user = user;
67
68        return fabric_client.setUserContext(member_user);
69    }).then(()=>{
70        console.log('User1 was successfully registered and enrolled and is ready to interact with the fabric network');
71
72    }).catch((err) => {
73        console.error('Failed to register: ' + err);
74        if(err.toString().indexOf('Authorization') > -1) {
75            console.error('Authorization failures may be caused by having admin credentials from a previous CA instance.\n'
76            'Try again after deleting the contents of the store directory '+store_path);
77        }
78    });
```

Figure 6.12

Note: If you are running your Hyperledger network on a remote VM, please specify the IP address of the remote VM instead of localhost (marked above).

We now have one user registered, enrolled, and set up for interacting with the Hyperledger network.

Let's save this file and run it in the property-node-client folder again:

node registerUser.js

If everything goes fine, we shall see the following output on the screen:

```
Successfully loaded admin from persistence
Successfully registered user1 - secret:ASlKHaJYMupr
Successfully enrolled member user "user1"
User1 was successfully registered and enrolled and is ready to interact with the
    fabric network
```

Figure 613

If you run ls inside the hfc-key-store folder, you can see a new file User1 and its corresponding keys are stored, along with the admin details:

```
1811bdf255487681e93e749741ed1b0c28265966d00f0a469c0ac0e4af0613f5-priv
1811bdf255487681e93e749741ed1b0c28265966d00f0a469c0ac0e4af0613f5-pub
admin
fca332ce96bd18b71ea6e52891b11beb50282b1410c3f0de56425eac84a60654-priv
fca332ce96bd18b71ea6e52891b11beb50282b1410c3f0de56425eac84a60654-pub
user1
```

Figure 6.14

Chaincode invoke and query

Next step in the process is to interact with the deployed chaincode in the network. We will be looking to run two scenarios: first to invoke the chaincode and second to query the chaincode. We can use this as a guide to run other operations with the network.

Invoking createProperty from the chaincode

The process of invoking the chaincode from the Fabric SDK is also a multi-step process:

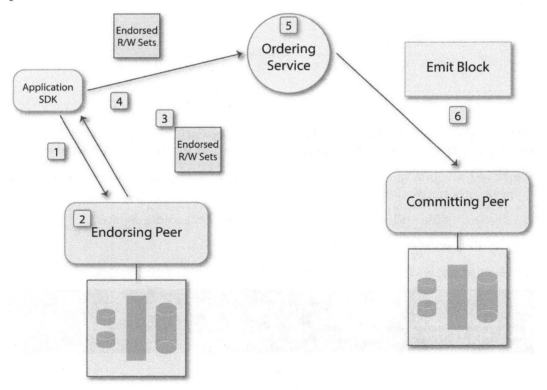

Figure 6.15

Following are the steps involved:

1. First, the application SDK sends a transaction proposal to the endorsing peer.

2. It then receives all the endorsing requests from the endorsing peers in the form of read-write sets.

3. It then verifies all read-write sets before sending them to the ordering service.

This summarizes the overall process of invoking a method from the chaincode. Keeping this in mind, let us start writing the logic for invoking the chaincode.

Start by creating a file named invoke.js.

Now, import the Fabric client and other in-built dependencies that will be required by this program. Then create an empty async function named invoke:

```
const Fabric_Client = require('fabric-client');
const path = require('path');
const util = require('util');
const os = require('os');
invoke();
async function invoke() {

};
```

Now that we have the skeleton ready, we have to start writing the logic to send the transactions we need. We can follow the steps below to achieve the same:

1. Get the instance of Fabric_Client.

2. Get the instance of the channel where the chaincode is installed, e.g., fabric_client.newChannel('mychannel');.

3. Get the peer instances that are part of this channel by passing the peer URL, e.g., fabric_client.newPeer('grpc://localhost:7051');.

4. Get the order instances by passing the orderer URL, e.g., fabric_client.newOrderer('grpc://localhost:7050');.

5. Then load the user details from state store. We will use these details to sign the transaction using the certificates.

6. Once we do so, we need to build the proposal request object that will send the transaction to the peer.

For example, the targets here lists the peer information, chaincode ID or name, function to be called, args to be provided for the method, and the channel ID.

Also, note that in our asset registry we had a function named createProperty as shown below:

```
public async createProperty(ctx: Context, propertyNumber: string,
propertyArea: string, cost: number, type: string, location:
string,value: number, ownerName: string) {
        const assetDetailsAsBytes = await ctx.stub.
getState(propertyNumber); // get the car from chaincode state
        const asset: AssetDetails = {
            propertyArea,

            location,

            propertyNumber,

            type,

            value,

            ownerName,

        };
        await ctx.stub.putState(propertyNumber, Buffer.from(JSON.
stringify(asset)));
    }
```

As you can see, it accepts a number of parameters and we need to pass all of those here:

```
const proposal_request = {
            targets: [peer],

            chaincodeId: asset,

            fcn: createProperty,

            args:["P1000003","howbe","2838","somehg","asdf","2323","som
eowner"],

            chainId: 'mychannel',

            txId: tx_id

    };
```

Once we do so, we need to send the transaction proposal:

```
  const endorsement_results = await          channel.sendTransactionPropos
al(proposal_request);
```

This will give all the transaction proposals back. The code for the same can be found below. You can paste it after the previous code written above:

```
const fabric_client = new Fabric_Client();
        const channel = fabric_client.newChannel('mychannel');
        console.log('Created client side object to represent the
channel');
        const peer = fabric_client.newPeer('grpc://localhost:7051');
        console.log('Created client side object to represent the peer');
        const orderer = fabric_client.newOrderer('grpc://
localhost:7050')
        console.log('Created client side object to represent the
orderer');
        const member_user = null;
        const store_path = path.join(__dirname, 'hfc-key-store');
        console.log('Setting up the user store at path:'+store_path);
        const state_store = await Fabric_Client.
newDefaultKeyValueStore({ path: store_path});
        fabric_client.setStateStore(state_store);
        const crypto_suite = Fabric_Client.newCryptoSuite();
        const crypto_store = Fabric_Client.newCryptoKeyStore({path:
store_path});
        crypto_suite.setCryptoKeyStore(crypto_store);
        fabric_client.setCryptoSuite(crypto_suite);
        const user = await fabric_client.getUserContext('user1', true);
        if (user && user.isEnrolled()) {
            console.log('Successfully loaded "user1" from user store');
        } else {
            throw new Error('\n\nFailed to get user1.... run
registerUser.js');
        }
        console.log('Successfully setup client side');
        console.log('\n\nStart invoke processing');
        const tx_id = fabric_client.newTransactionID();
        console.log(util.format("\nCreated a transaction ID: %s", tx_
id.getTransactionID()));
    const proposal_request = {
```

```
            targets: [peer],

            chaincodeId: 'asset',

            fcn: 'createProperty',

            args:["P1000003","howbe","2838","somehg","asdf","2323","som
eowner"],

            chainId: 'mychannel',

            txId: tx_id

    };

        const endorsement_results = await channel.sendTransactionProposa
l(proposal_request);

        const proposalResponses = endorsement_results[0];

        const proposal = endorsement_results[1];
```

Now that we have the endorsement results, let's verify whether these results are fine.

We first check if there was an error returned. If so, we can return the error without going to the orderer. So, paste the following in the file:

```
        if (proposalResponses[0] instanceof Error) {

            console.error('Failed to send Proposal. Received an error ::
' + proposalResponses[0].toString());

            throw proposalResponses[0];

        } else if (proposalResponses[0].response &&
proposalResponses[0].response.status === 200) {

            console.log(util.format(

                'Successfully sent Proposal and received response:
Status - %s',

                proposalResponses[0].response.status));

        } else {

            const error_message = util.format('Invoke chaincode
proposal:: %j', proposalResponses[i]);

            console.error(error_message);

            throw new Error(error_message);

        }
```

Next, we need to build the commit request with orderer information, proposal, responses and the proposal that was sent to peers. This commit request will be posted to the orderer:

```
        const commit_request = {
```

```
            orderer: orderer,
            proposalResponses: proposalResponses,
            proposal: proposal
        };
        const transaction_id_string = tx_id.getTransactionID();
        const promises = [];
        const sendPromise = channel.sendTransaction(commit_request);

        promises.push(sendPromise);
```

This completes the fourth step of *Figure 6.15* we have seen before. The work of client SDK is over here and it is up to the orderer to verify the transactions, put them into a block, and transmit to the other leader peers. Before we can send a transaction to the orderer, we need to register for events.

It is important to verify whether a transaction really went through before it gets committed into the block of the ledger. This can be achieved by listening to the events. So, we connect to the event hub for a particular channel by passing the peer information. We will also need to write, register, and unregister methods that will continuously listen to the channel events. Once done, they will be unregistered.

Then, we send the actual transaction and run this event listener by calling the Promise.all functions:

```
        let event_hub = channel.newChannelEventHub(peer);
            let txPromise = new Promise((resolve, reject) => {
            let handle = setTimeout(() => {
            event_hub.unregisterTxEvent(transaction_id_string);
            event_hub.disconnect();
            resolve({event_status : 'TIMEOUT'});
            }, 30000);
            event_hub.registerTxEvent(transaction_id_string, (tx, code)
=> {
            clearTimeout(handle);
                                const return_status = {event_status :
code, tx_id : transaction_id_string};
                if (code !== 'VALID') {
                console.error('There was an invalid transaction,
code = ' + code);
                resolve(return_status);                        } else {
                console.log('The transaction has successfully
```

```
committed on peer ' + event_hub.getPeerAddr());

                resolve(return_status);

            }
        }, (err) => {
            reject(new Error('A problem was encountered with the
eventhub ::'+err));
        },
            {disconnect: true}              );
        event_hub.connect();
        console.log('Registered transaction listener with the peer
event service for transaction ID:'+ transaction_id_string);
    });
        promises.push(txPromise);
    console.log('Sending endorsed transaction to the orderer');
    const results = await Promise.all(promises);
```

Once executed, we need to verify that the orderer accepted the request and committed it into the ledger.

This can be achieved by using the following code:

```
    if (results[0].status === 'SUCCESS') {
        console.log('Transaction successfully sent to the orderer');
    } else {
        const message = util.format('Failed to order the
transaction. Error code: %s', results[0].status);
        console.error(message);
        throw new Error(message);         }


    if (results[1] instanceof Error) {
        console.error(message);
        throw new Error(message);
    } else if (results[1].event_status === 'VALID') {
        console.log('Successfully committed the change to the ledger
by the peer');
        console.log('\n\n - try running "node query.js" to see the
results');
    } else {
```

```
        const message = util.format('Transaction failed to be
committed to the ledger due to : %s', results[1].event_status)

        console.error(message);

        throw new Error(message);

    }
```

Thus, the final file looks as shown in *Figure 6.16* to *Figure 6.21*:

```
 1    'use strict';
 2    /*
 3     * Copyright IBM Corp All Rights Reserved
 4     *
 5     * SPDX-License-Identifier: Apache-2.0
 6     */
 7    /*
 8     * Chaincode Invoke
 9     */
10
11    const Fabric_Client = require('fabric-client');
12    const path = require('path');
13    const util = require('util');
14    const os = require('os');
15
16    invoke();
17
18    async function invoke() {
19        console.log('\n\n --- invoke.js - start');
20        try {
21            console.log('Setting up client side network objects');
22            // fabric client instance
23            // starting point for all interactions with the fabric network
24            const fabric_client = new Fabric_Client();
25
26            // setup the fabric network
27            // -- channel instance to represent the ledger named "mychannel"
28            const channel = fabric_client.newChannel('mychannel');
29            console.log('Created client side object to represent the channel');
30            // -- peer instance to represent a peer on the channel
31            const peer = fabric_client.newPeer('grpc://localhost:7051');
32            console.log('Created client side object to represent the peer');
33            // -- orderer instance to reprsent the channel's orderer
34            const orderer = fabric_client.newOrderer('grpc://localhost:7050')
35            console.log('Created client side object to represent the orderer');
36
37            // This sample application uses a file based key value stores to hold
38            // the user information and credentials. These are the same stores as used
39            // by the 'registerUser.js' sample code
40            const member_user = null;
```

Replace with ip address

Figure 6.16

```
41    const store_path = path.join(__dirname, 'hfc-key-store');
42    console.log('Setting up the user store at path:'+store_path);
43    // create the key value store as defined in the fabric-client/config/default.json 'key-value-store' setting
44    const state_store = await Fabric_Client.newDefaultKeyValueStore({ path: store_path});
45    // assign the store to the fabric client
46    fabric_client.setStateStore(state_store);
47    const crypto_suite = Fabric_Client.newCryptoSuite();
48    // use the same location for the state store (where the users' certificate are kept)
49    // and the crypto store (where the users' keys are kept)
50    const crypto_store = Fabric_Client.newCryptoKeyStore({path: store_path});
51    crypto_suite.setCryptoKeyStore(crypto_store);
52    fabric_client.setCryptoSuite(crypto_suite);
53
54    // get the enrolled user from persistence and assign to the client instance
55    //    this user will sign all requests for the fabric network
56    const user = await fabric_client.getUserContext('user1', true);
57    if (user && user.isEnrolled()) {
58        console.log('Successfully loaded "user1" from user store');
59    } else {
60        throw new Error('\n\nFailed to get user1.... run registerUser.js');
61    }
62
63    console.log('Successfully setup client side');
64    console.log('\n\nStart invoke processing');
65
66    // get a transaction id object based on the current user assigned to fabric client
67    // Transaction ID objects contain more then just a transaction ID, also includes
68    // a nonce value and if built from the client's admin user.
69    const tx_id = fabric_client.newTransactionID();
70    console.log(util.format("\nCreated a transaction ID: %s", tx_id.getTransactionID()));
71
72
73    const proposal_request = {
74  targets: [peer],
75  chaincodeId: 'asset',
76  fcn: 'createProperty',
77  args:["P1000003","howbe","2838","somehg","asdf","2323","someowner"],
78  chainId: 'mychannel',
79  txId: tx_id
80 };
```

Figure 6.17

```
81
82
83        // notice the proposal_request has the peer defined in the 'targets' attribute.
84        // Send the transaction proposal to the endorsing peers.
85        // The peers will run the function requested with the arguments supplied.
86        // based on the current state of the ledger. If the chaincode successfully.
87        // runs this simulation it will return a positive result in the endorsement.
88        const endorsement_results = await channel.sendTransactionProposal(proposal_request);
89
90        // The results will contain a few different items
91        // first is the actual endorsements by the peers, these will be the responses
92        //     from the peers. In our sammple there will only be one results since
93        //     only sent the proposal to one peer.
94        // second is the proposal that was sent to the peers to be endorsed. This will
95        //     be needed later when the endorsements are sent to the orderer.
96        // second is the proposal that was sent
97        const proposalResponses = endorsement_results[0];
98        const proposal = endorsement_results[1];
99
100       // check the results to decide if we should send the endorsment to be orderered
101       if (proposalResponses[0] instanceof Error) {
102           console.error('Failed to send Proposal. Received an error :: ' + proposalResponses[0].toString());
103           throw proposalResponses[0];
104       } else if (proposalResponses[0].response && proposalResponses[0].response.status === 200) {
105           console.log(util.format(
106               'Successfully sent Proposal and received response: Status - %s',
107               proposalResponses[0].response.status));
108       } else {
109           const error_message = util.format('Invoke chaincode proposal:: %j', proposalResponses[i]);
110           console.error(error_message);
111           throw new Error(error_message);
112       }
113
114       // The proposal was good, now send to the orderer to have the transaction
115       // committed.
116
117       const commit_request = {
118           orderer: orderer,
119           proposalResponses: proposalResponses,
120           proposal: proposal
```

Figure 6.18

```
121          };
122
123          //Get the transaction ID string to be used by the event processing
124          const transaction_id_string = tx_id.getTransactionID();
125
126          // create an array to hold on the asynchronous calls to be executed at the
127          // same time
128          const promises = [];
129
130          // this will send the proposal to the orderer during the execuction of
131          // the promise 'all' call.
132
133          const sendPromise = channel.sendTransaction(commit_request);
134          //we want the send transaction first, so that we know where to check status
135
136          promises.push(sendPromise);
137
138          // get an event hub that is associated with our peer
139          let event_hub = channel.newChannelEventHub(peer);
140
141          // create the asynchronous work item
142
143          let txPromise = new Promise((resolve, reject) => {
144
145                  // setup a timeout of 30 seconds
146                  // if the transaction does not get committed within the timeout period,
147                  // report TIMEOUT as the status. This is an application timeout and is a
148                  // good idea to not let the listener run forever.
149                  let handle = setTimeout(() => {
150                          event_hub.unregisterTxEvent(transaction_id_string);
151                          event_hub.disconnect();
152                          resolve({event_status : 'TIMEOUT'});
153                  }, 30000);
154
155                  // this will register a listener with the event hub. THe included callbacks
156                  // will be called once transaction status is received by the event hub or
157                  // an error connection arises on the connection.
158
159                  event_hub.registerTxEvent(transaction_id_string, (tx, code) => {
160                          // this first callback is for transaction event status
```

Figure 6.19

```
161
162                              // callback has been called, so we can stop the timer defined above
163                              clearTimeout(handle);
164
165                              // now let the application know what happened
166                              const return_status = {event_status : code, tx_id : transaction_id_string};
167                              if (code !== 'VALID') {
168                                      console.error('The transaction was invalid, code = ' + code);
169                                      resolve(return_status); // we could use reject(new Error('Problem with the tranaction,
170                              } else {
171                                      console.log('The transaction has been committed on peer ' + event_hub.getPeerAddr());
172                                      resolve(return_status);
173                              }
174                      }, (err) => {
175                              //this is the callback if something goes wrong with the event registration or processing
176                              reject(new Error('There was a problem with the eventhub ::'+err));
177                      },
178                              {disconnect: true} //disconnect when complete
179                      );
180
181                      // now that we have a protective timer running and the listener registered,
182                      // have the event hub instance connect with the peer's event service
183                      event_hub.connect();
184                      console.log('Registered transaction listener with the peer event service for transaction ID:'+ transact
185              });
186
187              // set the event work with the orderer work so they may be run at the same time
188              promises.push(txPromise);
189
190              // now execute both pieces of work and wait for both to complete
191              console.log('Sending endorsed transaction to the orderer');
192              const results = await Promise.all(promises);
193
194              // since we added the orderer work first, that will be the first result on
195              // the list of results
196              // success from the orderer only means that it has accepted the transaction
197              // you must check the event status or the ledger to if the transaction was
198              // committed
199              if (results[0].status === 'SUCCESS') {
200                      console.log('Successfully sent transaction to the orderer');
```

Figure 6.20

```
201              } else {
202                      const message = util.format('Failed to order the transaction. Error code: %s', results[0].status);
203                      console.error(message);
204                      throw new Error(message);
205              }
206
207              if (results[1] instanceof Error) {
208                      console.error(message);
209                      throw new Error(message);
210              } else if (results[1].event_status === 'VALID') {
211                      console.log('Successfully committed the change to the ledger by the peer');
212                      console.log('\n\n - try running "node query.js" to see the results');
213              } else {
214                      const message = util.format('Transaction failed to be committed to the ledger due to : %s', results[1].
215                      console.error(message);
216                      throw new Error(message);
217              }
218      } catch(error) {
219              console.log('Unable to invoke ::'+ error.toString());
220      }
221      console.log('\n\n --- invoke.js - end');
222 };
```

Figure 6.21

Note: If you are running your Hyperledger network on a remote VM, please specify the IP address of the remote VM instead of localhost (marked above).

It might be worthwhile to put it all inside a try...catch in order to catch any exception that might occur in the process.

We now have the following program ready to execute or invoke a transaction in the network. To test it, let's run the following command on the terminal, from the property-node-client folder:

node invoke.js

Once successful, you should see an output similar to the one shown in *Figure 6.22*:

Note: If you faced any issues, we suggest you start the process all over again by deleting all the containers because sometimes fabric SDK seems to connect to an older instance of the chaincode deployed in the network.

```
--- invoke.js - start
Setting up client side network objects
Created client side object to represent the channel
Created client side object to represent the peer
Created client side object to represent the orderer
Setting up the user store at path:/Users/nakulshah/property-node-client/hfc-key-store
Successfully loaded "user1" from user store
Successfully setup client side


Start invoke processing

Created a transaction ID: b79f86a1c07c03f705f0d6ab4d33f5907c5c7b2e3524021b143debb202b0306b
Successfully sent Proposal and received response: Status - 200
Registered transaction listener with the peer event service for transaction ID:b79f86a1c07c03f705f0d6ab4d33f5907c5c7b2e3524021b143debb202b0306b
Sending endorsed transaction to the orderer
The transaction has been committed on peer 104.211.163.191:7051
Successfully sent transaction to the orderer
Successfully committed the change to the ledger by the peer
```

Figure 6.22

Alright, we now have the invoke functionality working. The next step is to create query functionality to verify that the invoke function worked.

Following are the steps to be followed for querying:

1. Connect to the state key store to load the user information.

2. Build a request object and pass the required parameters and query from a channel.

3. Verify if there was some error. If not, we print the query result.

So, let's get started.

Create a file named query.js and put the import statements shown below:

```
var Fabric_Client = require('fabric-client');

var path = require('path');

var util = require('util');

var os = require('os');
```

```
//
var fabric_client = new Fabric_Client();
var channel = fabric_client.newChannel('mychannel');
var peer = fabric_client.newPeer('grpc://localhost:7051');
channel.addPeer(peer);
//
var member_user = null;
var store_path = path.join(__dirname, 'hfc-key-store');
console.log('Store path:'+store_path);
var tx_id = null;
```

Then, load the user details from the state key store. After we have the user context, we need to build the request object, such as follows:

```
const request = {
    chaincodeId: 'fabcar',
    fcn: 'queryAllCars',
    args: ['']
};
```

Then, we need to query the chaincode using queryByChaincode and verify the query details.

The code is shown as follows:

```
Fabric_Client.newDefaultKeyValueStore({ path: store_path
}).then((state_store) => {
    fabric_client.setStateStore(state_store);
    var crypto_suite = Fabric_Client.newCryptoSuite();
    var crypto_store = Fabric_Client.newCryptoKeyStore({path: store_
path});
    crypto_suite.setCryptoKeyStore(crypto_store);
    fabric_client.setCryptoSuite(crypto_suite);
    return fabric_client.getUserContext('user1', true);
}).then((user_from_store) => {
    if (user_from_store && user_from_store.isEnrolled()) {
        console.log('Successfully loaded user1 from persistence');
        member_user = user_from_store;
    } else {
```

```
        throw new Error('Failed to get user1.... run registerUser.js');
    }
    const request = {
        chaincodeId: 'asset',
        fcn: 'queryAllAssets',
        args: ['P1000001','P100003']
    };
    return channel.queryByChaincode(request);
}).then((query_responses) => {
    console.log("Query has completed, checking results");
    if (query_responses && query_responses.length == 1) {
        if (query_responses[0] instanceof Error) {
            console.error("error from query = ", query_responses[0]);
        } else {
            console.log("Response is ", query_responses[0].toString());
        }
    } else {
        console.log("No payloads were returned from query");
    }
}).catch((err) => {
    console.error('Failed to query successfully :: ' + err);
});
```

Thus, the final file looks as shown in *Figure 6.23* and *Figure 6.24*:

```
1   'use strict';
2   /*
3   * Copyright IBM Corp All Rights Reserved
4   *
5   * SPDX-License-Identifier: Apache-2.0
6   */
7   /*
8    * Chaincode query
9    */
10
11  var Fabric_Client = require('fabric-client');
12  var path = require('path');
13  var util = require('util');
14  var os = require('os');
15
16  //
17  var fabric_client = new Fabric_Client();
18
19  // setup the fabric network
20  var channel = fabric_client.newChannel('mychannel');
21  var peer = fabric_client.newPeer('grpc://localhost:7051');
22  channel.addPeer(peer);
23
24  //
25  var member_user = null;
26  var store_path = path.join(__dirname, 'hfc-key-store');
27  console.log('Store path:'+store_path);
28  var tx_id = null;
29
30  // create the key value store as defined in the fabric-client/config/default.json 'key-value-store' setting
31  Fabric_Client.newDefaultKeyValueStore({ path: store_path
32  }).then((state_store) => {
33          // assign the store to the fabric client
34          fabric_client.setStateStore(state_store);
35          var crypto_suite = Fabric_Client.newCryptoSuite();
36          // use the same location for the state store (where the users' certificate are kept)
37          // and the crypto store (where the users' keys are kept)
38          var crypto_store = Fabric_Client.newCryptoKeyStore({path: store_path});
39          crypto_suite.setCryptoKeyStore(crypto_store);
40          fabric_client.setCryptoSuite(crypto_suite);
```

← **Replace with ip address**

Figure 6.23

```
41
42        // get the enrolled user from persistence, this user will sign all requests
43        return fabric_client.getUserContext('user1', true);
44    }).then((user_from_store) => {
45        if (user_from_store && user_from_store.isEnrolled()) {
46            console.log('Successfully loaded user1 from persistence');
47            member_user = user_from_store;
48        } else {
49            throw new Error('Failed to get user1.... run registerUser.js');
50        }
51
52        // queryCar chaincode function - requires 1 argument, ex: args: ['CAR4'],
53        // queryAllCars chaincode function - requires no arguments , ex: args: [''],
54        const request = {
55            //targets : --- letting this default to the peers assigned to the channel
56            chaincodeId: 'asset',
57            fcn: 'queryAllAssets',
58            args: ['P1000001','P100003']
59
60        };
61
62        // send the query proposal to the peer
63        return channel.queryByChaincode(request);
64    }).then((query_responses) => {
65        console.log("Query has completed, checking results");
66        // query_responses could have more than one  results if there multiple peers were used as targets
67        if (query_responses && query_responses.length == 1) {
68            if (query_responses[0] instanceof Error) {
69                console.error("error from query = ", query_responses[0]);
70            } else {
71                console.log("Response is ", query_responses[0].toString());
72            }
73        } else {
74            console.log("No payloads were returned from query");
75        }
76    }).catch((err) => {
77        console.error('Failed to query successfully :: ' + err);
78    });
```

Figure 6.24

Note: If you are running your Hyperledger network on a remote VM, please specify the IP address of the remote VM instead of localhost (marked above).

Let's test it by running the query.js command:

```
node query.js
```

You should see the following output:

```
Store path:/Users/nakulshah/property-node-client/hfc-key-store
Successfully loaded user1 from persistence
Query has completed, checking results
Response is  "[{\"Key\":\"P1000001\",\"Record\":{\"location\":\"12 avenue,richar
 street , california\",\"ownerName\":\"sam dave\",\"propertyArea\":\"1400 sqft.\
",\"propertyNumber\":\"P1000001\",\"type\":\"single\",\"value\":12332}},{\"Key\"
:\"P1000002\",\"Record\":{\"location\":\"12 avenue,richar street , california\",
\"ownerName\":\"sam dave\",\"propertyArea\":\"1400 sqft.\",\"propertyNumber\":\"
P1000002\",\"type\":\"single\",\"value\":12332}},{\"Key\":\"P1000003\",\"Record\
":{\"location\":\"asdf\",\"ownerName\":\"someowner\",\"propertyArea\":\"howbe\",
\"propertyNumber\":\"P1000003\",\"type\":\"somehg\",\"value\":\"2323\"}}]"
Nakuls-MacBook-Pro:property-node-client nakulshah$ █
```

Figure 6.25

We have successfully completed querying the network. Now, we move on to changing the property owner.

Invoking ChangePropertyOwner from Fabric SDK

This is similar to the invoke.js that we wrote earlier; however, it accepts a number of parameters.

Create changeOwner.js. and use the following code:

```
'use strict';
const Fabric_Client = require('fabric-client');
const path = require('path');
const util = require('util');
const os = require('os');
changeOwner('P1000003','nakul');
async function changeOwner(propertyId, OwnerName) {
    console.log('\n\n --- invoke.js - start');
    try {
        console.log('Setting up client side network objects');
        const fabric_client = new Fabric_Client();
        const channel = fabric_client.newChannel('mychannel');
        console.log('Created client side object to represent the
channel');
        const peer = fabric_client.newPeer('grpc://localhost:7051');
        console.log('Created client side object to represent the peer');
        const orderer = fabric_client.newOrderer('grpc://
localhost:7050')
        console.log('Created client side object to represent the
orderer');
        const member_user = null;
        const store_path = path.join(__dirname, 'hfc-key-store');
        console.log('Setting up the user store at path:'+store_path);
        const state_store = await Fabric_Client.
newDefaultKeyValueStore({ path: store_path});
        fabric_client.setStateStore(state_store);
        const crypto_suite = Fabric_Client.newCryptoSuite();
```

```
        const crypto_store = Fabric_Client.newCryptoKeyStore({path:
store_path});
        crypto_suite.setCryptoKeyStore(crypto_store);
        fabric_client.setCryptoSuite(crypto_suite);
        const user = await fabric_client.getUserContext('user1', true);
        if (user && user.isEnrolled()) {
            console.log('Successfully loaded "user1" from user store');
        } else {
            throw new Error('\n\nFailed to get user1.... run
registerUser.js');
        }
        console.log('Successfully setup client side');
        console.log('\n\nStart invoke processing');
        const tx_id = fabric_client.newTransactionID();
        console.log(util.format("\nCreated a transaction ID: %s", tx_
id.getTransactionID()));
        const proposal_request = {
            targets: [peer],
            chaincodeId: 'asset',
            fcn: 'changePropertyOwner',
            args:[propertyId,OwnerName],
            chainId: 'mychannel',
            txId: tx_id
    };
        const endorsement_results = await channel.sendTransactionProposa
l(proposal_request);
        const proposalResponses = endorsement_results[0];
        const proposal = endorsement_results[1];
        if (proposalResponses[0] instanceof Error) {
            console.error('Failed to send Proposal. Received an error ::
' + proposalResponses[0].toString());
            throw proposalResponses[0];
        } else if (proposalResponses[0].response &&
proposalResponses[0].response.status === 200) {
            console.log(util.format(
                'Successfully sent Proposal and received response:
```

```
Status - %s',
                proposalResponses[0].response.status));
        } else {
            const error_message = util.format('Invoke chaincode
proposal:: %j', proposalResponses[i]);
            console.error(error_message);
            throw new Error(error_message);
        }
        const commit_request = {
            orderer: orderer,
            proposalResponses: proposalResponses,
            proposal: proposal
        };
        const transaction_id_string = tx_id.getTransactionID();
        const promises = [];
        const sendPromise = channel.sendTransaction(commit_request);
        promises.push(sendPromise);
        let event_hub = channel.newChannelEventHub(peer);
        // Now, we create an asynchronous work item
        let txPromise = new Promise((resolve, reject) => {
            let handle = setTimeout(() => {
                event_hub.unregisterTxEvent(transaction_id_string);
                event_hub.disconnect();
                resolve({event_status : 'TIMEOUT'});
            }, 30000);
            event_hub.registerTxEvent(transaction_id_string, (tx, code)
=> {
                clearTimeout(handle);
                // now let the application know what happened
                const return_status = {event_status : code, tx_id :
transaction_id_string};
                if (code !== 'VALID') {
                    resolve(return_status);
                } else {
                    resolve(return_status);
```

```
            }
        }, (err) => {
            //this serves as the call back, in case anything goes
wrong with processing or event registration
        },
            {disconnect: true}
    //disconnect when complete
        );
        event_hub.connect();
        console.log('Registered transaction listener with the peer
event service for transaction ID:'+ transaction_id_string);
    });
    // set the event work with the orderer work so they can be run
at the same time
        promises.push(txPromise);
    // now execute both pieces of work and wait for them to complete
        console.log('Sending endorsed transaction to the orderer');
        const results = await Promise.all(promises);
        if (results[0].status === 'SUCCESS') {
            console.log('Successfully sent transaction to the orderer');
        } else {
            const message = util.format('Failed to order the
transaction. Error code: %s', results[0].status);
            console.error(message);
            throw new Error(message);
        }
        if (results[1] instanceof Error) {
            console.error(message);
            throw new Error(message);
        } else if (results[1].event_status === 'VALID') {
            console.log('\n\n - try running "node query.js" to see the
results');
        } else {
            const message = util.format('Transaction failed to be
committed to the ledger due to : %s', results[1].event_status)
            console.error(message);
```

```
        throw new Error(message);
    }
} catch(error) {
    console.log('Unable to invoke ::'+ error.toString());
}
console.log('\n\n --- invoke.js - end');
};
```

Thus, the final file looks as shown in *Figure 6.26* to *Figure 6.31*:

```
1   'use strict';
2   /*
3   * Copyright IBM Corp All Rights Reserved
4   *
5   * SPDX-License-Identifier: Apache-2.0
6   */
7   /*
8   * Chaincode Invoke
9   */
10
11  const Fabric_Client = require('fabric-client');
12  const path = require('path');
13  const util = require('util');
14  const os = require('os');
15
16  changeOwner('P1000003','nakul');
17
18  async function changeOwner(propertyId, OwnerName) {
19      console.log('\n\n --- invoke.js - start');
20      try {
21          console.log('Setting up client side network objects');
22          // fabric client instance
23          // starting point for all interactions with the fabric network
24          const fabric_client = new Fabric_Client();
25
26          // setup the fabric network
27          // -- channel instance to represent the ledger named "mychannel"
28          const channel = fabric_client.newChannel('mychannel');
29          console.log('Created client side object to represent the channel');
30          // -- peer instance to represent a peer on the channel
31          const peer = fabric_client.newPeer('grpc://localhost:7051');
32          console.log('Created client side object to represent the peer');
33          // -- orderer instance to reprsent the channel's orderer
34          const orderer = fabric_client.newOrderer('grpc://localhost:7050')
35          console.log('Created client side object to represent the orderer');
36
37          // This sample application uses a file based key value stores to hold
38          // the user information and credentials. These are the same stores as used
39          // by the 'registerUser.js' sample code
40          const member_user = null;
```

Replace with ip address

Figure 6.26

```
41    const store_path = path.join(__dirname, 'hfc-key-store');
42    console.log('Setting up the user store at path:'+store_path);
43    // create the key value store as defined in the fabric-client/config/default.json 'key-value-store' setting
44    const state_store = await Fabric_Client.newDefaultKeyValueStore({ path: store_path});
45    // assign the store to the fabric client
46    fabric_client.setStateStore(state_store);
47    const crypto_suite = Fabric_Client.newCryptoSuite();
48    // use the same location for the state store (where the users' certificate are kept)
49    // and the crypto store (where the users' keys are kept)
50    const crypto_store = Fabric_Client.newCryptoKeyStore({path: store_path});
51    crypto_suite.setCryptoKeyStore(crypto_store);
52    fabric_client.setCryptoSuite(crypto_suite);
53
54    // get the enrolled user from persistence and assign to the client instance
55    //    this user will sign all requests for the fabric network
56    const user = await fabric_client.getUserContext('user1', true);
57    if (user && user.isEnrolled()) {
58        console.log('Successfully loaded "user1" from user store');
59    } else {
60        throw new Error('\n\nFailed to get user1.... run registerUser.js');
61    }
62
63    console.log('Successfully setup client side');
64    console.log('\n\nStart invoke processing');
65
66    // get a transaction id object based on the current user assigned to fabric client
67    // Transaction ID objects contain more then just a transaction ID, also includes
68    // a nonce value and if built from the client's admin user.
69    const tx_id = fabric_client.newTransactionID();
70    console.log(util.format("\nCreated a transaction ID: %s", tx_id.getTransactionID()));
71
72
73    const proposal_request = {
74  targets: [peer],
75  chaincodeId: 'asset',
76  fcn: 'changePropertyOwner',
77  args:[propertyId,OwnerName],
78  chainId: 'mychannel',
79  txId: tx_id
80  };
```

Figure 6.27

```
81
82
83    // notice the proposal_request has the peer defined in the 'targets' attribute.
84    // Send the transaction proposal to the endorsing peers.
85    // The peers will run the function requested with the arguments supplied.
86    // based on the current state of the ledger. If the chaincode successfully.
87    // runs this simulation it will return a positive result in the endorsement.
88    const endorsement_results = await channel.sendTransactionProposal(proposal_request);
89
90    // The results will contain a few different items
91    // first is the actual endorsements by the peers, these will be the responses
92    //    from the peers. In our sammple there will only be one results since
93    //    only sent the proposal to one peer.
94    // second is the proposal that was sent to the peers to be endorsed. This will
95    //    be needed later when the endorsements are sent to the orderer.
96    // second is the proposal that was sent
97    const proposalResponses = endorsement_results[0];
98    const proposal = endorsement_results[1];
99
100   // check the results to decide if we should send the endorsment to be orderered
101   if (proposalResponses[0] instanceof Error) {
102       console.error('Failed to send Proposal. Received an error :: ' + proposalResponses[0].toString());
103       throw proposalResponses[0];
104   } else if (proposalResponses[0].response && proposalResponses[0].response.status === 200) {
105       console.log(util.format(
106           'Successfully sent Proposal and received response: Status - %s',
107           proposalResponses[0].response.status));
108   } else {
109       const error_message = util.format('Invoke chaincode proposal:: %j', proposalResponses[i]);
110       console.error(error_message);
111       throw new Error(error_message);
112   }
113
114   // The proposal was good, now send to the orderer to have the transaction
115   // committed.
116
117   const commit_request = {
118       orderer: orderer,
119       proposalResponses: proposalResponses,
120       proposal: proposal
```

Figure 6.28

```
121         };
122
123         //Get the transaction ID string to be used by the event processing
124         const transaction_id_string = tx_id.getTransactionID();
125
126         // create an array to hold on the asynchronous calls to be executed at the
127         // same time
128         const promises = [];
129
130         // this will send the proposal to the orderer during the exececution of
131         // the promise 'all' call.
132
133         const sendPromise = channel.sendTransaction(commit_request);
134         //we want the send transaction first, so that we know where to check status
135
136         promises.push(sendPromise);
137
138         // get an event hub that is associated with our peer
139         let event_hub = channel.newChannelEventHub(peer);
140
141         // create the asynchronous work item
142
143         let txPromise = new Promise((resolve, reject) => {
144
145             // setup a timeout of 30 seconds
146             // if the transaction does not get committed within the timeout period,
147             // report TIMEOUT as the status. This is an application timeout and is a
148             // good idea to not let the listener run forever.
149             let handle = setTimeout(() => {
150                 event_hub.unregisterTxEvent(transaction_id_string);
151                 event_hub.disconnect();
152                 resolve({event_status : 'TIMEOUT'});
153             }, 30000);
154
155             // this will register a listener with the event hub. THe included callbacks
156             // will be called once transaction status is received by the event hub or
157             // an error connection arises on the connection.
158
159             event_hub.registerTxEvent(transaction_id_string, (tx, code) => {
160                 // this first callback is for transaction event status
```

Figure 6.29

```
161
162             // callback has been called, so we can stop the timer defined above
163             clearTimeout(handle);
164
165             // now let the application know what happened
166             const return_status = {event_status : code, tx_id : transaction_id_string};
167             if (code !== 'VALID') {
168                 console.error('The transaction was invalid, code = ' + code);
169                 resolve(return_status); // we could use reject(new Error('Problem with the tranaction,
170             } else {
171                 console.log('The transaction has been committed on peer ' + event_hub.getPeerAddr());
172                 resolve(return_status);
173             }
174         }, (err) => {
175             //this is the callback if something goes wrong with the event registration or processing
176             reject(new Error('There was a problem with the eventhub ::'+err));
177         },
178         {disconnect: true} //disconnect when complete
179         );
180
181         // now that we have a protective timer running and the listener registered,
182         // have the event hub instance connect with the peer's event service
183         event_hub.connect();
184         console.log('Registered transaction listener with the peer event service for transaction ID:'+ transact
185     });
186
187     // set the event work with the orderer work so they may be run at the same time
188     promises.push(txPromise);
189
190     // now execute both pieces of work and wait for both to complete
191     console.log('Sending endorsed transaction to the orderer');
192     const results = await Promise.all(promises);
193
194     // since we added the orderer work first, that will be the first result on
195     // the list of results
196     // success from the orderer only means that it has accepted the transaction
197     // you must check the event status or the ledger to if the transaction was
198     // committed
199     if (results[0].status === 'SUCCESS') {
200         console.log('Successfully sent transaction to the orderer');
```

Figure 6.30

```
201         } else {
202             const message = util.format('Failed to order the transaction. Error code: %s', results[0].status);
203             console.error(message);
204             throw new Error(message);
205         }
206
207         if (results[1] instanceof Error) {
208             console.error(message);
209             throw new Error(message);
210         } else if (results[1].event_status === 'VALID') {
211             console.log('Successfully committed the change to the ledger by the peer');
212             console.log('\n\n - try running "node query.js" to see the results');
213         } else {
214             const message = util.format('Transaction failed to be committed to the ledger due to : %s', results[1].
215             console.error(message);
216             throw new Error(message);
217         }
218     } catch(error) {
219         console.log('Unable to invoke ::'+ error.toString());
220     }
221     console.log('\n\n --- invoke.js - end');
222 };
```

Figure 6.31

Note: If you are running your Hyperledger network on a remote VM, please specify the IP address of the remote VM instead of localhost (marked above).

Now let's invoke the changeOwner function:

```
node changeOwner.js
```

Here, as you can see, we are setting up the name nakul as the new owner for the property ID P1000003.

In order to check if this was successful, we need to query all the properties again:

```
node query.js
```

```
Store path:/Users/nakulshah/property-node-client/hfc-key-store
Successfully loaded user1 from persistence
Query has completed, checking results
Response is   "[{\"Key\":\"P1000001\",\"Record\":{\"location\":\"12 avenue,richar
  street , california\",\"ownerName\":\"sam dave\",\"propertyArea\":\"1400 sqft.\
",\"propertyNumber\":\"P1000001\",\"type\":\"single\",\"value\":12332}},{\"Key\"
:\"P1000002\",\"Record\":{\"location\":\"12 avenue,richar street , california\",
\"ownerName\":\"sam dave\",\"propertyArea\":\"1400 sqft.\",\"propertyNumber\":\"
P1000002\",\"type\":\"single\",\"value\":12332}},{\"Key\":\"P1000003\",\"Record\
":{\"location\":\"asdf\",\"ownerName\":\"nakul\",\"propertyArea\":\"howbe\",\"pr
opertyNumber\":\"P1000003\",\"type\":\"somehg\",\"value\":\"2323\"}}]"
Nakuls-MacBook-Pro:property-node-client nakulshah$ ▮
```

Figure 6.32

As see in *Figure 6.32*, we have the owner name set as nakul for property ID P1000003.

Summary

In this chapter, we learnt the process of registering and interacting with the network. We extended our asset-registry use case by writing the Fabric SDK integration for it. In the next chapter, we will be completing our use case by integrating it with a Rest API server and creating a simple front end to interact with it using a browser. We will also see some other functionalities related to Fabric SDK like creating channels, installing chaincodes, and so on.

## CHAPTER 7

Fabric SDK: Building End-to-End Application with Fabric Network

In this chapter, we will further extend our asset-registry use case. We will complete the use case by building a Rest API layer and a front end. The chapter will also extend our knowledge of Fabric use case by describing other important concepts like creating a channel, installing a chaincode, and more using Fabric.

Finally, the completed application will look as shown in *Figure 7.1*:

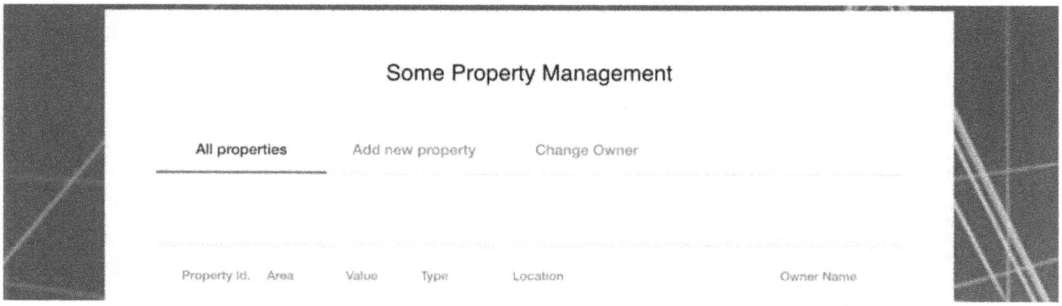

Figure 7.1

Through this application, we can view a list of all the properties, add a new property, and change the owner of an existing property. This application can also have an authentication mechanism in place for admin and user; however, building that is out of the scope of this chapter.

So, let's get started. First, we need to clone the repository or copy the project that we built in the last chapter as we will extend the same to include the APIs.

Prerequisite

Before starting this chapter, please ensure that you have the network running, as we had done in the previous chapter. If the network is unavailable, use the commands below to bring it up:

```
cd startup
./startup.sh typescript
```

Creating the API project

```
mkdir asset-registry-app
cd asset-registry-app
npm init
```

Accept the default option and hit *Enter*.

Now, we need some dependencies to build a Rest service on Node.js. Though it can be very complex adhering to a design pattern available for Node.js, for now, we will build a simple application using Node.js.

Replace the following code with the one in your package.json file:

```
{
  "name": "property-node-client",
  "version": "1.0.0",
  "description": "",
  "main": "server.js",
  "dependencies": {
    "body-parser": "latest",
    "cors": "^2.8.5",
    "express": "latest",
    "fabric-ca-client": "~1.4.0",
    "fabric-client": "~1.4.0",
    "grpc": "^1.6.0"
  },
```

```
"keywords": [],
"author": "",
"license": "ISC"
}
```

Express is a web framework for Node.js that makes writing web application in Node.js seamless.

Body parser helps us parse the request body coming from the front end.

Let's start by creating an entry point file named server.js that will start our Node.js server. This is a standard file that needs to be written in order to start the server. To do so, paste the following content in the file:

```
var express        = require('express');
var app            = express();
var bodyParser     = require('body-parser');
var http           = require('http')
var fs             = require('fs');
var Fabric_Client  = require('fabric-client');
var path           = require('path');
var util           = require('util');
var os             = require('os');
var cors = require('cors')
var app = express();
app.use(cors());
app.use(bodyParser.urlencoded({ extended: true }));
app.use(bodyParser.json());
app.get('/healthcheck', async (req, res) => res.sendStatus(200));
var port = process.env.PORT || 8000;
app.listen(port,function(){
  console.log("Live on port: " + port);
});
```

This is a standard Node.js server file where we have written middleware in order to parse the body that comes along with the request object. It also has a middleware to handle cores. This is the file where our routes will be loaded, which are used to handle API requests.

We will be writing the following APIs to handle the requests:

- **Get localhost:8000/property**: This is used to return the list of properties from Hyperledger. It expects query strings that we will need to query our network.

- **Post localhost:8000/property**: This API will be used to create a new property and add it to the existing ledger.

- **Put localhost:8000/property**: This API will be used to change the owner of the property. This is the Postman Collection that you can import for testing the APIs and to know the expected request and response.

```
{
  "info": {
    "_postman_id": "ab1d89df-d61e-40d7-9cd5-5ecfb6347c78",
    "name": "works",
    "schema": "https://schema.getpostman.com/json/
collection/v2.1.0/collection.json"
  },
  "item": [
    {
      "name": "property",
      "request": {
        "method": "GET",
        "header": [],
        "body": {
          "mode": "raw",
          "raw": ""
        },
        "url": {
          "raw": "localhost:8000/property?startIndex=P100000
1&endIndex=P1000002",
          "host": [
            "localhost"
          ],
          "port": "8000",
          "path": [
            "property"
```

```
      ],
      "query": [
        {
          "key": "startIndex",
          "value": "P1000001"
        },
        {
          "key": "endIndex",
          "value": "P1000002"
        }
      ]
    },
    "description": "test"
  },
  "response": []
},
{
  "name": "localhost:8000/property",
  "request": {
    "method": "PUT",
    "header": [
      {
        "key": "Content-Type",
        "name": "Content-Type",
        "value": "application/json",
        "type": "text"
      }
    ],
    "body": {
      "mode": "raw",
      "raw": "{\n\t\"newOwner\": \"test\",\n\
t\"propertyId\": \"P1000002\"\n}"
    },
    "url": {
```

```
        "raw": "localhost:8000/property",
        "host": [
          "localhost"
        ],
        "port": "8000",
        "path": [
          "property"
        ]
      }
    },
    "response": []
  },
  {
    "name": "post property",
    "request": {
      "method": "POST",
      "header": [
        {
          "key": "Content-Type",
          "name": "Content-Type",
          "value": "application/json",
          "type": "text"
        }
      ],
      "body": {
        "mode": "raw",
        "raw": "{\n\t\"propertyId\": \"P1000006\",\
n\t\"area\": \"123*200\",\n\t\"cost\": \"12020\",\
n\t\"type\": \"some\",\n\t\"location\": \"2990\",\n
\"ownerName\":\"Bill Gates\",\n\t\"value\": \"38382\"\n}"
      },
      "url": {
        "raw": "localhost:8000/property",
        "host": [
          "localhost"
```

```
      ],
      "port": "8000",
      "path": [
        "property"
      ]
    }
  },
  "response": []
}
]
}
```

Now, we have a server.js file ready and our routes defined. Thus, we can start building it. In our previous project, we had created a Node.js Fabric SDK and written a number of codes to support functionalities like invoking, querying, and changing the owner. Now, we will have to modify these files. Ideally, a Fabric SDK can exist as a separate microservice realized through container technology and the API microservice can call this API service using a standard HTTP call. A standard microservice architecture may look as shown in *Figure 7.2*:

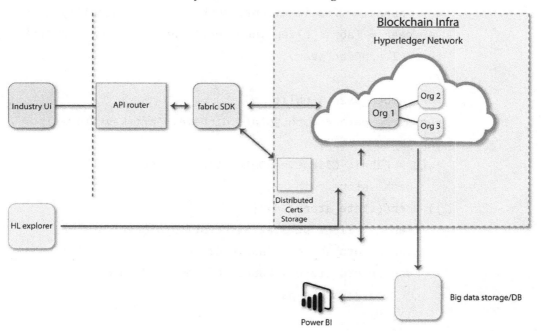

Figure 7.2: Docker Swarm Cluster

This is a standard and production-level microservice architecture that can be used to build a scalable Hyperledger network and an application built over it.

However, we will be building a simple application where we can have the Fabric SDK and API in the same service.

Modifying our previous project files

We will be using the same files that we wrote in the previous chapters, namely, query.js, invoke.js, and changeOwner.js, in order to call these within our routes. Thus, we will export these functions in order to enable other files to import the same.

Create a new file query.js, and paste the following content:

```
'use strict';
var Fabric_Client = require('fabric-client');
var path = require('path');
var util = require('util');
var os = require('os');
module.exports = function(start, end) {
        var fabric_client = new Fabric_Client();
        var channel = fabric_client.newChannel('mychannel');
        var peer = fabric_client.newPeer('grpc://localhost:7051');
        channel.addPeer(peer);
        //
        var member_user = null;
        var store_path = path.join(__dirname, 'hfc-key-store');
        var tx_id = null;
        return Fabric_Client.newDefaultKeyValueStore({
            path: store_path
        }).then((state_store) => {
            fabric_client.setStateStore(state_store);
            var crypto_suite = Fabric_Client.newCryptoSuite();
            var crypto_store = Fabric_Client.newCryptoKeyStore({
                path: store_path
            });
            crypto_suite.setCryptoKeyStore(crypto_store);
            fabric_client.setCryptoSuite(crypto_suite);
```

```
            return fabric_client.getUserContext('user1', true);
        }).then((user_from_store) => {
            if (user_from_store && user_from_store.isEnrolled()) {
                console.log('Successfully loaded user1 from
persistence');
                member_user = user_from_store;
            } else {
                throw new Error('Failed to get user1.... run
registerUser.js');
            }
            const request = {
                chaincodeId: 'asset',
                fcn: 'queryAllAssets',
                args: [start, end]
            };
            return channel.queryByChaincode(request);
        }).then((query_responses) => {
            console.log("It ran succesfully, checking results");

            if (query_responses && query_responses.length == 1) {
                if (query_responses[0] instanceof Error) {
                    console.error("error occured  = ", query_
responses[0]);
                } else {
                    return query_responses[0].toString();
                }
            } else {
                console.log("Nothing returned");
            }
        }).catch((err) => {
            console.error('Failed to run: ' + err);
        });
    }
```

Now, create one more file named invoke.js that will create a property for us. Since we have made this dynamic, it expects input from the front end to create a property, like cost, property ID, location, and more. So, paste the following:

```
'use strict';
const Fabric_Client = require('fabric-client');
const path = require('path');
const util = require('util');
const os = require('os');
module.exports = (function () {
    return {
        invokeChaincode: async function invoke(p,r,o,m,a,i,n) {
            console.log('\n\n --- invoke.js - start');
            try {
                console.log('Setting up client side network objects');
                const fabric_client = new Fabric_Client();
                const channel = fabric_client.newChannel('mychannel');
                console.log('Created client side object to represent the channel');
                const peer = fabric_client.newPeer('grpc://localhost:7051');
                console.log('Created client side object to represent the peer');
                const orderer = fabric_client.newOrderer('grpc://localhost:7050');
                console.log('Created client side object to represent the orderer');
                const member_user = null;
                const store_path = path.join(__dirname, 'hfc-key-store');
                console.log('Setting up the user store at path:'+store_path);
                const state_store = await Fabric_Client.newDefaultKeyValueStore({ path: store_path});
                fabric_client.setStateStore(state_store);
                const crypto_suite = Fabric_Client.newCryptoSuite();
                const crypto_store = Fabric_Client.newCryptoKeyStore({path: store_path});
```

```
            crypto_suite.setCryptoKeyStore(crypto_store);
            fabric_client.setCryptoSuite(crypto_suite);
            const user = await fabric_client.getUserContext('user1',
true);
            if (user && user.isEnrolled()) {
                console.log('Successfully loaded "user1" from user
store');
            } else {
                throw new Error('\n\nFailed to get user1.... run
registerUser.js');
            }
            console.log('Successfully setup client side');
            console.log('\n\nStart invoke processing');
            const tx_id = fabric_client.newTransactionID();
            console.log(util.format("\nCreated a transaction ID:
%s", tx_id.getTransactionID()));
            console.log(p,r,o,m,a,i,n);
            const proposal_request = {
                targets: [peer],
                chaincodeId: 'asset',
                fcn: 'createProperty',
                args:[p,r,o,m,a,i,n],
                chainId: 'mychannel',
                txId: tx_id
        };
            const endorsement_results = await channel.sendTransactio
nProposal(proposal_request);
            const proposalResponses = endorsement_results[0];
            const proposal = endorsement_results[1];
            if (proposalResponses[0] instanceof Error) {
                console.error('Failed to send Proposal. Received an
error :: ' + proposalResponses[0].toString());
                throw proposalResponses[0];
            } else if (proposalResponses[0].response &&
proposalResponses[0].response.status === 200) {
                console.log(util.format(
```

```
                            'Successfully sent Proposal and received
response: Status - %s',
                    proposalResponses[0].response.status));
            } else {
                const error_message = util.format('Invoke chaincode
proposal:: %j', proposalResponses[i]);
                console.error(error_message);
                throw new Error(error_message);
            }
            const commit_request = {
                orderer: orderer,
                proposalResponses: proposalResponses,
                proposal: proposal
            };
            const transaction_id_string = tx_id.getTransactionID();

            const promises = [];
            const sendPromise = channel.sendTransaction(commit_
request);
            promises.push(sendPromise);
            let event_hub = channel.newChannelEventHub(peer);
            let txPromise = new Promise((resolve, reject) => {
                let handle = setTimeout(() => {
                    event_hub.unregisterTxEvent(transaction_id_
string);
                    event_hub.disconnect();
                    resolve({event_status : 'TIMEOUT'});
                }, 30000);
                event_hub.registerTxEvent(transaction_id_string,
(tx, code) => {
                    clearTimeout(handle);
                    const return_status = {event_status : code, tx_
id : transaction_id_string};
                    if (code !== 'VALID') {
                        console.error('Invalid Txn with code= ' +
code);
```

```
                          resolve(return_status);
                  } else {
                          console.log('The txn committed for' + event_
hub.getPeerAddr());

                          resolve(return_status);
                  }
          }, (err) => {

                  reject(new Error('Problem occurred with' +err));
          },
                  {disconnect: true}
          );
          event_hub.connect();
          console.log('Registered txn listener for txn ID:'+
transaction_id_string);
      });
      promises.push(txPromise);
      const results = await Promise.all(promises);
      if (results[0].status === 'SUCCESS') {
          console.log('Successfully Sent txn to the orderer');
      } else {
          const message = util.format('Failed to order the
txn.: %s', results[0].status);
          console.error(message);
          return false;
      }
      if (results[1] instanceof Error) {
          console.error(message);
          return false;
      } else if (results[1].event_status === 'VALID') {
          ;
                                  return true;
      } else {
          return false;
      }
```

```
            } catch(error) {
            }
            console.log('\n\n end');
        }
    }
})()
```

The invoke file has been modified to accept parameters dynamically and export the function that can be imported from APIs. Next, create the changeOwner.js file and paste the following in it:

```
'use strict';
const Fabric_Client = require('fabric-client');
const path = require('path');
const util = require('util');
const os = require('os');
module.exports = (function () {
    return {
        changeOwner: async function changeOwner(OwnerName,propertyId) {
            console.log('\n\n --- invoke.js - start');
            var changeSuccess = false;
            try {
                const fabric_client = new Fabric_Client();
                const channel = fabric_client.newChannel('mychannel');
                const peer = fabric_client.newPeer('grpc://
localhost:7051');
                const orderer = fabric_client.newOrderer('grpc://
localhost:7050');
                const member_user = null;
                const store_path = path.join(__dirname, 'hfc-key-
store');
                const state_store = await Fabric_Client.
newDefaultKeyValueStore({ path: store_path});
                fabric_client.setStateStore(state_store);
                const crypto_suite = Fabric_Client.newCryptoSuite();
                const crypto_store = Fabric_Client.
newCryptoKeyStore({path: store_path});
                crypto_suite.setCryptoKeyStore(crypto_store);
```

```
            fabric_client.setCryptoSuite(crypto_suite);
            const user = await fabric_client.getUserContext('user1',
true);

            if (user && user.isEnrolled()) {

    ;

            } else {
                throw new Error('\n\nFailed FOR user1.... run
registerUser.js');
            }
            const tx_id = fabric_client.newTransactionID();
            const proposal_request = {
                targets: [peer],
                chaincodeId: 'asset',
                fcn: 'changePropertyOwner',
                args:[propertyId,OwnerName],
                chainId: 'mychannel',
                txId: tx_id
        };
            const endorsement_results = await channel.sendTransactio
nProposal(proposal_request);
            const proposalResponses = endorsement_results[0];
            const proposal = endorsement_results[1];
            if (proposalResponses[0] instanceof Error) {
                                throw proposalResponses[0];
            } else if (proposalResponses[0].response &&
proposalResponses[0].response.status === 200) {
                console.log(util.format(
                    'Successfully sent Proposal, Status , %s',
                    proposalResponses[0].response.status));
            } else {
                const error_message = util.format('Invoke chaincode
proposal:: %j', proposalResponses[i]);
                console.error(error_message);
                throw new Error(error_message);
            }
```

```
                const commit_request = {
                    orderer: orderer,
                    proposalResponses: proposalResponses,
                    proposal: proposal
                };
                const transaction_id_string = tx_id.getTransactionID();
                const promises = [];
                const sendPromise = channel.sendTransaction(commit_
request);
                promises.push(sendPromise);
                let event_hub = channel.newChannelEventHub(peer);
                let txPromise = new Promise((resolve, reject) => {
                    let handle = setTimeout(() => {
                        event_hub.unregisterTxEvent(transaction_id_
string);
                        event_hub.disconnect();
                        resolve({event_status : 'TIMEOUT'});
                    }, 30000);
                    event_hub.registerTxEvent(transaction_id_string,
(tx, code) => {
                        clearTimeout(handle);
                        const return_status = {event_status : code, tx_
id : transaction_id_string};
                        if (code !== 'VALID') {
                                            resolve(return_
status);
                        } else {
                            resolve(return_status);
                        }
                    }, (err) => {

                        return false;
                    },
                        {disconnect: true}
                    );
```

```
                    event_hub.connect();
                                });
            promises.push(txPromise);
            const results = await Promise.all(promises);
            if (results[0].status === 'SUCCESS') {
                } else {
                const message = util.format('Failed Error code: %s',
results[0].status);
                console.error(message);
                return false;
            }
            if (results[1] instanceof Error) {
                console.error(message);
                return false;
            } else if (results[1].event_status === 'VALID') {
                console.log('\n\n - RUN "node query.js" to see the
results');
                return true;
            } else {
                const message = util.format('TXN failed,: %s',
results[1].event_status)
                console.error(message);
                changeSuccess=false
                return changeSuccess;
            }
        } catch(error) {
            console.log('FAILED ::'+ error.toString());
        }
        console.log('\n\n - end');
    }
  }
})()
```

Now that we have written our utility files to interact with the network, we can start writing our APIs that will use the methods that we imported here.

Creating the APIs

Let's create a file named routes.js that will have all our routes.

Now, we can import our modules:

```
var query = require('./query.js');
var invoke = require('./invoke');
var changeOwner = require('./changeOwner');
var bodyParser    = require('body-parser');
```

Create an empty function, and export the same:

```
module.exports = function(app){

}
```

Now, inside this, we will add our routes one by one. Let's first write the Get Property route inside the exported function:

```
  app.get('/property', function(req, res){
    var startIndex = req.query.startIndex;
    var endIndex = req.query.endIndex;
    var data = query(startIndex, endIndex).then((data)=>{
        if(!data) {
            return res.status(400).send({'error':'not found'})
        }
        var body = JSON.parse(data);
        return res.json(body);
    })
  });
```

Here, we are first defining the route path, i.e., /property. It takes a callback function that requires two parameters req and res.

Now, from req.query we will first get the start index and end index, and then call our query function written inside query.js. This returns the promise so we can use .then to wait for it to resolve, and then we check to see if we get any data from Hyperledger. If the data is not returned, that is, if any error or exception is thrown, we can return 400 status with error message; else, we return the data.

Now, we can write the logic for POST Property route, which will create a new property. We have this logic to create the property written in invoke.js so let's write this route as shown below:

```
app.post('/property',function(req,res){
  console.log('--------',req.body)
  var data = req.body;
  console.log('register Data....',data);
    var data =   invoke.invokeChaincode(data.propertyId,data.area,data.
cost,data.type,data.location,data.ownerName,data.value).then((data)=>{
      if(!data) {
          return res.status(400).send({'error':'not found'})
      }
      return res.json({"result": "added new property to ledger!"});
  })
})
```

Since it is a POST request, the request object can be retrieved from request.body that is populated because of the bodyparser middleware. Once we have the body data, we need to invoke the chaincode and pass the parameters like propertyId, area, cost, type, and more, as shown below:

```
invoke.invokeChaincode(data.propertyId,data.area,data.cost,data.
type,data.location,data.ownerName,data.value)
```

Then, based on the returned response from Hyperledger, we can return the corresponding status and response.

Let's write the Put Property route, which will change the owner:

```
app.put('/property',function(req,res){
  var data = req.body;
  console.log(data);
    var data =   changeOwner.changeOwner(data.newOwner, data.
propertyId).then((data)=>{
      if(!data) {
          return res.status(400).send({'error':'not found'})
      }
      return res.json({"result": "change owner success"});
  })
})
```

Thus, the final file looks as shown in *Figure 7.3* and *Figure 7.4*:

```
1   //SPDX-License-Identifier: Apache-2.0
2
3
4   var query = require('./query.js');
5   var invoke = require('./invoke');
6   var changeOwner = require('./changeOnwer');
7   var bodyParser    = require('body-parser');
8
9
10
11
12  module.exports = function(app){
13
14    app.get('/property', function(req, res){
15      var startIndex = req.query.startIndex;
16      var endIndex = req.query.endIndex;
17
18      var data = query(startIndex, endIndex).then((data)=>{
19          if(!data) {
20              return res.status(400).send({'error':'not found'})
21          }
22
23          var body = JSON.parse(data);
24          return res.json(body);
25
26      })
27
28    });
29
30    app.post('/property',function(req,res){
31      console.log('--------',req.body)
32      var data =  req.body;
33      console.log('register Data....',data);
34
35      var data =   invoke.invokeChaincode(data.propertyId,data.area,data.cost,data.type,data.location,data.ownerName,data.value)
36          if(!data) {
37              return res.status(400).send({'error':'not found'})
38          }
39
40
```

Figure 7.3

```
41              return res.json({"result": "added new property to ledger!"});
42
43      })
44
45    })
46
47    app.put('/property',function(req,res){
48
49      var data =  req.body;
50      console.log(data);
51
52      var data =   changeOwner.changeOwner(data.newOwner, data.propertyId).then((data)=>{
53          if(!data) {
54              return res.status(400).send({'error':'not found'})
55          }
56
57
58          return res.json({"result": "change owner success"});
59
60      })
61    })
62  }
```

Figure 7.4

This looks like the Invoke POST route, but here we only take the property ID and new owner name. It calls the changeOwner function inside changeOwner.js, which changes the owner's name.

Save this file and import, and use this file inside server.js.

Paste the following line below app.use(bodyParser.json()):

```
require('./routes.js')(app);
```

```
15
16    app.use(bodyParser.urlencoded({ extended: true }));
17    app.use(bodyParser.json());
18    require('./routes.js')(app);
19
20    app.get('/healthcheck', async (req, res) => res.sendStatus(200));
21
22    var port = process.env.PORT || 8000;
23
```

Figure 7.5

This will register our routes inside the app that we have built.

Before we can start using this application, we have to generate the certificates for admin and user like we did in the previous chapters.

You can copy the files enrollAdmin.js and registerUser.js from the previous chapter and paste them inside the new project.

Now run the following command on cmd:

```
npm i
```

This will install all the dependencies.

The next step is to start your network.

If you are running the network on a remote VM, note down the IP address and replace the localhost in query.js, invoke.js, changeOwner.js, enrollAdmin.js, and registerUser.js with the IP address.

Copy the enrollAdmin.js and registerUser.js files from the folders created in the previous chapter:

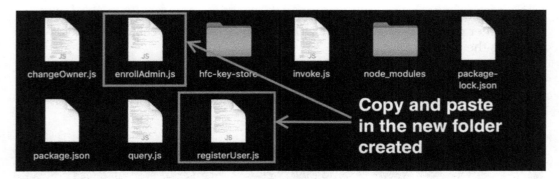

Figure 7.6

Let's first generate the certificates for admin:

`node enrollAdmin.js`

Then, run the following command:

`node registerUser.js`

Next, start your server:

`node server.js`

This should provide an output that reads **Live on port: 8000**.

Now, let's test our APIs in Postman. Install Postman, if you don't have it already, and then import the collection that we shared above by saving the JSON in a file named asset-registry.postman.json. Then, you can use **Import** button on the right-hand corner of Postman.

Let's invoke the GET property API, and the response should be an array, as shown in *Figure 7.7*:

Figure 7.7

Now, we will invoke the POST property API, and the response should be as shown in *Figure 7.8*:

Figure 7.8

Lastly, we invoke the PUT Property API, and the response should be as shown in *Figure 7.9*:

Figure 7.9

Now, test the POST and PUT APIs in a similar manner.

Once we have everything in place, we can move on to the last piece of the project, that is to build the front end of the application.

We will be building our front end in Angular: https://angular.io/.

Note, you can use https://github.com/SateDev/asset-registry-ui repo to pull the UI code or create the application from scratch.

- Let's start creating the front-end application.

- Create a new Angular application by following the steps. Open a new terminal and install ng CLI, which is a command line tool to create Angular applications.

  ```
  mkdir asset-property-front-end
  cd asset-property-front-end
  npm install -g @angular/cli
  ```

- Create a new app by using the following command.

  ```
  ng new property-front-end
  ```

- Select **css** and hit *Enter*:

```
CREATE property-front-end/README.md (1033 bytes)
CREATE property-front-end/.editorconfig (246 bytes)
CREATE property-front-end/.gitignore (629 bytes)
CREATE property-front-end/angular.json (3915 bytes)
CREATE property-front-end/package.json (1317 bytes)
CREATE property-front-end/tsconfig.json (435 bytes)
CREATE property-front-end/tslint.json (1621 bytes)
CREATE property-front-end/src/favicon.ico (5430 bytes)
CREATE property-front-end/src/index.html (303 bytes)
CREATE property-front-end/src/main.ts (372 bytes)
CREATE property-front-end/src/polyfills.ts (2841 bytes)
CREATE property-front-end/src/styles.css (80 bytes)
CREATE property-front-end/src/test.ts (642 bytes)
CREATE property-front-end/src/browserslist (388 bytes)
CREATE property-front-end/src/karma.conf.js (1031 bytes)
CREATE property-front-end/src/tsconfig.app.json (166 bytes)
CREATE property-front-end/src/tsconfig.spec.json (256 bytes)
CREATE property-front-end/src/tslint.json (244 bytes)
CREATE property-front-end/src/assets/.gitkeep (0 bytes)
CREATE property-front-end/src/environments/environment.prod.ts (51 bytes)
CREATE property-front-end/src/environments/environment.ts (662 bytes)
CREATE property-front-end/src/app/app-routing.module.ts (245 bytes)
CREATE property-front-end/src/app/app.module.ts (393 bytes)
```

Figure 7.10

This will create a number of files for you. Install all the packages that are required.

Some of the packages we need for this project are different from the ones installed here, so let's change our package.json by replacing it with the following code:

```
{
  "name": "asset-registry",
  "version": "0.0.1",
  "scripts": {
    "ng": "ng",
```

```
    "start": "ng serve",
    "build": "ng build",
    "test": "ng test",
    "lint": "ng lint",
    "e2e": "ng e2e"
},
"private": true,
"dependencies": {
    "@angular/animations": "^6.1.10",
    "@angular/cdk": "^7.0.2",
    "@angular/common": "^6.0.0",
    "@angular/compiler": "^6.0.0",
    "@angular/core": "^6.0.0",
    "@angular/forms": "^6.0.0",
    "@angular/http": "^6.0.0",
    "@angular/material": "^7.0.2",
    "@angular/platform-browser": "^6.0.0",
    "@angular/platform-browser-dynamic": "^6.0.0",
    "@angular/router": "^6.0.0",
    "core-js": "^2.5.4",
    "ng-http-loader": "^3.2.0",
    "rxjs": "6.0.0",
    "zone.js": "^0.8.26"
},
"devDependencies": {
    "@angular/compiler-cli": "^6.0.0",
    "@angular-devkit/build-angular": "~0.6.1",
    "typescript": "~2.7.2",
    "@angular/cli": "~6.0.1",
    "@angular/language-service": "^6.0.0",
    "@types/jasmine": "~2.8.6",
    "@types/jasminewd2": "~2.0.3",
    "@types/node": "~8.9.4",
    "codelyzer": "~4.2.1",
```

```
"jasmine-core": "~2.99.1",
"jasmine-spec-reporter": "~4.2.1",
"karma": "~1.7.1",
"karma-chrome-launcher": "~2.2.0",
"karma-coverage-istanbul-reporter": "~1.4.2",
"karma-jasmine": "~1.1.1",
"karma-jasmine-html-reporter": "^0.2.2",
"protractor": "~5.3.0",
"ts-node": "~5.0.1",
"tslint": "~5.9.1"
    }
}
```

Save the new package.json and delete node_modules. Then, run the following command:

```
cd property-front-end
rm -rf node_modules
npm i
```

In order to build the front end, we will use angular-material and angular-flex dependencies.

Inside src/app, run the following command:

```
cd src/app
ng generate module property
```

This will be our property module. In this, we can define the component logic, HTML template, and style CSS.

Let's create a component by giving the following command inside ./src/app/property:

```
ng generate component property
```

The output should look as shown in *Figure 7.11*:

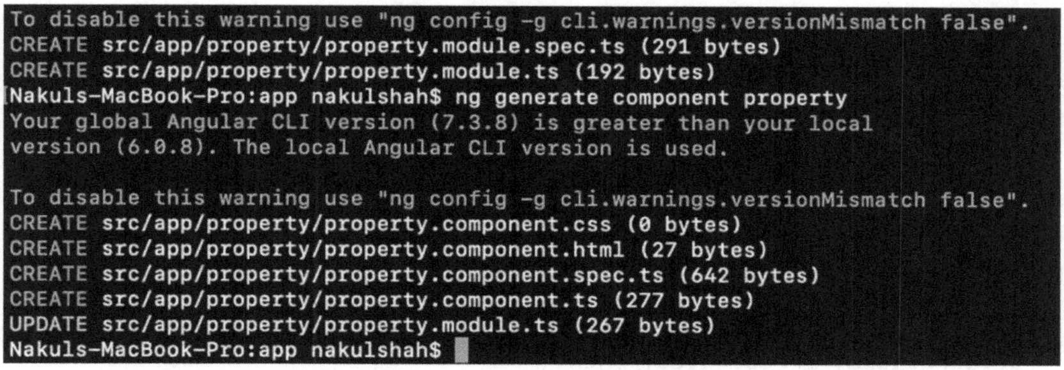

```
To disable this warning use "ng config -g cli.warnings.versionMismatch false".
CREATE src/app/property/property.module.spec.ts (291 bytes)
CREATE src/app/property/property.module.ts (192 bytes)
[Nakuls-MacBook-Pro:app nakulshah$ ng generate component property
Your global Angular CLI version (7.3.8) is greater than your local
version (6.0.8). The local Angular CLI version is used.

To disable this warning use "ng config -g cli.warnings.versionMismatch false".
CREATE src/app/property/property.component.css (0 bytes)
CREATE src/app/property/property.component.html (27 bytes)
CREATE src/app/property/property.component.spec.ts (642 bytes)
CREATE src/app/property/property.component.ts (277 bytes)
UPDATE src/app/property/property.module.ts (267 bytes)
Nakuls-MacBook-Pro:app nakulshah$
```

Figure 7.11

Now, replace the content inside property.module.ts with the following content:

```
import { NgModule } from '@angular/core';

import { CommonModule } from '@angular/common';

import { PropertyComponent } from './property.component';

import { RouterModule } from '@angular/router';

import { MatTabsModule, MatFormFieldModule, MatButtonModule,
MatInputModule, MatDatepickerModule, MatNativeDateModule, MatTableModule
} from '@angular/material';

import { ReactiveFormsModule } from '@angular/forms';

const routes = [
  {
    path: 'property',
    component: PropertyComponent
  },
  {
    path      : '**',
    redirectTo: 'property'
  }
];

@NgModule({
  imports: [
    MatTabsModule,
    MatFormFieldModule,
    MatButtonModule,
```

```
    ReactiveFormsModule,

    MatTableModule,

    MatDatepickerModule,

    MatNativeDateModule,

    MatInputModule,

    RouterModule.forChild(routes),

    CommonModule

  ],

  declarations: [PropertyComponent]

})

export class PropertyModule { }
```

Then, inside the property.component.ts file, replace the content with the following code:

```
import { Component, OnInit } from '@angular/core';

import { FormGroup, FormBuilder, Validators } from '@angular/forms';

import { PropertyService } from './../services/property.services';

import { MatSnackBar, MatTableDataSource } from '@angular/material';

@Component({

  selector: 'app-property',

  templateUrl: './property.component.html',

  styleUrls: ['./property.component.css']

})

export class PropertyComponent implements OnInit {

  singleUpdateForm: FormGroup;

  changeOwnerForm: FormGroup;

  displayedColumns: string[] = ['index', 'position', 'name', 'weight',
'symbol','test'];

  dataSource;

  allRates;

  constructor(private formBuilder: FormBuilder, private propertyService:
PropertyService, private snackbarService: MatSnackBar) { }


  ngOnInit() {

    this.singleUpdateForm = this.formBuilder.group({
```

```
      propertyId   : ['', [Validators.required]],
      area : ['', [Validators.required]],
      cost : ['' , [Validators.required]],
      type : ['' , [Validators.required]],
      location : ['' , [Validators.required]],
      ownerName : ['' , [Validators.required]],
      value : ['' , [Validators.required]],
      });
      this.changeOwnerForm = this.formBuilder.group({
        newOwner   : ['', [Validators.required]],
        propertyId : ['', [Validators.required]]
        });
        this.getAllRates();
  }
  submitRate() {
    this.propertyService.submitProperty(this.singleUpdateForm.value)
    .subscribe((res) => {
      this.snackbarService.open('Successfully saved the properties');
      this.getAllRates();
    }, (err) => {
      this.snackbarService.open('Some error occurred', 'dismiss');
      this.singleUpdateForm.reset();
    });
  }
  changeOwner() {
    this.propertyService.changeOwner(this.changeOwnerForm.value)
    .subscribe((res) => {
      this.snackbarService.open('Successfully changed owner',
'dismiss');
      this.changeOwnerForm.reset();
      this.getAllRates();
    }, (err) => {
      this.snackbarService.open('Some error occurred');
    });
```

```
  }
  getAllRates() {
    this.propertyService.getProperties()
    .subscribe((res: any) => {
      if (res) {
        const properties = JSON.parse(res);
        console.log(properties);
        this.allRates = properties['map']((property) => {
              return property['Record'];
        });
        console.log(this.allRates);
        this.buildTable();
      }
    }, (err) => {
    });
  }
  buildTable() {
    this.dataSource = new MatTableDataSource<any>(this.allRates);
  }
}
```

Next, replace the file content of property.component.html with the following code:

```
<mat-tab-group>
  <mat-tab label="All properties">
    <table mat-table [dataSource]="dataSource" class="mat-elevation-z8">
      <ng-container matColumnDef="index">
        <th mat-header-cell *matHeaderCellDef> Property Id. </th>
        <td mat-cell *matCellDef="let element; let i = index" >
{{element.propertyNumber}} </td>
      </ng-container>
      <ng-container matColumnDef="position">
        <th mat-header-cell *matHeaderCellDef> Area </th>
        <td mat-cell *matCellDef="let element"> {{element?.propertyArea
}} </td>
      </ng-container>
```

```html
        <ng-container matColumnDef="name">
          <th mat-header-cell *matHeaderCellDef>Value </th>
          <td mat-cell *matCellDef="let element"> {{element?.value }} </td>
        </ng-container>
        <ng-container matColumnDef="weight">
          <th mat-header-cell *matHeaderCellDef> Type </th>
          <td mat-cell *matCellDef="let element"> {{element?.type}} </td>
        </ng-container>
      <ng-container matColumnDef="symbol">
          <th mat-header-cell *matHeaderCellDef> Location </th>
          <td mat-cell *matCellDef="let element"> {{element?.location}} </td>
        </ng-container>
        <ng-container matColumnDef="test">
          <th mat-header-cell *matHeaderCellDef> Owner Name </th>
          <td mat-cell *matCellDef="let element"> {{element?.ownerName}} </td>
        </ng-container>
        <tr mat-header-row *matHeaderRowDef="displayedColumns"></tr>
        <tr mat-row *matRowDef="let row; columns: displayedColumns; let i = index"></tr>
      </table>
  </mat-tab>
  <mat-tab label="Add new property">
     <form name="singleUpdateForm" [formGroup]="singleUpdateForm" novalidate>
          <mat-form-field class="tfs-block">
              <input matInput placeholder="Enter property id" formControlName="propertyId">
            </mat-form-field>
          <mat-form-field class="tfs-block">
              <input matInput placeholder="Add new property" formControlName="area">
            </mat-form-field>
            <mat-form-field class="tfs-block">
```

```
                <input matInput placeholder="Enter cost(initial)
property" formControlName="cost">
            </mat-form-field>
            <mat-form-field class="tfs-block">
                <input matInput placeholder="Type of property"
formControlName="type">
            </mat-form-field>
            <mat-form-field class="tfs-block">
                <input matInput placeholder="Enter cost(current)
property" formControlName="value">
            </mat-form-field>
            <mat-form-field class="tfs-block">
                <input matInput placeholder="location of property"
formControlName="location">
            </mat-form-field>
            <mat-form-field class="tfs-block">
                <input matInput placeholder="Owner of property"
formControlName="ownerName">
            </mat-form-field>
        <button mat-raised-button color="accent" class="tfs-block
submit-button " aria-label="rate"
            [disabled]="singleUpdateForm.invalid"
(click)="submitRate()">Save</button>
    </form>
  </mat-tab>
  <mat-tab label="Change Owner">
    <form name="changeOwnerForm" [formGroup]="changeOwnerForm"
novalidate>
            <mat-form-field class="tfs-block">
                <input matInput placeholder="Enter property Id"
formControlName="propertyId">
            </mat-form-field>
            <mat-form-field class="tfs-block">
                <input matInput placeholder="Enter new owner"
formControlName="newOwner">
            </mat-form-field>
        <br>
```

```
        <button mat-raised-button color="accent" class="tfs-block
submit-button " aria-label="rate"
        [disabled]="changeOwnerForm.invalid"
(click)="changeOwner()">Save</button>
    </form>
</mat-tab>
</mat-tab-group>
```

Then, replace the content of property.component.css with the following CSS:

```
form{
    text-align: center;
}
table{
    width:100%;
    margin-top:10%;
}
```

Now we need to use this in src/app/app.module.ts. To do so, replace the content of app.module.ts with the following content:

```
import { BrowserModule } from '@angular/platform-browser';
import { NgModule } from '@angular/core';
import { RouterModule, Routes, Router } from '@angular/router';


import { AppComponent } from './app.component';
import { PropertyService } from './services/property.services';
import { HttpClientModule } from '@angular/common/http';
import { NgHttpLoaderModule } from 'ng-http-loader';
import { MatIconModule, MatTabsModule, MatSnackBarModule} from '@
angular/material';
import { BrowserAnimationsModule } from '@angular/platform-browser/
animations';
const appRoutes: Routes = [
  {
    path        : 'change',
    loadChildren: './property/property.module#PropertyModule'
  },
  {
```

```
    path        : '**',
    redirectTo: 'change'
}
];
@NgModule({
  declarations: [
    AppComponent
  ],
  imports: [
    BrowserModule,
    MatIconModule,
    MatSnackBarModule,
    BrowserAnimationsModule,
    MatTabsModule,
    HttpClientModule, // <============ (Perform http requests with this
module)
    NgHttpLoaderModule, // <============
    RouterModule.forRoot(appRoutes)
  ],
  providers: [PropertyService],
  bootstrap: [AppComponent]
})
export class AppModule { }
```

Then, replace the content of app.component.css with the following CSS:

```
:host .flex-container {
    height: 100%;
    padding: 0;
    margin: 0;
    display: -webkit-box;
    display: -moz-box;
    display: -ms-flexbox;
    display: -webkit-flex;
    display: flex;
    align-items: center;
```

```
    justify-content: center;
  }
  :host .row {
    width: auto;
  }
  :host .flex-item {
    padding: 5px;
    width: 20px;
    height: 20px;
    margin: 10px;
  }
  :host #login {
    width: 100%;
    height: 100%;
    overflow: hidden;
    background: url('/assets/images/backgrounds/dark-material-bg.jpg')
no-repeat;
    background-size: cover;
  }
  :host #login #login-intro {
    padding: 128px;
    color: white;
  }
  :host #login #login-intro .logo {
    width: 128px;
    margin-bottom: 32px;
  }
  :host #login #login-intro .title {
    font-size: 42px;
    font-weight: 300;
    line-height: 1;
  }
  :host #login #login-intro .description {
    padding-top: 16px;
```

```css
    font-size: 14px;
    max-width: 600px;
    color: rgba(255, 255, 255, 0.54);
}
:host #login #login-form-wrapper {
    overflow: auto;

    background: #fff;
}
:host #login #login-form-wrapper #login-form {
    padding: 48px 48px 48px 48px;
    min-height: 400px;
    height: auto;
    width: 700px;
}


:host #login #login-form-wrapper #login-form .logo {
    width: 128px;
    height: 128px;
    line-height: 128px;
    font-size: 86px;
    font-weight: 500;
    text-align: center;
    margin: 32px auto;
    color: #fff;
    border-radius: 2px;
}
:host #login #login-form-wrapper #login-form .title {
    font-size: 21px;
}
:host #login #login-form-wrapper #login-form .description {
    padding-top: 8px;
}
:host #login #login-form-wrapper #login-form form {
```

```
    width: 100%;
    padding-top: 32px;
  }
  :host #login #login-form-wrapper #login-form form mat-form-field {
    width: 100%;
  }
  :host #login #login-form-wrapper #login-form form mat-checkbox {
    margin: 0;
  }
  :host #login #login-form-wrapper #login-form form .remember-forgot-
password {
    font-size: 13px;
    margin-top: 8px;
  }
  :host #login #login-form-wrapper #login-form form .remember-forgot-
password .remember-me {
    margin-bottom: 16px;
  }
  :host #login #login-form-wrapper #login-form form .remember-forgot-
password .forgot-password {
    font-size: 13px;
    font-weight: 500;
    margin-bottom: 16px;
  }
  :host #login #login-form-wrapper #login-form form .submit-button {
    width: 100%;
    margin: 16px auto;
    display: block;
  }
  :host #login #login-form-wrapper #login-form .separator {
    font-size: 15px;
    font-weight: 600;
    margin: 24px auto;
    position: relative;
    overflow: hidden;
```

```
    width: 100px;
    text-align: center;
    color: rgba(0, 0, 0, 0.54);
  }
  :host #login #login-form-wrapper #login-form .separator .text {
    display: inline-flex;
    position: relative;
    padding: 0 8px;
    z-index: 9999;
  }
  :host #login #login-form-wrapper #login-form .separator .text:before,
:host #login #login-form-wrapper #login-form .separator .text:after {
    content: '';
    display: block;
    width: 30px;
    position: absolute;
    top: 10px;
    border-top: 1px solid rgba(0, 0, 0, 0.12);
  }
  :host #login #login-form-wrapper #login-form .separator .text:before {
    right: 100%;
  }
  :host #login #login-form-wrapper #login-form .separator .text:after {
    left: 100%;
  }
  :host #login #login-form-wrapper #login-form button.google, :host
#login #login-form-wrapper #login-form button.facebook {
    width: 70%;
    text-transform: none;
    color: #fff;
    font-size: 13px;
  }
  :host #login #login-form-wrapper #login-form button.google mat-icon,
:host #login #login-form-wrapper #login-form button.facebook mat-icon {
    color: #fff;
```

```
    margin: 0 8px 0 0;
  }
  :host #login #login-form-wrapper #login-form button.google {
    background-color: #d73d32;
    margin-bottom: 8px;
  }
  :host #login #login-form-wrapper #login-form button.facebook {
    background-color: #3f5c9a;
  }
  :host #login #login-form-wrapper #login-form .register {
    margin: 32px auto 24px auto;

    font-weight: 500;
  }
  :host #login #login-form-wrapper #login-form .register .text {
    margin-right: 8px;
  }
```

Next, replace the content of app.component.html with the following HTML:

```
<div class="flex-container" id="login">
  <div class="row">
      <div id="login-form-wrapper"  >
        <div class="">
        </div>
        <div id="login-form">
          <div class="">
          </div>
          <div class="title tfs-text-center"> Some Property Management</
div>
          <br>
          <br>
          <div class="content">
            <router-outlet></router-outlet>
          </div>
        </div>
```

```
    </div>
  </div>
</div>

<ng-http-loader></ng-http-loader>
```

Thus, router outlet is where the property module will load. Now we need to create a service to call our property API that we have built in the previous section.

Create a folder named services inside src/app, and create a file named property. services.ts. Paste the following code in it:

```
import { HttpClient, HttpHeaders } from '@angular/common/http';
import { Injectable } from '@angular/core';
@Injectable()
export class PropertyService {
  propertyApiUrl = '//localhost:8000/property';
  constructor(private http: HttpClient) { }
  submitProperty(body) {
    console.log(body);
    const httpOptions = {
      headers: new HttpHeaders({
        'Content-Type': 'application/json'
      })
    };
    return this.http.post(this.propertyApiUrl, body, httpOptions);
  }
  changeOwner(body) {
    console.log(body);
    const httpOptions = {
      headers: new HttpHeaders({
        'Content-Type': 'application/json'
      })
    };
    return this.http.put(this.propertyApiUrl, body, httpOptions);
  }
  getProperties() {
    const httpOptions = {
```

```
    headers: new HttpHeaders({
      'Content-Type': 'application/json'
    })
  };
  return this.http.get(this.propertyApiUrl + '?startIndex=P1000001&end
Index=P1000101', httpOptions);
  }
}
```

Here, in order to create a property, we are calling our back-end API service that is running on port 8000, as shown below:

```
submitProperty(body) {
  console.log(body);
  const httpOptions = {
    headers: new HttpHeaders({
      'Content-Type': 'application/json'
    })
  };
  return this.http.post(this.propertyApiUrl, body, httpOptions);
}
```

We are using Angular httpClient to call this API and are passing the request body and options. Similarly, this has to be done inside getProperties and changeOwner functions as well.

Do note that in app.module.ts we have already imported this service, so it becomes available to all the components.

```
providers: [PropertyService],
```

Let's change index.html to include some styles to have a decent design.

Replace the content of index.html with the following code:

```
<!doctype html>
<html lang="en">
<head>
  <meta charset="utf-8">
  <title> Property Management</title>
  <base href="/">
  <meta name="viewport" content="width=device-width, initial-scale=1">
```

```
<link rel="icon" type="image/x-icon" href="favicon.ico">
<style type="text/css">
  body {
    -webkit-font-smoothing: antialiased;
    text-rendering: optimizeLegibility;
    font-family: "proxima-nova-soft", sans-serif;
    overflow-x: hidden;
  background-image: url(http://alfaroproperties.com/wp-content/
uploads/2014/04/drawing-at-home-on-blue-background-900x400.jpg)
!important;
    background-repeat: no-repeat;
    background-size: 100% 140%;
    height: 100%;
    width: 100%;
  }
  body .icon,
  body .secondary-text,
  body i {
    color: rgba(0, 0, 0, .54);
  }
  body .vertical-centered-box {
    position: absolute;
    width: 100%;
    height: 100%;
    text-align: center;
  }
</style>
</head>
<body>
  <app-root>
  </app-root>
</body>
</html>
```

In style.css put the following code:

```css
@import "~@angular/material/prebuilt-themes/indigo-pink.css";
.tfs-block{
    width: 100%;
    margin: 16px auto;
    display: block;
}
.tfs-text-center{
    text-align: center
}
```

Now, add the following line in polyfills.ts:

```
import 'core-js/es7/reflect';
```

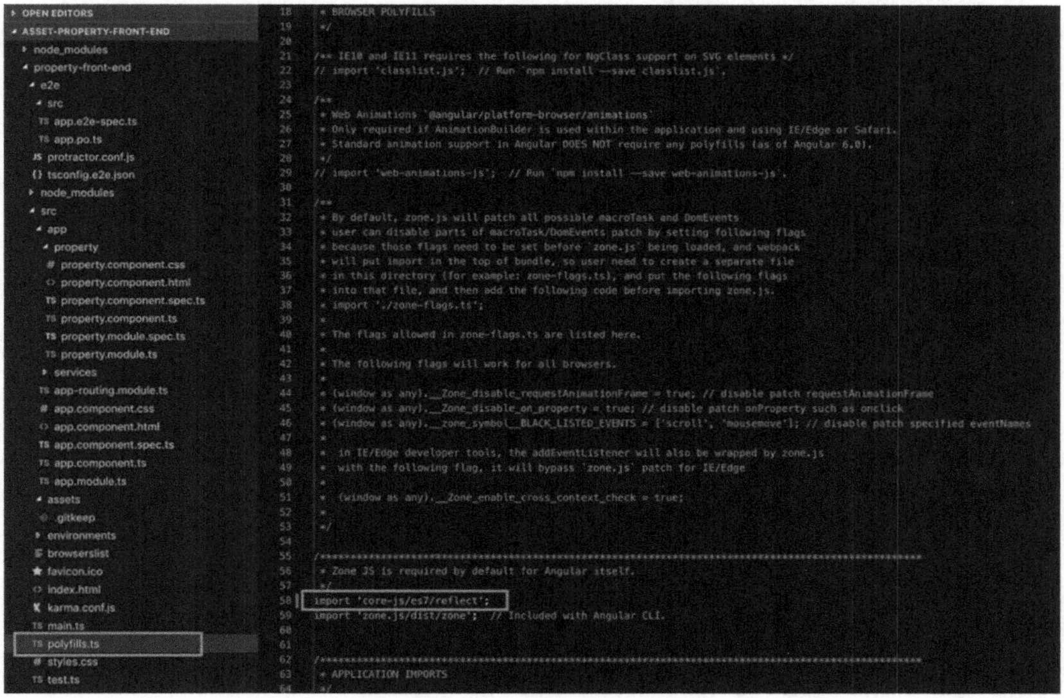

Figure 7.12

Enter the folder property-front-end.

Now, let's run this application and test it. To do so, run the following command:

```
ng serve
```

If you encounter an error, replace the code in the angular.json file with the following code:

```
{
  "$schema": "./node_modules/@angular/cli/lib/config/schema.json",
  "version": 1,
  "newProjectRoot": "projects",
  "projects": {
    "tfs-form": {
      "root": "",
      "sourceRoot": "src",
      "projectType": "application",
      "prefix": "app",
      "schematics": {},
      "architect": {
        "build": {
          "builder": "@angular-devkit/build-angular:browser",
          "options": {
            "outputPath": "dist/tfs-form",
            "index": "src/index.html",
            "main": "src/main.ts",
            "polyfills": "src/polyfills.ts",
            "tsConfig": "src/tsconfig.app.json",
            "assets": [
              "src/favicon.ico",
              "src/assets"
            ],
            "styles": [
              "src/styles.css"
            ],
            "scripts": []
          },
          "configurations": {
            "production": {
              "fileReplacements": [
```

```
          {
            "replace": "src/environments/environment.ts",
            "with": "src/environments/environment.prod.ts"
          }
        ],
        "optimization": true,
        "outputHashing": "all",
        "sourceMap": false,
        "extractCss": true,
        "namedChunks": false,
        "aot": true,
        "extractLicenses": true,
        "vendorChunk": false,
        "buildOptimizer": true
      }
    }
  },
  "serve": {
    "builder": "@angular-devkit/build-angular:dev-server",
    "options": {
      "browserTarget": "tfs-form:build"
    },
    "configurations": {
      "production": {
        "browserTarget": "tfs-form:build:production"
      }
    }
  },
  "extract-i18n": {
    "builder": "@angular-devkit/build-angular:extract-i18n",
    "options": {
      "browserTarget": "tfs-form:build"
    }
  },
```

```
    "test": {
      "builder": "@angular-devkit/build-angular:karma",
      "options": {
        "main": "src/test.ts",
        "polyfills": "src/polyfills.ts",
        "tsConfig": "src/tsconfig.spec.json",
        "karmaConfig": "src/karma.conf.js",
        "styles": [
          "src/styles.css"
        ],
        "scripts": [],
        "assets": [
          "src/favicon.ico",
          "src/assets"
        ]
      }
    },
    "lint": {
      "builder": "@angular-devkit/build-angular:tslint",
      "options": {
        "tsConfig": [
          "src/tsconfig.app.json",
          "src/tsconfig.spec.json"
        ],
        "exclude": [
          "**/node_modules/**"
        ]
      }
    }
  }
},
"tfs-form-e2e": {
  "root": "e2e/",
```

```
    "projectType": "application",
    "architect": {
      "e2e": {
        "builder": "@angular-devkit/build-angular:protractor",
        "options": {
          "protractorConfig": "e2e/protractor.conf.js",
          "devServerTarget": "tfs-form:serve"
        }
      },
      "lint": {
        "builder": "@angular-devkit/build-angular:tslint",
        "options": {
          "tsConfig": "e2e/tsconfig.e2e.json",
          "exclude": [
            "**/node_modules/**"
          ]
        }
      }
    }
  },
  "defaultProject": "tfs-form"
}
```

Now, enter the ng serve command again.

The output should look as shown in *Figure 7.12*, if no errors occur:

```
Your global Angular CLI version (7.3.8) is greater than your local
version (6.0.8). The local Angular CLI version is used.

To disable this warning use "ng config -g cli.warnings.versionMismatch false".
** Angular Live Development Server is listening on localhost:4200, open your bro
wser on http://localhost:4200/ **
                                                                              u
Date: 2019-04-12T16:53:41.769Z
Hash: d2bc0676cd5185bbed32
Time: 8387ms
chunk {main} main.js, main.js.map (main) 362 kB [entry] [rendered]
chunk {polyfills} polyfills.js, polyfills.js.map (polyfills) 582 kB [entry] [ren
dered]
chunk {property-property-module} property-property-module.js, property-property-
module.js.map (property-property-module) 13.4 kB [rendered]
chunk {runtime} runtime.js, runtime.js.map (runtime) 8.02 kB [entry] [rendered]
chunk {styles} styles.js, styles.js.map (styles) 422 kB [entry] [rendered]
chunk {vendor} vendor.js, vendor.js.map (vendor) 6.89 MB [initial] [rendered]
i [wdm]: Compiled successfully.
```

Figure 7.13

Now, move to **localhost:4200** in order to load the UI. It will load all the properties from the **All Properties** tab.

Next, click on the **Add new property** tab and enter the details in order to add a new property.

Enter all the fields and click **Save**. You should see the success response.

You can go to the **All Properties** tab to see the newly added property in the list.

Now, you can go to the **Change Owner** tab and try changing the owner. Check the **List property** tab to see the updated owner.

Thus, we have completed an end-to-end application on Hyperledger Fabric using Node.js, Angular, and Fabric:

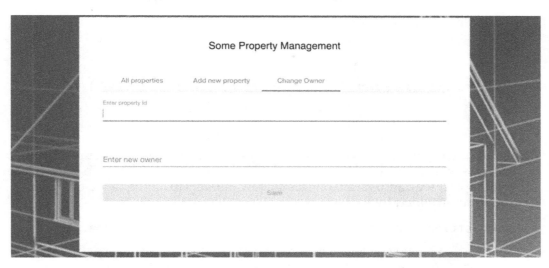

Figure 7.14

Using Fabric SDK for advanced use cases

In this section, we will learn to use the Fabric SDK for more advance functionalities like creating a channel, collecting private data, and so on. We will also look into other advanced use cases like calling a chaincode from within another chaincode.

Creating a channel using Fabric SDK

In this section, we will learn to create a channel using the Fabric SDK. The process requires the artefacts of the channel to be present. Thus, we first need to take the instance of a Fabric client and connect to our orderer using the configuration:

```
// this is orderer configuration
var ordererOrg ={
    "mspid": "OrdererMSP",
    "url": "grpcs://localhost:7050",
    "server-hostname": "orderer.example.com",
    "tls_cacerts": "../network/crypto-config/ordererOrganizations/
trade.com/orderers/orderer.trade.com/msp/tlscacerts/tlsca.trade.com-
cert.pem"
},

var client = new Client();
var orderer = client.newOrderer(
```

```
ordererOrg.url,
{
  'pem': caroots, // in case you are using ssl
  'ssl-target-name-override': ordererOrg['server-hostname']
}
);
```

Since we have our connection to the orderer, we need to get the current world ledger state. We can save the same in our file system or a database. To set it in the key-value pair, we can use setConfigSetting available inside the fabric-client/fabric-utils module provided by Fabric.

```
setConfigSetting('key-value-store', 'path to FileKeyValueStore.js');
```

Next, in order to create a channel, we require the admin user to be enrolled in the network. This process is similar to the one we followed in the previous section. If you have three organizations in the channel, the admin user needs to be enrolled for each of these organizations. Moreover, if there is an orderer organization, you need the admin user enrolled in the orderer organization as well.

Then, once the admin users are enrolled, you will have to collect the signature from each organization and push them in an array in order to use it to create a channel involving these organizations and orderer.

You can use the client.signChannelConfig(config); function to get the signature.

The next step in the process of setting up a channel is to create a request object like we had for invoke and query chaincode in the previous SDK example. Thus, creating a channel from a Fabric SDK is also a transaction. Following is an example of the object:

```
let tx_id = client.newTransactionID();
var request = {
  config: config,
  signatures : signatures,
  name : channel-name,
  orderer : orderer,
  txId : tx_id
};
```

- config: It is the configuration that we loaded from channel.tx using client. extractChannelConfig. Do remember that we had used the configtxgen tool to generate channel.tx.

- signatures: It refers to the list of signatures that we got from each of the organizations and orderer.
- channel_name: It refers to the user-defined channel name.
- orderer: It stands for the configuration of the orderer that we will send transaction details to.
- tx_id: It is the user-generated transaction ID.

Now you can create a channel using the createChannel function:

```
return client.createChannel(request);
```

Creating the channel may take some time as it requires initializing the ledger and creating the genesis block based on the channel configuration file that we generated multiple times before using the configtexgen tool.

Joining the channel using SDK

Since we have created the channel, the next step is to add our organizations to it. This will make our channel ready to have the chaincode installed and instantiated.

We first need to connect to our channel instance using client.newChannel('channel-name').

Next, we need to add the orderer using addOrderer:

```
channel.addOrderer(
  client.newOrderer(
    ORGS.orderer.url,
    {
      'pem': caroots,
      'ssl-target-name-override': ORGS.orderer['server-hostname']
    }
  )
);
```

Once the orderer has been added, we need to get the genesis block from the orderer. This can be done by sending a transaction request to the orderer:

```
tx_id = client.newTransactionID();
let request = { txId : tx_id };
return channel.getGenesisBlock(request);
```

Before sending the join request, we need to have the signing information of the client. The next step is to send the join request to all the organizations that are going to be a part of this channel, as specified in the channel config file.

The following is an example to show the request:

```
tx_id = client.newTransactionID();
let request = {
  targets : targets,
  block : genesis_block,
  txId : tx_id
};
channel.joinChannel(request).then….
```

- targets: It refers to the list of peer instances where we need to send our channel join request.
- block: It is genesis_block, i.e., the block that we got from the previous step through the orderer.

This will also take some time to execute.

Installation of a chaincode is similar to copying the content of the chaincode to each of the organization peers. This is also a transaction similar to the send transaction that we executed at the time of invoking the chaincode.

Now, let's understand the process.

First, get the client instance. Then, get the channel instance and connect to the orderer instance. Once we have all this set up, we will also need to get an admin user context for each of these organizations. Then we can send the transaction request to all the peers of target organizations.

Following is an example of the request object:

```
var request = {
  targets: targets,
  chaincodePath: chaincode_path,
  chaincodeId: Constants.CHAINCODE_ID,
  chaincodeVersion: chaincode_version
};
client.installChaincode(request);
```

- targets: It is the list of peer organization details.

- chaincodePath: It is the local path.

- chaincodeId: It is the unique ID associated with the chaincode that can be used later in order to send transactions to invoke a function from the chaincode installed here.

Internally, in the SDK, the installation request packages the chaincode's source code into a prescribed format called **ChaincodeDeploymentSpec (CDS)**. This package is signed by the administrator of the organization that is associated with the client object to create a signed CDS. It is then sent for installation to the **LSCC**.

The above procedure is a description of a simple case where each instance of a signed CDS just has the signature of the identity associated with the client that issues the installation request. Fabric can also support other complex scenarios, e.g., a CDS (out-of-band) is passed to different clients (of various organizations) and prior to the installation requests being received, it is signed by each organization.

In order to complete the installation successfully, the chaincode folder must contain a subfolder named src. The chaincode path sent in the installation proposal should be pointing to the actual code in the folder.

To check the installation, we can review the proposal requests as shown in the following code:

```
if    (proposalResponses    &&    proposalResponses[i].response    &&
proposalResponses[i].response.status === 200) {
  logger.info('proposal was good');
}
```

Instantiate the chaincode

We now have all the endorsing peers with the chaincode installed. The next step is to instantiate the chaincode.

The process remains the same as shown in the previous step, but with a small difference. Here, the request object is different and may look as shown below:

```
var tx_id = client.newTransactionID();
var request = {
  chaincodePath: chaincode_path,
  chaincodeId: CHAINCODE_ID,
  chaincodeVersion: version,
  fcn: funcName,
  args: argList,
  txId: tx_id,
```

```
'endorsement-policy': TRANSACTION_ENDORSEMENT_POLICY
};
channel.sendInstantiateProposal(request, 300000);
```

As you can see, most of the fields are self-explanatory. We also have the endorsement policy defined in this step. Let's see how a sample policy looks like:

```
var TWO_ORG_MEMBERS_AND_ADMIN = [
  { role: { name: 'member', mspId: 'Org1MSP' } },
  { role: { name: 'member', mspId: 'Org2MSP' } },
  { role: { name: 'admin', mspId: 'OrdererMSP' } }
];
var ALL_TWO_ORG_MEMBERS = {
  identities: FOUR_ORG_MEMBERS_AND_ADMIN,
  policy: {
    '2-of': [{ 'signed-by': 0 }, { 'signed-by': 1}]
  }
};
```

This is similar to the one we might have used in the CLI container while instantiating the chaincode from it. We first define the identity of the organizations in a separate variable and then use it in identities object. Thus, the policy object inside ALL_ TWO_ORG_MEMBERS, defines that two organizations should sign.

Summary

In this chapter, we learnt to build a complete use case by developing a Rest API layer and front end for our asset-registry project.

CHAPTER 8

Fabric in Production

In this chapter, we will learn to manage and deploy a network in the production scenario. We will also look into the scalability and security perspective of Hyperledger.

Additionally, we will look into some examples to understand the process of upgrading network components in real time, like adding a new organization to an existing channel, upgrading channel configuration, and more.

Let's start with understanding the tools leveraged in order to deploy Fabric. These tools can include Docker Swarm and Kubernetes (k8s), but this chapter only includes Swarm.

This chapter primarily covers the following topics:

- Deployment using Swarm
- Explorer
- Cloud deployment of Fabric

Objective: This chapter will conclude our book on Hyperledger by reviewing certain aspects of production environment that are essential to deploy Fabric-based solutions in real-world scenarios.

Fabric deployment using Swarm

So far, network deployment was done in one host machine. However, in the real-world scenario this is the not the case. Organizations are located across multiple cities and countries, making it essential to have multiple host setups, where each organization can have a node for the network in its premises. Let's understand the overall view of a sample network.

Docker is the technology that facilitates the deployment of local services in your application for testing them with the help of a single host orchestration tool like Compose. But in the real world, a more helpful and robust orchestration tool is required in order to enable deployment in multiple host machines. Swarm and Kubernetes serve as tools to facilitate the same. There are a lot of differences between these tools in terms of their usage and functionality, but their core purpose is the same. k8s, donated by Google, has built-in functionalities like autoscaling, whereas multiple tools are required to be configured with Swarm to enable the same. However, once configured and used with the add-ons in the network, it is similar to Kubernetes in its usability. So, let's keep the debate aside and begin with Swarm.

Before you move forward, please ensure that the dependencies listed below are available:

- Docker
- Swarm
- At least three virtual machines

Figure 8.1 below shows the overall strategy for Swarm:

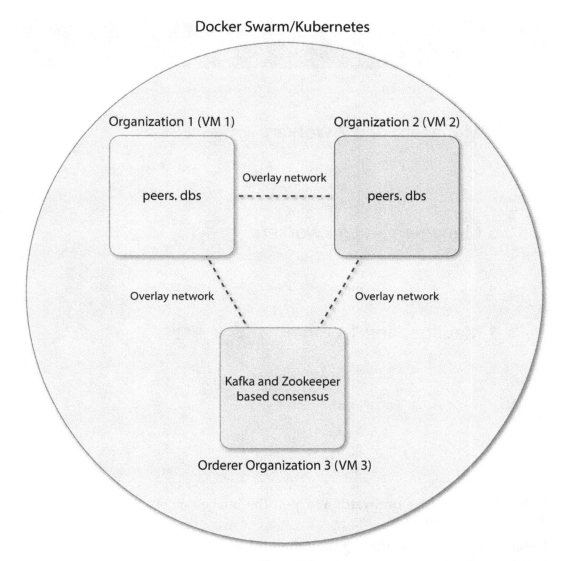

Figure 8.1

Prior to starting, you need to set up a cluster of Swarm.

We can leverage Docker labs to understand this. Open Docker labs and click on the tool icon in the left panel. In the pop-up window, you should select 3 Managers and 2 Workers:

Templates ✕

3 Managers and 2 Workers

5 Managers and no workers

1 Manager and 1 Worker

CLOSE

Figure 8.2

Let's set up a cluster of Swarm and pull the images required. To pull images, follow these commands:

Note: We shall start deploying the following codes in Manager 1 and consider that as our host.

```
sudo su
```

Fabric tools:

```
docker pull hyperledger/fabric-tools:x86_64-1.1.0
```

Fabric orderer:

```
docker pull hyperledger/fabric-orderer:x86_64-1.1.0
```

Fabric peer:

```
docker pull hyperledger/fabric-peer:x86_64-1.1.0
```

Fabric chaincode environment:

```
docker pull hyperledger/fabric-ccenv:x86_64-1.1.0
```

Fabric CA:

```
docker pull hyperledger/fabric-ca:x86_64-1.1.0
```

Fabric CouchDB:

```
docker pull hyperledger/fabric-couchdb:x86_64-0.4.6
```

Now, you can execute the command to view the Docker images:

```
docker images
```

Tag these images as mentioned in the following list:

- docker tag hyperledger/fabric-ca:x86_64-1.1.0 hyperledger/fabric-ca:latest
- docker tag hyperledger/fabric-tools:x86_64-1.1.0 hyperledger/fabric-tools:latest
- docker tag hyperledger/fabric-orderer:x86_64-1.1.0 hyperledger/fabric-orderer:latest
- docker tag hyperledger/fabric-peer:x86_64-1.1.0 hyperledger/fabric-peer:latest
- docker tag hyperledger/fabric-ccenv:x86_64-1.1.0 hyperledger/fabric-ccenv:latest
- docker tag hyperledger/fabric-couchdb:x86_64-0.4.6 hyperledger/fabric-couchdb:latest

```
git clone https://github.com/SateDev/hlf-docker-swarm
 cd hyperledger -swarm
```

Let's move forward:

```
./create_network.sh
```

The next step, once the setup for the network is complete, is to move the crypto material:

```
./move_crypo.sh
```

This will migrate all the crypto material to a desired location where your Docker service can read the same.

Open the file with .env extension and change the hostname to the hostname/IP addresses of your VMs:

```
vi .env,
```

Replace ORG1, ORG2, and ORG3 on the screen with the following, as shown in *Figure 8.3* and *Figure 8.4*:

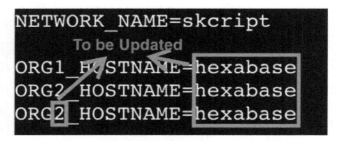

Figure 8.3

Change the hostnames:

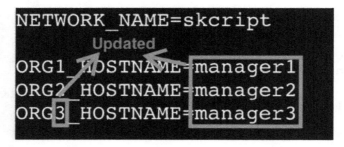

Figure 8.4

Now, quit out of vi editor by using :wq.

Thus, our service will get created in these nodes:

```
./populate_hostname.sh
```

Before we begin, let's copy the crypto material in each VM.

Go to the second VM and clone the same repository:

```
Sudo su

git clone https://github.com/SateDev/hlf-docker-swarm

cd hyperledger-swarm

./move_crypto.sh
```

Repeat the preceding procedure for the third VM as well.

Now, go to the master VM (`manager1` in our case), and use the below command to begin all the containers:

`./start_all.sh`

To verify that the services are running, you can run the following command:

`docker service ls | grep "0/1"`

This command will inform you about the services that have failed or are in process of starting. When the command does not return any value, it means all the services are running fine and you are good to move forward.

We are now ready to interact with this network.

Firstly, let us set up the channel:

`./scripts/create_channel.sh`

If it fails to start, the orderer might not be up and running. In order to debug the same, follow the commands below:

`cd scripts`

`cd channel`

`vi create_channel.sh`

Enter echo $ORDERER_NAME under set -ev:

```
#!/bin/bash
GLOBAL_ENV_LOCATION=$PWD/scripts/.env
source $GLOBAL_ENV_LOCATION

set -ev
echo $ORDERER_NAME
# ===========================
# CREATING THE CHANNEL mychannel
# ===========================
docker exec "$CLI_NAME" peer channel create -o "$ORDERER_NAME":7050 -c "$CHANNEL_NAME" -f "$CHANNEL_TX_LOCATION" --tls --cafile $ORDERER_C
```

Figure 8.5

Exit out of the editor.

Go into the folder titled Network and run the following command again:

`./scripts/create_channel.sh`

Then, let us install the chaincode:

`./scripts/install_chaincodes.sh`

Now that the chaincode is installed, you can begin interacting with it in real time.

The command shall fail if the organizations are more than three in number (for our example) as our setup has been done for only three organizations. If more than three VMs are set up, it can run on them as well.

Integrating solution for monitoring Hyperledger Explorer

Hyperledger Explorer: It serves as a blockchain module and open-source browser used to see the activity on underlying blockchain networks.

Let's understand the process involved.

Install it on Ubuntu and Hyperledger Fabric.

Requirements:

The prerequisites for installing the required development tools are as follows:

- Nodejs 8.11.x (v9 not supported)
- PostgreSQL 9.5 or greater
- Jq [https://stedolan.github.io/jq/]

Hyperledger Explorer works with Hyperledger Fabric 1.2. Install the software dependencies as mentioned below to manage the Fabric network.

- docker-ce
- docker-compose
- GO

Step 1: Set up Hyperledger Fabric.

```
curl -O https://hyperledger.github.io/composer/latest/prereqs-ubuntu.sh
chmod u+x prereqs-ubuntu.sh
./prereqs-ubuntu.sh
```

Install Golang required for Fabric:

```
wget https://dl.google.com/go/go1.11.2.linux-amd64.tar.gz

tar -xzvf go1.11.2.linux-amd64.tar.gz

mv go/ /usr/local
```

The next step is to set up the concerned program on a start-up file:

```
nano ~/.bashrc
```

Add the following:

```
export GOPATH=/usr/local/go

export PATH=$PATH:$GOPATH/bin
```

Run the startup file again:

```
source ~/.bashrc
```

Always download the latest version for curl, unless you have it already, or if you face issues while executing the curl commands mentioned.

```
sudo apt-get install curl
```

Clone Hyperledger Fabric:

```
git clone -b master https://github.com/hyperledger/fabric-samples.git
```

Download the Hyperledger Fabric Docker images:

```
cd fabric-samples
```

```
curl -sSL http://bit.ly/2ysbOFE | bash -s 1.2.1 1.2.1 0.4.10
```

Step 2: Set up Hyperledger Explorer.

Once the images have been pulled, clone Hyperledger Explorer:

```
cd ..
```

```
git clone https://github.com/hyperledger/blockchain-explorer.git
```

Step 3: Install PostgreSQL.

```
sudo apt-get update
```

```
sudo apt-get install postgresql postgresql-contrib
```

Database setup:

```
cd blockchain-explorer/app
```

You can modify explorerconfig.json to update the PostgreSQL properties:

```
{
    "persistence": "postgreSQL",
    "platforms": ["fabric"],
    "postgreSQL": {
        "host": "127.0.0.1",
        "port": "5432",
        "database": "fabricexplorer",
        "username": "hppoc",
        "passwd": "password"
    },
    "sync": {
        "type": "local",
        "platform": "fabric",
        "blocksSyncTime": "3"
    }
}
```

Figure 8.6

You may need to apply permission to db/ in some cases:

```
cd blockchain-explorer/app/persistence/fabric/postgreSQL
chmod -R 775 db/
```

Run the script to create the database:

```
cd blockchain-explorer/app/persistence/fabric/postgreSQL/db
./createdb.sh
sudo -u postgres psql
```

Step 4: Generate the Hyperledger Fabric network.

Run the following commands:

```
cd fabric-samples/first-network/
./byfn.sh -m generate
./byfn.sh -m up
```

A success message should appear.

Step 5: Configure Hyperledger Explorer on Fabric.

We will change config.json to update network-configs.

Change the directory fabric-path to your Fabric network path as shown in *Figure 8.7*:

Figure 8.7

Open config.json and update the network settings depending on your Hyperledger Fabric network that you have running:

```
cd blockchain-explorer/app/platform/fabric
nano config.json
```

Step 6: Build Hyperledger Explorer.

Run the following commands:

```
cd blockchain-explorer
npm install
cd blockchain-explorer/app/test
npm install
npm run test
cd client/
npm install
npm test -- -u --coverage
npm run build
```

You will see the following screenshot:

```
root@enter-traning:/var/blockchain-explorer/client# npm test -- -u --coverage
> hyperledger-explorer-client@0.3.7 test /var/blockchain-explorer/client
> react-scripts test --env=jsdom "-u" "--coverage"
 PASS  src/state/redux/charts/tests.spec.js
 PASS  src/components/Lists/Blocks.spec.js
 PASS  src/components/Charts/ChartStats.spec.js
 PASS  src/components/Lists/Transactions.spec.js
 PASS  src/state/redux/tables/tests.spec.js
 PASS  src/components/Header/HeaderView.spec.js
 PASS  src/components/Lists/Peers.spec.js
 PASS  src/components/View/DashboardView.spec.js
 PASS  src/components/Lists/Chaincodes.spec.js
  ● Console
    console.error node_modules/@material-ui/core/node_modules/warning/warning.js:36
      Warning: Material-UI: the key `hash` provided to the classes property is not implemented in ChaincodeModal.
      You can only override one of the following: code,cubeIcon,source
    console.error node_modules/@material-ui/core/node_modules/warning/warning.js:36
      Warning: Material-UI: the key `hash` provided to the classes property is not implemented in ChaincodeModal.
      You can only override one of the following: code,cubeIcon,source
 PASS  src/components/Main.spec.js
 PASS  src/components/View/BlocksView.spec.js
 PASS  src/components/View/TransactionView.spec.js
 PASS  src/components/View/TransactionsView.spec.js
 PASS  src/components/Lists/TimelineStream.spec.js
 PASS  src/components/Lists/Channels.spec.js
 RUNS  src/components/View/LandingPage.spec.js
/var/blockchain-explorer/client/node_modules/react-scripts/scripts/test.js:20
  throw err;
  ^

TypeError: getBlockActivity is not a function
    at LandingPage.componentDidMount (/var/blockchain-explorer/client/src/components/View/LandingPage.js:136:5)
    at <anonymous>
npm ERR! Test failed.  See above for more details.
```

Figure 8.8

Step 7: Run Hyperledger Explorer.

Run the following commands:

```
cd blockchain-explorer/
./start.sh
```

You can view Hyperledger Explorer on your browser http://localhost:8080:

Figure 8.9

Hyperledger Fabric in Clouds

In this section, we will look into the deployment of Hyperledger Fabric on major cloud providers like Azure, Amazon, and IBM Bluemix.

Fabric in AWS

Amazon has been working extensively in the race of **blockchain technology as a service** and has come up with the blockchain service https://aws.amazon.com/managed-blockchain/ that currently supports Hyperledger Fabric.

Click on the Get Started button, which will take you to the AWS console page. On the page, you can sign up and select the proper region:

Figure 8.10

Once done, you shall see the screen as shown in *Figure 8.10*:

Figure 8.11

We can select a plan and click on Create a network, which will take you to the screen as shown in *Figure 8.12*:

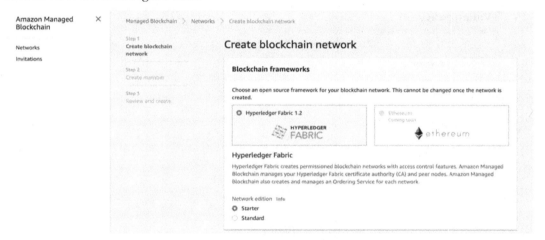

Figure 8.12

Select Hyperledger Fabric 1.2 for now and enter the Network name, Description, and leave the Voting policy as shown in *Figure 8.13*. Then click on Next:

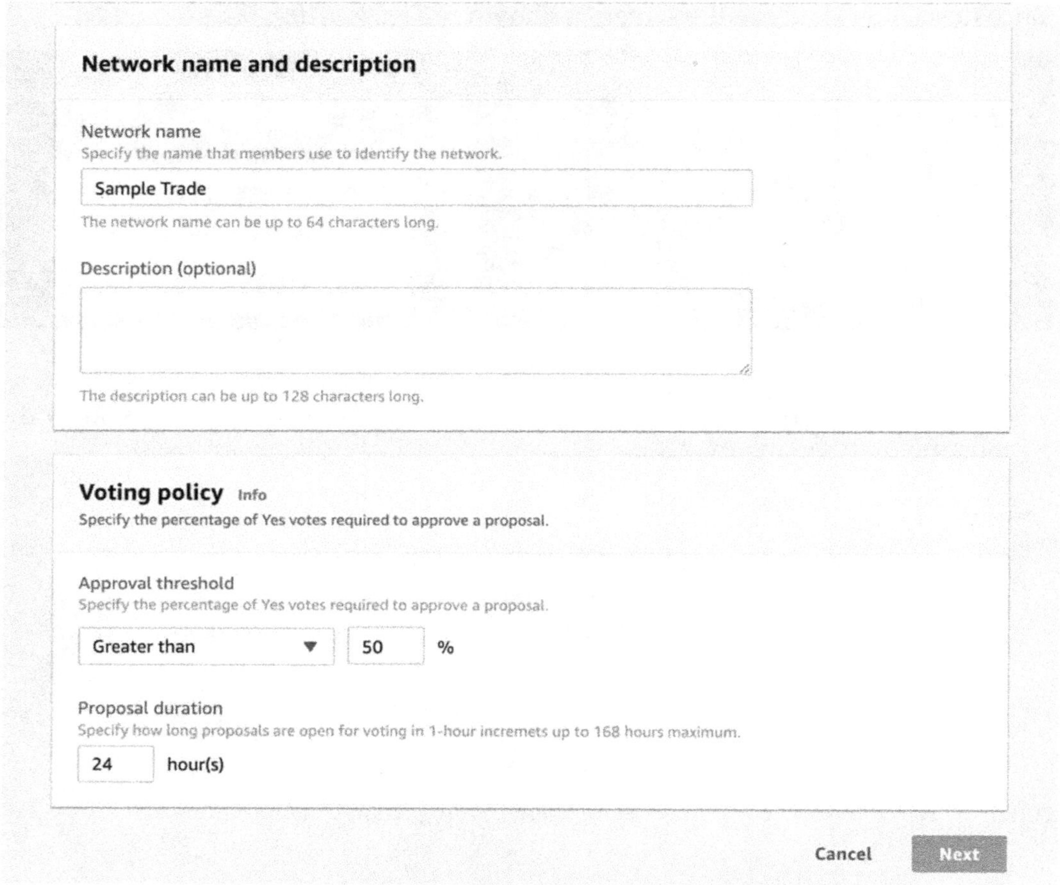

Figure 8.13

This will then lead you to the next screen where you can enter the member details:

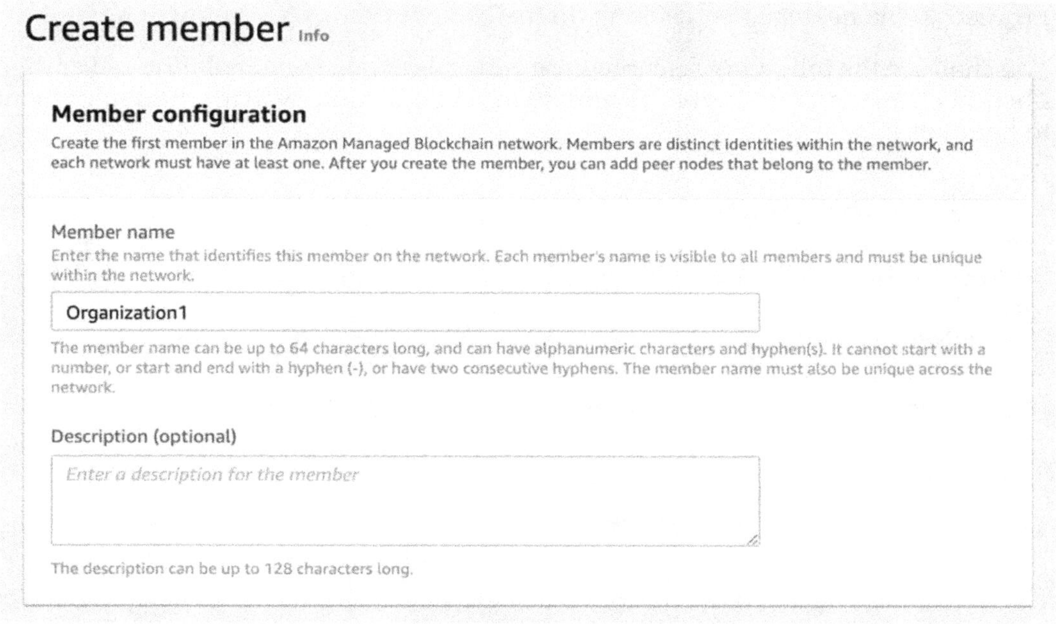

Create member Info

Member configuration

Create the first member in the Amazon Managed Blockchain network. Members are distinct identities within the network, and each network must have at least one. After you create the member, you can add peer nodes that belong to the member.

Member name

Enter the name that identifies this member on the network. Each member's name is visible to all members and must be unique within the network.

> Organization1

The member name can be up to 64 characters long, and can have alphanumeric characters and hyphen(s). It cannot start with a number, or start and end with a hyphen (-), or have two consecutive hyphens. The member name must also be unique across the network.

Description (optional)

> Enter a description for the member

The description can be up to 128 characters long.

Figure 8.14

Enter the first member's details here, such as organization name and some optional description.

Next, we have to choose CA username and password:

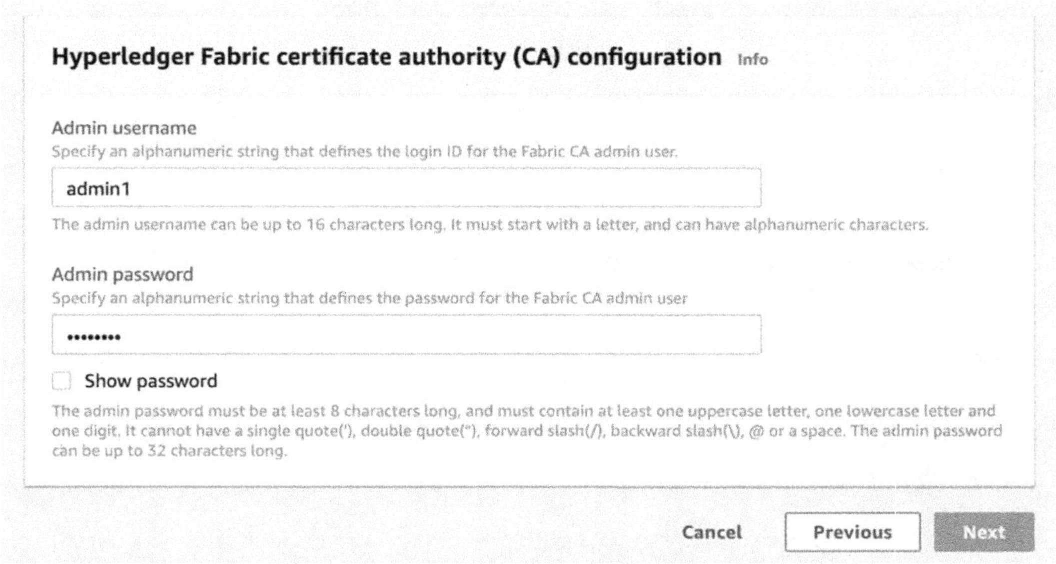

Hyperledger Fabric certificate authority (CA) configuration Info

Admin username

Specify an alphanumeric string that defines the login ID for the Fabric CA admin user.

> admin1

The admin username can be up to 16 characters long. It must start with a letter, and can have alphanumeric characters.

Admin password

Specify an alphanumeric string that defines the password for the Fabric CA admin user

> ••••••••

☐ Show password

The admin password must be at least 8 characters long, and must contain at least one uppercase letter, one lowercase letter and one digit. It cannot have a single quote('), double quote("), forward slash(/), backward slash(\), @ or a space. The admin password can be up to 32 characters long.

Cancel   Previous   Next

Figure 8.15

Proceed to the next step by clicking on the Next button.

You shall see the following screen where you can review the details entered earlier. Then, click on the **Create network and member** button and wait for the deployment to happen:

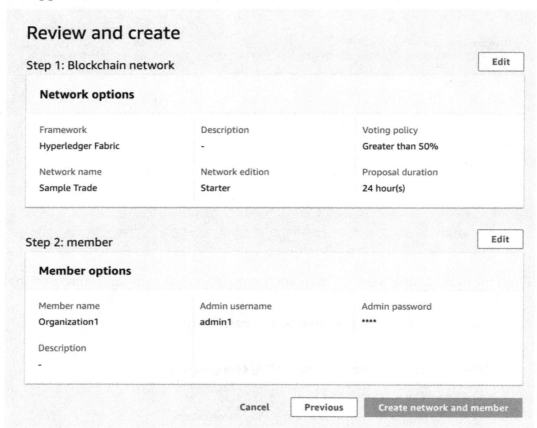

Figure 8.16

Once created, you will have the network listed as shown in *Figure 8.17*:

Figure 8.17

Click on the existing network and go to the members. You can click on the existing member to see their details and do things like add peers and so on.

Now click on one of the members and you can see the information as shown below in *Figure 8.18*:

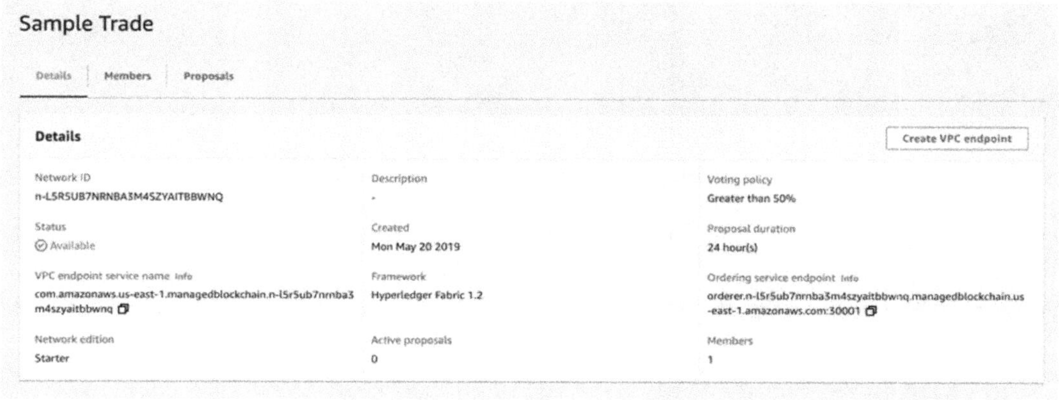

Sample Trade

Details | Members | Proposals

Details   [Create VPC endpoint]

Network ID   Description   Voting policy
n-L5R5UB7NRNBA3M4SZYAITBBWNQ   -   Greater than 50%

Status   Created   Proposal duration
⊘ Available   Mon May 20 2019   24 hour(s)

VPC endpoint service name Info   Framework   Ordering service endpoint Info
com.amazonaws.us-east-1.managedblockchain.n-l5r5ub7nrnba3   Hyperledger Fabric 1.2   orderer.n-l5r5ub7nrnba3m4szyaitbbwnq.managedblockchain.us
m4szyaitbbwnq ▢   -east-1.amazonaws.com:30001 ▢

Network edition   Active proposals   Members
Starter   0   1

Figure 8.18

From here you can create peer nodes for this existing organization.

After you have put a request to create a new node, it shall show a list of peers being created. From here you can also take the CA end point to get certificates for your Node.js SDK client.

Once created, you shall see the following. Click on this peer to get information about it.

Similarly, to add new members, you can click on Create invitation proposal:

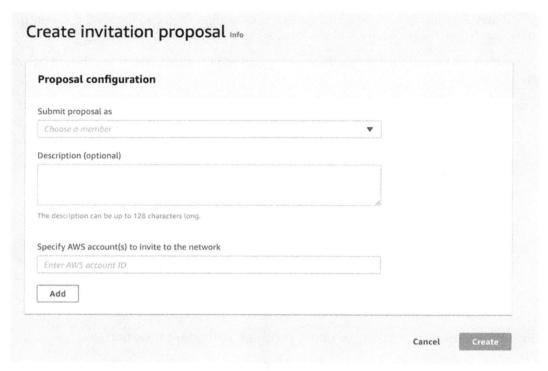

Figure 8.19

Members can create their identity in the platform and add it in the network from here.

Now, you can start interacting with the network.

Hyperledger Fabric in Azure Cloud

Now, let's begin with the Azure cloud. Azure provides a number of solutions for enterprises to try the blockchain technology. Some of these are listed here: https://azure.microsoft.com/en-in/solutions/blockchain/.

Azure is a complete blockchain suite that enables development, testing, and deployment of the major enterprise blockchain platforms like Hyperledger, Corda, Ethereum, and so on.

https://azure.microsoft.com/en-in/features/blockchain-workbench/.

The Microsoft Workbench solution provides a prebuilt and pre-deployed network for easy development.

Navigate to the link mentioned below in order to get started with Hyperledger Fabric deployment:

https://azuremarketplace.microsoft.com/en-in/marketplace/apps/microsoft-azure-blockchain.azure-blockchain-hyperledger-fabric?tab=PlansAndPrice.

Clicking it will take you to the official portal of Azure as shown in the following screenshot:

Home > Hyperledger Fabric on Azure

Hyperledger Fabric on Azure
Microsoft

Hyperledger Fabric on Azure
Microsoft .

| Create | ♡ Save for later |

We are excited to support Blockchain on Microsoft Azure with a set of solution templates that deploy and configure your choice of blockchain network with minimal Azure and blockchain knowledge.

With a handful of user inputs and a simple single-click deployment through the Azure portal, you can provision a fully configured blockchain network topology in minutes, using Microsoft Azure compute, networking, and storage services across the globe. Rather than spending hours building out and configuring the infrastructure, we have automated these time-consuming pieces to allow you to focus on building out your scenarios and applications. You are only charged for the underlying infrastructure resources consumed, such as compute, storage, and networking. There are no incremental charges for the solution itself.

For questions related to this offering, please refer to our support forum.

Useful Links
Technical Walkthroughs

Figure 8.20

Now click on the Create button. It will open the dialog box for inputs and configuration required to spin up Hyperledger Fabric on Azure.

First, enter the resource prefix that will be used for all your resources, like peers, orders, and so on. Then set up the credentials or SSH and choose the username and password. Create a new resource group for this deployment by clicking on the Create New button and enter a resource name of your choice.

Then choose the location and click OK:

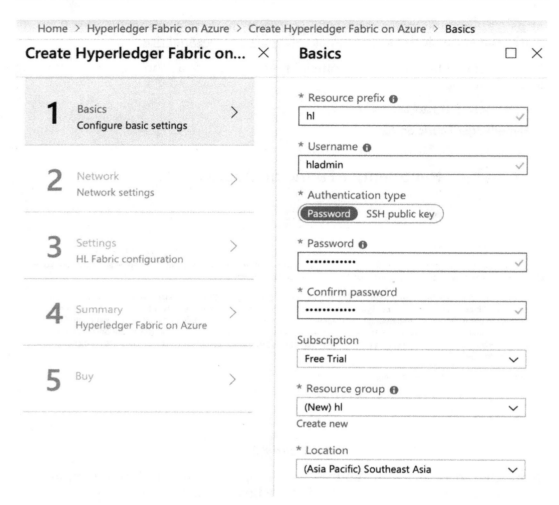

Figure 8.21

Now, you will have the network settings tab available. You will have an option to either set up a new Fabric network or join an existing one by providing the essential network settings from other deployments. This network can even exist in other cloud providers like Bluemix.

For now, choose the default New network. This will create a CA instance for which you need to choose the CA password.

Next is the organization setup. For now, choose Default. Next is VPN; if you want your network to be behind a VPN, you can choose the setup. However, we are choosing No for the current case.

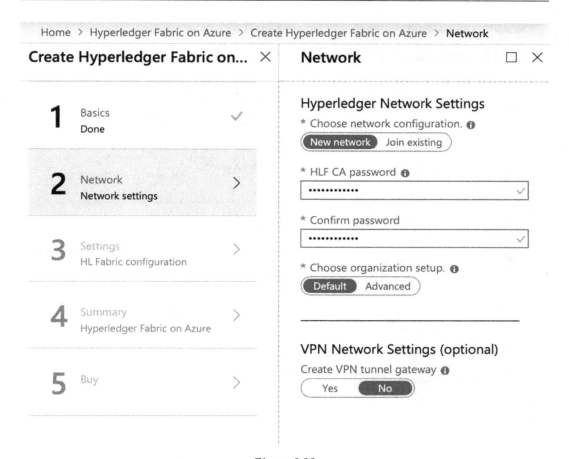

Home > Hyperledger Fabric on Azure > Create Hyperledger Fabric on Azure > **Network**

Create Hyperledger Fabric on... ×

1 Basics
Done ✓

2 Network
Network settings >

3 Settings
HL Fabric configuration >

4 Summary
Hyperledger Fabric on Azure >

5 Buy >

Network □ ×

Hyperledger Network Settings
* Choose network configuration. ❶
(New network) Join existing)

* HLF CA password ❶
[••••••••••••] ✓

* Confirm password
[••••••••••••] ✓

* Choose organization setup. ❶
(Default) Advanced)

VPN Network Settings (optional)
Create VPN tunnel gateway ❶
(Yes (No))

Figure 8.22

When you proceed, next, it will ask you about the network configuration required for fabric, i.e., whether you want a Single VM development setup or multi VM production setup, which will have more options and settings. Choose Multi VM and the screen should look as shown in *Figure 8.23*. You shall now see various options to set up the network. First choose VM disk type to be standard SSD for this example. You can also choose Premium SSD.

Then, enter the number of order nodes. For Multi VM it uses Kafka and Zookeeper. Also, choose the number of peer nodes; we are choosing two peer nodes. For all the peer nodes, you can choose the storage type, i.e., LevelDB or CouchDB. Click OK to proceed. It will run some final validation, and after that click OK to proceed:

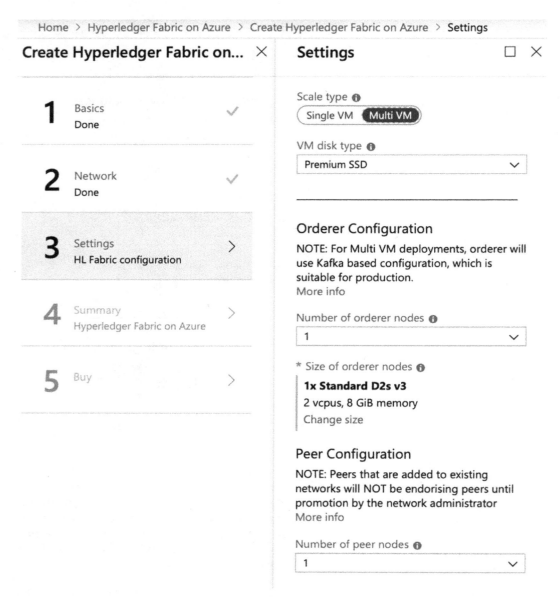

Figure 8.23

Last screen should show all the other steps in green to proceed. Then, click on Create to create this deployment.

Once done, wait for the deployment to complete. You can view the progress by clicking on Notifications.

IBM blockchain platform

IBM has been a major contributor when it comes to blockchain innovations. Hyperledger Fabric itself has been IBM's baby, which has got immense popularity. IBM now provides these solutions as part of its cloud infrastructure.

Recently, it has come up with https://cloud.ibm.com/catalog/services/blockchain-platform-20. It is a powerful blockchain service based on Hyperledger Fabric. It can provide scalability, flexibility, and more control in the network. It also provides a number of tools for development like Visual Studio code.

Ideally, you will be using Enterprise plans or above for production, but for preview we can use Starter plan as well, which has network configuration similar to that of Hyperledger first network consisting of two networks.

A typical process of using Fabric for production includes the following steps:

- Build the consortium
- Develop application over it
- Operate and govern

Summary

In this chapter, we translated our knowledge of Hyperledger Fabric into production deployment. We understood the process of deploying Fabric in a multi-host production environment using orchestration tools like Docker Swarm. We also reviewed the steps to perform common operations like adding new organizations to an existing network, attaching Hyperledger Explorer to our Fabric network, and more. Finally, we studied some performance aspects of Hyperledger Fabric network in production and common remedies to improve its transactions per second (tps).

Index

A

addresses 4
API project
  creating 230-235
  files, modifying 236-242
APIs
  creating 246-276
application blockchain
        interface (ABCI) 113

B

bitcoin
  about 3
  working 5
blockchain
  about 3, 54, 55
  basics 6
  bitcoin 3
  bitcoin, working 4, 5
  blocks 9
  building blocks 9
  consensus 11

cryptocurrency 2
defining 2, 4
mining 6, 7
node 10
peer-to-peer (P2P) network 10
smart contracts 10
state machine 11
structure 11
transaction 9
used, for decentralization 17
virtual machine 10
working 13
blockchain business networks
  about 30, 31
  advantages 30
blockchain business networks,
        concepts
  consensus 31
  privacy 31
  shared ledger 30
  smart contracts 30
blockchain, components
  blockchain program 8

P2P network 8
private key cryptography 8
blockchain, structure
  header 12
  merkle root 12
  transaction list 12
blockchain technology, features
  anonymity 14
  automated operations 14
  distributed 14
  double spending 14
  flexible 14
  global reach 13
  non-repudiation of transactions 14
  open source 14
  secure 13
blockchain technology, problems
  anonymity 31
  cryptocurrency 32
  privacy, lacking 32
  slow transactions 31
blockchain, types
  about 23
  private blockchain 24
  public blockchain 23
blocks 6, 9
business network
  assets, modeling 39, 40
  participants, modeling 39, 40
  transaction, modeling 39, 40
business network definition (BND)
    39
Byzantine generals problem
  about 23
  blockchain, types 23

C

Certificate Revocation Lists (CRL) 88
chaincode
  best practices 164, 165
createProperty, invoking 202-218
demystifying 145, 146
deploying 159-164
for developers 146-158
for operators 177
initiating 179
instantiating 179
invoking 202
package, creating 178
package, installing 178
package, signing 178
packaging 177
query 202
stopping 179
testing 159-164
upgrading 179
used, for writing unit test 170, 171
used, in Node.js 94
chaincode development
  IBM blockchain platform, used 172-
    177
chaincode, method
  about 95, 97
  init(stub) asynchronous 95
  invoke(stub) asynchronous 95-98
ChangePropertyOwner
  invoking, from Fabric SDK 219-228
consensus 11
consortium
  chaincode, installing 109
  channel 107, 108
  client/application, installing 109
  defining 106, 107
  ledgers, adding to network 108
  peers, adding to network 108
convector tool
  used, for creating token 166-170
Corda 21
cryptocurrency
  about 2

features 3
cryptography 8
cryptography keys
  private key 8
  public key 8

D

decentralization
  about 15, 16
  blockchain, used 17
  history 16
  working, in blockchain 17
decentralization application (Dapps)
  about 18
  features 18
  gems 17
  lighthouse 17
  OpenBazaar 16, 17
  popcorn time 17
  requisites 19
decentralized autonomous
      organization (DAO) 19
decentralized ecosystem
  about 18
  communication 18
  computation 18
  disadvantages 20
  storage 18
distributed model
  versus decentralized model 15
distributed system 22, 23
Docker 118
Docker Compose tool
  URL, for installing 121
Docker, terminologies
  containers 120
  Docker Compose 121, 122
  Docker Swarm 121, 122
  Golang 124
  images 118-120

Kubernetes 121, 122
Node.js 123, 124

E

Elliptic Curve Digital
      Signature Algorithm (ECDSA)
      8
encryptions, cryptography
  asymmetric cryptography 8
  symmetric cryptography 8
enterprise blockchain 20, 55-57
enterprise blockchain platforms
  about 20
  differences 21
  Ethereum 20
  features 21
  Hyperledger Fabric 20
  Quorum 21
  R3 Corda 21
  Ripple 21
enterprise blockchain
      platforms, considerations
  about 22
  disintermediation 22
  efficiency 22
  integrity 22
  robustness 22
  security 22
  transparency 22
ERC-20 token
  reference link 166

F

Fabric
  deploying, Swarm used 283-288
Fabric 0.6 72-74
Fabric 1.0
  about 74, 75
  key issues and features 75

Fabric 1.1 75-77
Fabric 1.2 77-81
Fabric 1.4 LTS
  about 81, 82
  key updates 82
Fabric CA client
  reference link 89
Fabric client
  reference link 89
Fabric Composer playground 47-51
Fabric network
  admin enrolment, using
      CA server 188-196
  admin registration, using
      CA server 188-196
  Node.js, installing 187
  Node.js SDK project, creating 187
  NPM, installing 187
  npm modules, installing 187
  prerequisites 184-186
  process, working 188
  reference link 89
  user enrolment 196-201
  user enrolment, using CA server
      188-196
  user registration 196-201
  user registration, using
      CA server 188-196
Fabric network, npm modules
  CA client 188
  client 187
  gRPC module 188
Fabric SDK
  chaincode, instantiate 281, 282
  ChangePropertyOwner,
      invoking 219-228
  used, for advanced use cases 277
  used, for creating channel 277-279
  used, for joining channel 279-281

G

Get Certificate workflow 113

H

Hyperledger
  about 54, 55
  channels 117
  company network 101, 102
  consensus in 32, 33
  encryption 117
  private data collection 117
  transaction privacy 116
  transaction security 116
  zero-knowledge proofs (ZKP) 117
Hyperledger application
  boilerplate angular
      application, generating 43
  business network, defining 39
  business network, deploying 41, 42
  business network, generating 41
  business network structure, creating
      39
  Hyperledger Composer, used 38
  REST server, creating 42
Hyperledger application model 102
Hyperledger Burrow 113
Hyperledger Burrow, components
  API gateway 114
  consensus engine 113
  permissioned EVM 114
Hyperledger Caliper
  about 34
  reference link 34
Hyperledger Cello
  about 34
  reference link 34
Hyperledger Composer
  about 34, 35
  advantages 35

query language 43
reference link 34
used, in Hyperledger application 38
Hyperledger Composer, components
about 36
command line interface 37
connection profile 37
execution runtime 37
Javascript SDK 37
LoopBack connector 37
playground web user interface 37
REST server 37
Yeoman code generator 37
Hyperledger Composer, query
language
business network archive,
regenerating 46
business network, updating 43-45
query definition file, creating 45
REST server, generating 47
skeleton angular
application, generating 47
updated business network,
deploying 46
Hyperledger Explorer
about 33
building 293
configuring, on Hyperledger Fabric
292
executing 293
Hyperledger Fabric
network, generating 292
Hyperledger Fabric, setting up 290
monitoring 290
PostgreSQL, installing 291
setting up 291
Hyperledger Fabric
about 59, 63, 64, 111
bitcoin, versus Ethereum 67
bitcoin, versus permissioned

blockchain 67
blockchain ledger, concept 83
chain code 70
chaincode 69
components 59-64
core functionalities 112
difference between, by
Linux foundation 69
difference between, by R3
consortium 69
difference between, Quorum
by JP Morgan 69
differences 70, 71
Ethereum, versus bitcoin 67
Ethereum, versus permissioned
blockchain 67
IBM blockchain platform 305
in AWS 294-300
in Azure Cloud 300-303
in cloud 294
Node.js SDK, used 89-94
permissioned blockchain, versus
bitcoin 67
permissioned blockchain, versus
Ethereum 67
permissioned parties 69
pre-requisites 117
releases 70, 71
smart contracts 69, 70
structure 83, 84
transaction 65, 66
world state 83
Hyperledger Fabric, advantages
digital keys, protection 31
modular architecture 31
performance and scalability 31
permissioned data 31
rich queries 31
sensitive data, protection 31
Hyperledger Fabric architecture 32

Hyperledger Fabric network, nodes
  about 60
  MSP and CA services 62
  orderer node 62, 112
  peer node 61, 112
  services 62
Hyperledger Fabric, technical stack
  Apache Kafka and Zookeeper 60
  Docker 59
  Go language 59
  gRPC and protobuffs 60
  Node.js 59
Hyperledger frameworks
  about 57, 110
  Hyperledger Burrow 57, 113
  Hyperledger Caliper 58
  Hyperledger Cello 58
  Hyperledger Composer 58
  Hyperledger Explorer 58
  Hyperledger Fabric 57, 111
  Hyperledger Indy 57, 112, 113
  Hyperledger Iroha 57, 114-116
  Hyperledger Quilt 59
  Hyperledger Sawtooth 58, 110, 111
  YAC consensus algorithm 116
Hyperledger Indy 112, 113
Hyperledger Iroha
  about 114-116
  architecture 114
Hyperledger Iroha, layers
  API level 115
  chain business logic level 115
  peer interaction level 115
  storage level 115
Hyperledger Iroha, validations
  stateful validation 115
  stateless validation 115
Hyperledger network
  about 102
  blockchain network 103

certificate authority 105
  creating, from scratch 104
  network administration node 106
  sample network, building 103, 104
  setting up 127-142
Hyperledger network process
  binaries, pulling 126
  creating 125
  crypto files, generating 126
  Docker images, pulling 127
  initiating 127
  pre-requisites, installing 125
Hyperledger Quilt
  about 35
  reference link 35
Hyperledger Sawtooth 110, 111
Hyperledger Sawtooth,
      consensus implementation
  Dev mode 110
  PoET simulator 110
  Proof of elapsed time (PoET) 110
Hyperledger tools
  about 33, 57
  Hyperledger Caliper 34
  Hyperledger Cello 34
  Hyperledger Explorer 33
  Hyperledger Quilt 35
  Hyperledger URSA 35
Hyperledger URSA
  about 35
  reference link 35

I

IBM blockchain platform
  about 305
  reference link 305
  used, in chaincode development
      172-177
init(stub) asynchronous
  stub.getArgs() 95

stub.getFunctionAndParameters() 95

Interplanetary file system (IPFS) 18

invoke(stub) asynchronous 95-98

L

leverage blockchain technology 22

M

membership service provider (MSP)
  about 84-86
    certificates, generating 87, 88
    signing keys, generating 87, 88
membership services provider (MSP) 105
Merkle directed acyclic graph (DAG) 18

N

node 10
Node.js
  chaincode, used 94
Node.js modules
  reference link 124
Node.js SDK
  used, for Hyperledger Fabric 89-94
NPM modules
  composer-admin 37
  composer-client 37

O

operating system (OS) 118

P

peer network
  consensus 115
  simulator 115
  validator 115
peers
  about 61
  anchor peer 61
  endorser peer 61
  validating 62
PoW 20
Privacy Enhanced Mail (PEM) 88
Proof-of-Concepts (POCs) 31
Proof-of-Stake 20
public blockchain, versus private blockchain
  differences 24
public networks
  versus permissioned networks 67, 68

S

secure transaction processing
  fundamentals 14
services, Hyperledger Fabric network nodes
  CLI 62
  CouchDB 63
smart contracts 4 ,10
state machine 11
Swarm
  used, for deploying Fabric 283-288
system chaincode 180

T

token
  creating, convector tool used 166-170
Torii 115
transaction 9
Transport Layer Security/Secure Socket Layer (TLS/SSL) 87

U

unit test
  writing, for chaincode 170, 171

V

virtual machine 10

W

wallet 5
wallet, types
  cold wallet 5
  hardware wallet 6
  multi-signature wallet 6
  software wallet 5
  web wallet 5

Y

YAC consensus algorithm
  about 116
  consensus 116
  ordering 116
  validation 116

Z

zero-knowledge proof (ZKP) 35

CPSIA information can be obtained
at www.ICGtesting.com
Printed in the USA
FSHW010504190819
61179FS

9 789388 511650